THE PROBLEM OF PARTITION:
PERIL TO WORLD PEACE

THE PROBLEM OF PARTITION: PERIL TO WORLD PEACE

RAND McNALLY
EUROPEAN
HISTORY SERIES

THOMAS E. HACHEY

Marquette University

RAND McNALLY & COMPANY . Chicago

INITIAL BOOKS IN
THE RAND McNALLY EUROPEAN HISTORY SERIES
George L. Mosse, advisory editor

GEORGE FASEL, Europe in Upheaval: The Revolutions of 1848
BRISON D. GOOCH, The Reign of Napoleon III
HANS J. HILLERBRAND, Men and Ideas in the Sixteenth Century
BARBARA JELAVICH, The Habsburg Empire in European Affairs, 1814–1918
HARRY J. MAGOULIAS, Byzantine Christianity: Emperor, Church and the West
JOHN B. WOLF, Toward a European Balance of Power, 1620–1715
THOMAS E. HACHEY, The Problem of Partition: Peril to World Peace

To Jane

Editor's Preface

It used to be thought that the sole object of history was to discover and set forth the facts. When the *English Historical Review* was founded it recommended such a procedure, for through it one "can usually escape the risk of giving offense." While much of this tradition has remained active in the teaching and writing of history, it has led, in turn, to a sharp reaction against such timidity and narrowness. History became a branch of philosophy or of the social sciences, and scholarship was in danger of being displaced by the search for general laws that might govern the development of all mankind. There is a hunger for history abroad in the land, but many of those who want to know about the past are rightly dissatisfied with arid narrations of fact (and turn to the historical novel instead), while others are bewildered by abstruse generalizations that seem to ignore the particular for the universal.

The books in the Rand McNally European History Series do not place themselves in either of these traditions. Instead, they recognize both the importance of accurate and detailed scholarship and the obligation to place such scholarship within a meaningful historical setting. They do not shun general ideas and assumptions; they test them in a crucible of research. This combination is always exciting, because it penetrates historical development; and this development, in each of its stages, illuminates a new dimension of mankind. A prominent historian once wrote, "What man is, only history tells."

Here "what man is" is told by scholars who have researched and reflected upon a significant period of history. They have taken this opportunity to present their conclusions in a manner that will attract and stimulate those who long for a lively account of the past. All of the authors in this series are specialists presenting their original insights, making it possible for all those interested in history to partake of their work.

George L. Mosse, *advisory editor*
Rand McNally European History Series

Preface

The intent of this book is to illustrate the causes, character and consequences of the six most significant political partitions in the twentieth century. Arranged in chronological sequence, the partition experiences examined in each of these chapters are studies in failure. Too frequently partition was embraced as a temporary expedient which invariably became a permanent condition whereby national and/or ethnic groups were tragically separated by artificial divisions. In other instances, partition was used as a palliative, an ill-considered response to nationalist movements complicated by religious and/or racial differences. In a world in which separatist movements are very much alive—in Middle East countries with Kurdish minorities, in southern Sudan, in French Canada, et cetera—it would seem that future secessionists might use the partition experiences of recent history as their guide in avoiding at least some of the pitfalls of the past. Surely it is a subject worthy of the consideration of today's student, who should try to profit from yesterday's experience when the time comes for him to deal with tomorrow's problems.

THOMAS E. HACHEY

August, 1972
Higgins Beach
Scarborough, Maine

Acknowledgments

I am indebted to the Marquette University Committee on Research for the generous grant which provided welcome support during my preparation of this book. Equally valuable was the splendid cooperation afforded me by each of the authors who cheerfully contributed to this study with their time and energy. Special thanks is owed to two loyal friends, Professor Ralph E. Weber of Marquette University and Joseph F. Marcey, Jr. of The Viking Press, for reading parts of the manuscript and offering useful suggestions. Throughout the preparation of this work, Rand McNally editor Ted Tieken was especially obliging and always encouraging. Laurette Hupman and Henrietta Pons, also of Rand McNally, made this author's task infinitely simpler by their expert assistance and kind collaborations. Lastly, I am most grateful to my wife Jane who proofed the entire copy, typed the manuscript in its final form and lent me moral support in bringing this volume to completion.

THOMAS E. HACHEY

Contents

Introduction

History is replete with examples of nations and empires seizing control over foreign lands and populations. Some ethnic groups have been completely assimilated by their conquerors; other groups retained for centuries their separate cultural identities within alien states or empires. There have also been instances of ethnic communities which shared a common heritage, language and culture, but not a common nationality because they were absorbed by two or more foreign powers. Such divisions frequently produced mixed allegiances among these minorities: one to the state in which they were sometimes accorded citizenship, the other to the race or ethnic group with which they shared a cultural bond and special affinity. Compulsory separations and unnatural divisions among various peoples and nationalities have been a recurrent theme throughout most of recorded history. There is a notable difference, however, between the assimilations and divisions which traditionally have derived from racial imperialism or conquests for economic and strategic gain, and the relatively recent partitioning of the peoples and countries discussed in this book.

The creation of new states through the geographical and political partition of older ones is not novel to the twentieth century. It is rather the circumstances which prompted modern-day partitions that make them a unique phenomenon of the contemporary world. Partition has never occurred with such frequency over so short a span of time, nor has it ever involved so many millions of people in such different areas of the globe. Whether undertaken as an expedient or as a panacea, the outcome of recent political/ geographical partitions has been generally uniform: they have either proven inadequate and sometimes dangerous as expedients, or, instead of providing panaceas, have frequently compounded the very problems they were intended to resolve. The six studies which follow include every partition of major significance in this century. Except for Ireland, which was partitioned in 1921, all of the partitions followed in the wake of World War II. Religious differences were a major factor in the partitioning of three regions: India, Ireland and Palestine. The elements which contributed to the partition of the other three, Germany, Korea and Vietnam, are more complicated since these divisions were in large measure a by-product of the Cold War.

There are both similarities and differences in the partition experiences of six such culturally and geographically diverse regions. India, Ireland and Palestine provide the colonial models in this study of recently partitioned lands. Each shared the common experience of British imperial administration. The British government's policy of furthering its own ends by playing off one side against the other, as in the instances of Hindus and Muslims, Protestants and Catholics, and Jews and Arabs, only served to exacerbate existing sectarian frictions and render inevitable the segregation, and ultimately the partition, of antagonist populations. Immigrations gave a religious character to the geographical borders which delineated the political partitions in all three British-controlled territories. Muslim invaders entered India through the passes of the northwest frontier and, together with Hindu converts, gradually took control over the area which later would roughly correspond with the future state of Pakistan. England's sponsored settlement of Anglican and Scot Presbyterians in Ulster permanently altered the socioreligious features of that region. Jewish immigration before and after World War II was both a cause of and a catalyst in the subsequent partition of Palestine.

Perhaps the most striking parallel between the experiences of the three British administered lands is the manner in which partition was implemented. Unlike Germany, where partition was made to appear accidental when it was perhaps intentional, the British government openly recommended partition as the most plausible solution to the divisive problems endemic to India, Ireland, and Palestine. Britain was therefore responsible for the consequences of these policies, and they were considerable. Although nationalist movements on both sides in all three countries included men who sought change through constitutional means, those men who preached change through violence and/or resistance prevailed. Riots which destroyed lives and property preceded partition in India, Ireland, and Palestine, and continued afterwards as well. Even when hostilities ended, neither side in any of the three partitioned countries was reconciled to the new geographical and political boundaries.

Differences between the three colonial models are also important. While "Big Power" rivalry played a significant part in the background of the Palestinian partition crisis, it was far less perceptible in the Indian experience and was virtually nonexistent in the instance of Ireland. Furthermore, while there were cultural and religious differences between nationalists and Unionists in Ireland, they nevertheless shared a common Irish heritage. But there was no such common ground between Jews and Arabs in Palestine. The former community was predominantly European, the latter predominantly Asiatic. They differed not only in religion and language, but also in their ways of thought and conduct. In India, linguistic and religious differences placed greater barriers between the Hindu and the Muslim than did racial or ethnic distinctions. And after the partition of the subcontinent into India and Pakistan, the chasm between West and East Pakistan involved more than the one thousand miles of physical separation. Muslim nationalism was defeated by regionalism as the racially, culturally and linguistically different East Pakistanis seceded from West Pakistan and established the nation of Bangladesh. Neither the Catholic population in Ulster nor the Palestinian Arabs in Israel represents any real parallel to these circumstances in Pakistan.

Germany, Korea and Vietnam, unlike India, Ireland and Pakistan, were not partitioned by a colonial power belatedly attempting to placate rival religious and racial groups. Their divisions were more a result of Cold War maneuverings between the West and the Communist bloc. Partition in these three instances has created unnatural divisions against the majority will, with boundaries which bear no relation to ethnic or linguistic groupings. Perhaps the most tragic feature of these national separations is that the populations of the divided countries have been compelled to join opposing international alliances.

As in the case of the colonial models, there are similarities and differences among the three major Cold War partitions. In Germany, Korea and Vietnam it was expected that geographical and political divisions would be temporary. But in each instance partition was made permanent by the unilateral establishment of governments with national pretensions under regimes supported by the West. Both the West and the Communist bloc subsequently sacrificed the national interests of the partitioned countries in global power plays. Refugees were a particular problem for all three nations and they frequently became little more than pawns in the ideological conflict between East and West.

Korea's national existence as a homogeneous unit extends back to the seventh century and, although long dominated by powerful neighbors like China and Japan, the cultural ties and identification between the peoples of North and South remain intact. Vietnam has never been a united country but its population has often joined in a common effort to resist foreign rule in Indochina. The present states of North and South Vietnam are not parts of a divided whole. Indeed, the regimes of both North and South Vietnam are presently attempting to create this unified "whole." But Vietnamese and Koreans in both parts of their divided countries look toward a future unification of their peoples. Germans, by contrast, seem more reconciled to partition as West and East appear to be gradually developing their own separate identities. Except for the East German harassment of West Berlin, however, there is no parallel between the German experience and North Korean and North Vietnamese attempts to end partition by conquest, whether by invasion or guerrilla warfare.

Colonial partitions, then, were usually provoked by religious and separatist elements which sought the establishment of a nationalist state. Cold War partitions, in contrast, divided existing nations and peoples without reference to either the needs or the desires of the resident populations. While the partition experience has been generally an unhappy one for the peoples involved, it seems to have been due, in the colonial context, to the *native* prejudices and hatreds which were cultivated *before* partition and, in the Cold War context, to the suspicions and rivalries of *outside* parties *after* partition. However distinct these six partition experiences may be in origin, evolution, and results, they share the human consequences of individual and familial suffering, national trauma and trauma, repercussions.

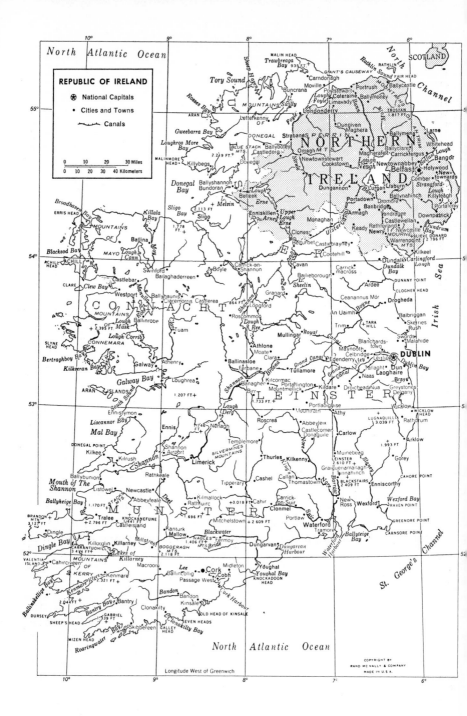

Chapter 1.

The Partition of Ireland and the Ulster Dilemma

Thomas E. Hachey
Marquette University

THE HISTORIC ROOTS OF THE IRISH PROBLEM

In a post-World War II society grown accustomed to crises in Berlin, the Middle East, and parts of Asia, Ireland in the 1970s seems an improbable setting for yet another international trouble spot. But such a judgment derives more from prevailing misconceptions about that country than from an informed view of the real circumstances of Irish life, or the historical conditions which produced them. Popular folklore, the ballads of romantic patriots, and Irish travel brochures frequently convey a blissful image of an idyllic pastoral land, the Emerald Isle of saints and scholars. There is another Ireland, however, historic Ireland, a country deeply scarred by centuries of oppression, imperialist exploitation, institutional racism, and religious bigotry. Its people and its problems today are victims and by-products of that legacy. Hence, any meaningful understanding of contemporary Ireland demands some knowledge of the early English and Scottish settlements in

Ireland; of the historic highlights from that time to the climactic event in Irish history, the Irish War of Independence, 1916–22; and an examination of how the political partition which followed produced a spiritual schism in the national soul.

Ireland's troubled and frequently tragic relations with England over the past 800 years have been substantially influenced by two elements: geography and religion. It was perhaps inevitable that the geographical proximity of the two island countries would lead the more populous and powerful England to expand her interests at the expense of her Irish neighbor. English colonizers and adventurers began settling and plundering Ireland in the twelfth century, shortly after the Norman conquest of England, but it was not until the reign of Henry VIII (1509–1547) that all Ireland was brought under English control. In the Protestant Reformation which convulsed much of Europe, a cruel twist of fate created further tensions for the future of Anglo-Irish relations as England became Protestant while Ireland remained Roman Catholic. England's emergence as a dominant maritime power in an age of colonization and mercantilism doubtlessly would have forced Ireland into a dependent status in any circumstance. But Ireland's sympathy for and cooperation with the Catholic powers of Spain and France in their religious wars with England in the sixteenth and seventeenth centuries had lasting consequences. The English determined that the security of their country required a totally subjugated Ireland. In 1601, an English army dispatched by Queen Elizabeth achieved that objective with a ruthless determination which included destroying crops by way of reducing the Irish peasants to starvation.

Ireland's present religious division dates from the land settlement which followed. Since Ulster clan chiefs had raised the most effective resistance to religious and political Anglicization, their province was singled out by the wrathful conquerors. Under James I in 1608 scores of choice Ulster plantations were forfeited for treason and given to Scots and English settlers. The town of Derry was awarded to a company of Londoners who promptly renamed it Londonderry, a name Ulster Catholics refuse to recognize even today. Besides the estates confiscated by the nobility, mostly English, thousands of Presbyterian farmers from Scotland were settled throughout Ulster as tillers of the soil. These Scots received comparatively small plots of land but they took a much stronger hold than the absentee English landlords who lived handsomely in England off the rents paid by Irish tenants. The plantation policy left Ulster as the only province in Ireland with a significantly large Protestant garrison. It was also during this period that the Irish Parliament in Dublin was enlarged with a majority of Protestants in order to check the power of the Catholic nobility, Anglo-Irish as well as Irish, in the other three provinces of Leinster, Munster and Connaught.

Fearing further property confiscations and religious persecution, Irish Catholics turned to violence in 1641 and massacred thousands of native Protestants. England was horrified but helpless, for she was trembling on the brink of her own civil war between Puritans and royalist supporters of Charles I. Fearing the Puritans more, the Irish vainly attempted to aid King Charles but Oliver Cromwell's Puritan army defeated the Stuart forces and executed the king. Puritan fury then turned upon Catholic Ireland as Cromwell's veterans descended upon that country not only for conquest, but for revenge. After Catholic Ireland had been subdued, however, Puritan ferocity diminished and comparatively few were executed for their part in the rebellion. The poor were left unmolested and, under the terms of a general pardon, were permitted to return to their ordinary lives without fear of punishment. Severe penalties were reserved for the wealthy. Catholic landowners in Ireland were divided into two groups: those who had participated in the rebellion and those who had not. The former promptly lost their estates and all their property rights. The latter were allowed to retain land but were forced to settle in the western province of Connaught. Their former holdings were then divided among the officers and men of Cromwell's army, a policy which all but completed the destruction of the Irish gentry.

Another tragic chapter in Irish history resulted from Ireland's support of James II, the Catholic King of England who was deposed in the Revolution of 1688. James landed in Ireland with French money and arms in 1689. William of Orange, the new King of England and leader of the Protestant forces, arrived in Ulster the following year which set the scene for an epic battle between English kings fought on Irish soil. Although the Catholics were not finally defeated until the signing of the Treaty of Limerick in 1691, the psychological turning point and most memorable event of the war was the battle of the Boyne River where William's army defeated the Catholic forces under James. The victory all but assured the ultimate triumph of the Protestant cause. The Battle of the Boyne is fondly remembered among the Protestant community of Northern Ireland where it is annually celebrated on July 12, Orangeman's Day, with parades and festivities.

Neither the Tudor plantation policy nor the Cromwellian settlement had as devastating an effect upon Ireland as did the Penal Laws which were passed in the last few years of the seventeenth century and in the early decades of the eighteenth. Protestant ascendancy was maintained by an Irish Parliament controlled by agents of English absentee landlords. Presbyterians as well as Catholics suffered from the economic exploitation. A flourishing wool industry was destroyed when export from the country was forbidden. The resultant poverty forced many Presbyterian merchants and craftsmen to emigrate. It also reduced the vast majority of the Catholic population into craven, demoralized and impoverished serfs.

During the late eighteenth century, Irish Protestants, more confident of their position, less frightened of the beaten Catholic masses, resentful of British mercantilist restrictions, and anxious to free the Irish Parliament from English domination, developed a patriotism of their own. Active opposition was made possible by French assistance to the American Revolution which provided an excuse for the formation of a supposedly defensive volunteer Protestant army. With these volunteers behind him, Irish nationalist Henry Grattan demanded and obtained trade concessions and an independent Irish Parliament. But middle-class Protestants were still unhappy with a parliament which served primarily, if not exclusively, the interests of the landed gentry. The Society of United Irishmen, founded in Belfast in 1791, moved the reform movement to the political left. Its leader, Theobold Wolfe Tone, was a Dublin Protestant but the heart of this national movement was in revolutionary Ulster. United Irishmen saw themselves as culturally distinct from other British ethnic groups. Moreover, they hoped to unite Catholics and Protestants under the banner of liberty and found their inspiration in the French Revolution. Their goal was a democratic republic and they regarded the exploited Catholic peasantry as natural revolutionary allies of the nonconformist Ulster middle class in achieving that end. In the ill-prepared and disastrous risings of 1798, Protestants in Armagh died no differently from Catholics in Wexford.

A major factor contributing to the failure of the United Irishmen movement was that most Irish Protestants preferred keeping the system of ascendancy, with all its shortcomings, rather than extending political equality to the Catholic majority. Limited Catholic gains toward equality, the fear of a French invasion supported by an Irish conspiracy, and the impact of the Evangelical movement in Britain and Ireland revived militant Protestantism and provided Anglicans and Presbyterians with a common no-popery position. The success of the Orange Order in the late 1790s was a manifestation of this new Protestant spirit. Orangeism was the outgrowth of an Ulster Protestant tenant farmer secret society, the Peep O'Day Boys, rivals to the Defenders, a Catholic agrarian secret society. Protestant farmers resented papist competition for the limited land available, particularly in Ulster communities with large Catholic populations. Beginning in 1795, the Orange Order rapidly grew in size and was soon terrorizing Catholics in southern Ulster counties, driving some of them into the wild and sparsely settled regions of Connaught. Recognizing the antirevolutionary potential of the Orangemen, members of the gentry class took command of the movement, armed its membership, and persuaded government authorities that no-popery was an effective tool of law and order. Orangeism spread throughout Ireland into Britain where it won adherents in the highest quarters, including members of the royal family. Comparable to Anglo-Saxon Protestant nativist movements in both England and America, Orangeism remains today a vital force in the Protestant power structure in Northern Ireland: a divisive, irrational, hate movement in Irish life.[1]

After the United Irishmen rising of 1798, England and Ireland were joined in a legislative union which abolished the Dublin Parliament in 1800 and gave the Irish representation in the British Parliament at Westminster. Ulster Protestants were the most bitter opponents of the Act of Union for they feared a remote British Parliament might be more responsive to Catholic grievances and agitations. It was indeed British Prime Minister William Pitt's in-

---

[1]Lawrence J. McCaffrey, "The Catholic Minority in the North" in *Divided Ireland,* ed. Francis William O'Brien (Rockford, Illinois, 1971), pp. 48–49.

tention to remove the remaining disabilities of the Penal Laws against Catholics. King George III denied Pitt royal assent, however, and Catholic emancipation was delayed until 1829 when it was accomplished largely through the efforts of Daniel O'Connell. O'Connell also succeeded in creating modern Irish nationalism on the foundations of Catholic civil rights. His achievements changed the attitudes of nineteenth century Ulster Protestants who now became the most militant champions of maintaining the Union. Orange leaders came to view British power as the best guarantee of Protestant ascendancy in Ireland. Furthermore, since Ulster was the only section of Ireland to participate in the Industrial Revolution, linen factories and Belfast shipyards were assimilated into the British urban industrial complex. Protestant merchants and industrialists were convinced that a revived Irish Parliament dominated by a priest-ridden Catholic peasantry would destroy Ulster's economy and persecute their religion.

Beginning in 1845, Ireland's eight and one-half million people (twice the present population) either witnessed or suffered the ravages of famine. During the next six years, about a million people died of starvation and disease; and from 1847 to 1854 nearly two million others emigrated, most of them to the United States, where they continued their embittered opposition to the British government and organized the Fenian movement. Other than a few border attacks against Canada, the Fenians limited their activities to anti-British propaganda and provided moral and some financial assistance to the organization's counterpart in Ireland, the Irish Republican Brotherhood. The latter wished to overthrow British rule in Ireland through violent revolution, but the Irish people were not ready for it. The more moderate movement of constitutional nationalism commanded the support of a majority of Irishmen, particularly with the emergence of the Irish Parliamentary party under the inspired and brilliant leadership of Charles Stewart Parnell.

Parnell's quest for dominion home rule was a political manifestation of the cultural nationalism which was emerging in Ireland. Taking their inspiration from the Young Ireland movement of the 1840s, cultural nationalists asked: what would be accomplished if Ireland had her own parliament in Dublin even though Irishmen remained British in culture and values? To be truly free, Ireland would have to be de-Anglicized. She would have to revive

her own language, culture, and traditions; she would have to re-
cover her own identity. Cultural nationalism inspired three significant movements: the Gaelic League, the Gaelic Athletic
Association, and the literary revival. The first sought to revive the
Irish language; the second sponsored ancient Irish sports like hurl-
ing and Gaelic football, and also promoted a hostile attitude toward English sports like lawn tennis, polo, and cricket; and the
third produced a literary renaissance led by Anglo-Irish Protestants like William Butler Yeats, John Millington Synge, George
Russell and Lady Gregory, who rejected the class, religious and
political prejudices of their background and embraced cultural
nationalism. The Gaelic emphasis was also reflected in political
organizations like Sinn Fein (Ourselves Alone) founded by Arthur
Griffith in 1905. Griffith's party argued that the Act of Union had
been illegal and embraced the view that Ireland and England
should exist as two independent nations under the same British
Crown, a dual monarchy on the Austro-Hungarian model. Harsh
reality would transform these romantic visionaries into hardened
revolutionaries a short time later.

From 1886, when Parnell and British Prime Minister William
Gladstone concluded the alliance between Irish nationalism and
British Liberalism, the Conservative Party in England used Ulster's resistance to Irish Home Rule as a weapon to maintain power
and frustrate Liberalism. They used the Union as a symbol of
Protestant principles, traditional institutions, aristocratic power,
private property, and the permanence of the Empire. British Conservatives in the Parliament and in the army endorsed and encouraged Ulster Protestant threats in order to defeat the
constitutional inevitability of Home Rule through civil war. Liberal Prime Minister Herbert Asquith had promised the Irish Parliamentary Party that England would grant Home Rule to Ireland
in return for its support of the Liberal Party at Westminster. The
Irish kept their bargain but Asquith was threatened by civil war
in Ulster and a mutiny among British army officers if he attempted
to implement what was demonstrably the will of a majority of the
British electorate. Asquith asked, and Irish nationalist party leader
John Redmond agreed, to postpone Home Rule when war with
Germany erupted in August 1914.

In order to win Irish nationalist support for the war effort, Home
Rule was placed on the statute books, but with Redmond's consent

the Prime Minister sought to appease Unionists with a suspensory bill delaying the operation of Home Rule until after the war was over. For the moment, Britain had narrowly escaped a constitutional crisis, and possibly civil war. But British politicians had not solved the Irish question; they had only postponed a decision. Neither Asquith nor Redmond realized how the stalemate of August 1914 would alter the character of Irish nationalism. Although most of Ireland responded favorably to Redmond's appeal that the Irish join the British in fighting the common enemy, there were men in Ireland who believed their common enemy was England, and they waited for an opportunity to strike out at her.

THE PERIOD OF "THE TROUBLES"

Irish nationalists drew two lessons from the events of 1914: that the English could not be trusted to honor promises, and that force rather than peaceful or constitutional methods would bring results. These attitudes were reflected in the declining support given to John Redmond's Irish Nationalist party, and in the corresponding growth of popularity which the more aggressive Sinn Fein movement enjoyed after 1914. Originally committed to a policy of passive resistance, Sinn Fein by this date was becoming increasingly militant in its demand for independence under a dual monarchy in which England and Ireland would share a common crown. The more radical Irish Republican Brotherhood sought the establishment of an Irish Republic by physical force, and it was the I.R.B. whose members controlled the key positions in the Irish Volunteers. The latter were predominantly Catholic and nationalist and their immediate objective was to check the power of the Ulster Volunteers, who were Protestant and Unionist. James Connolly's small Citizen Army was another militant force, but with a difference. A dual monarchy or a change of flags did not interest Connolly for he viewed the struggle against Britain as a part of the socialist battle against capitalism. In these circumstances, the I.R.B. republicans provided the strongest link in bringing such diverse elements as the Volunteers, Sinn Fein and the Citizen Army into an anti-British effort which reached its climax with the Easter Rising of 1916.

Romantic nationalism in Ireland was given its ultimate expression in the Rising of 1916. The sabotage, terrorism and assassinations which would characterize future Irish rebel activities were not a part of the 1916 insurrection. The Rising was led by poets and visionaries who hoped by their example to shake the apathy of the Irish people rather than attempt a real but impossible military victory over the British. The participants were uniformed and followed the conventions of war in acting out what they intended as a "blood sacrifice"; they did not indulge in the guerrilla tactics which typified subsequent liberation efforts in Ireland. Not surprisingly, the rebellion went poorly for the Irish idealists. A German ship containing a cargo of arms, timed to arrive just before the Rising, was intercepted by British warships off the coast of County Cork. The German captain scuttled his ship and the consignment of obsolete Russian rifles went to the bottom of the sea. Plans went further awry when Irish Volunteer chief Eoin Mac Neill called off the rebellion and some Dublin leaders refused to accept that order. What was to have been a national rising became a local insurrection limited to Dublin. On Easter Monday, 1916, rebellion leader Padraic Pearse and fifteen hundred rebels seized several strategic positions in the center of Dublin and declared the establishment of an Irish Republic. British troops suppressed the rebellion in a week of bloody fighting which left the heart of the Irish capital in ruins. Over one hundred British soldiers died, and more than three hundred were wounded. Only fifty-two members of the Volunteers and Citizen Army were killed, but over four hundred and fifty Dublin civilians lost their lives and 2,614 were wounded by stray bullets and shells.

Ireland had not responded to the Rising as Pearse had expected. During the chaos and turmoil of the battle, many Dubliners took advantage of the breakdown of authority and looted stores and shops. At Westminster, John Redmond condemned the Rising as a German plot involving only a fanatical and misguided minority of the Irish population. The majority of Irishmen agreed and many condemned the Republicans and Sinn Feiners as traitors. It was not an unreasonable sentiment in view of the fact that a quarter million Irish men served voluntarily in the British army during World War I and their families supported them if not their cause. When Republican prisoners were led through the Dublin streets to prison they were cursed by the people who lined the way.

Padraic Pearse and his comrades may have won little more than the ridicule and contempt of their countrymen, and they might have been forgotten by both Ireland and history if they had been sentenced to long terms in prison.

Reprisal was the immediate response of the English Government to the Rising. It was a tactic which would be repeatedly employed over the decades by the British in Ireland, almost always with disastrous results. Over a period of ten days the leaders of the rebellion were court-martialed and executed. James Connolly was so badly wounded that he was executed while strapped to a stretcher. Thirteen others fell before a firing squad before the volume of public protest spared seventy-five others who also had been condemned to death. More than two thousand Sinn Feiners and Republicans were imprisoned in Ireland and Britain, many of them without trials. The viciousness of the executions and the imprisonment of so many men made the Government appear cruel and arbitrary. The "dirty traitors" of Easter week became gallant martyrs and national heroes. Their portraits adorned the walls of Irish homes and pubs; their speeches and poems were widely sold, read, and quoted. In the space of a few short weeks the Irish national mood had changed as the British unwittingly fulfilled Padraic Pearse's wish; a blood sacrifice had shaken Ireland from her apathy.[2]

England's war with Germany and the angry Irish reaction to the Easter vengeance almost certainly prompted the London Government to adopt a more conciliatory policy toward the Irish in the hope of pacifying that disruptive internal problem. Sinn Fein and Republican prisoners were gradually released over the next two years so that all had been freed by the end of the war. Eamon de Valera, a mathematics teacher who had commanded a Volunteer unit during the Easter week rebellion, was among those released from jail. He and his comrades immediately began reorganizing the Volunteer Army and promoting candidates for political office under the Sinn Fein party label. Meanwhile, British Prime Minister Lloyd George summoned an Irish Convention representing all shades of opinion—Sinn Fein, Home Rule, and Unionist—to work out an acceptable plan for Home Rule. Southern Unionists were

---

[2]Lawrence J. McCaffrey, *The Irish Question* (Lexington, Kentucky, 1968), pp. 166–67.

prepared to cooperate in establishing an Irish Parliament but Ulster Unionists, encouraged by their sympathizers in Britain, refused. John Redmond's Irish Parliamentary Party failed to establish a consensus in the face of a Sinn Fein boycott and Ulster's veto and the Convention, which held its first session in July 1917, ended in failure in April 1918. To London it may have seemed that neither vengeance nor pardon was very effective in dealing with the Irish; in truth, it was more a matter of too little too late. Radicalism was spreading in Ireland and the British Home Rule proposals which enjoyed the support of an overwhelming Irish majority in 1914 had considerably less appeal to Irishmen by 1918.

British manpower resources were seriously depleted by the heavy toll taken in the fighting on the Western Front in 1917 and, with the Russian withdrawal from the War, the London Government was in desperate need for more soldiers. In April 1918, Parliament authorized Lloyd George to extend conscription to Ireland. The immediate reaction of Catholic Ireland produced an uncommon unity as the different factions joined ranks against conscription; the Irish Party walked out of the House of Commons and the Irish trade unions, Sinn Fein, and the Catholic Church joined ranks in opposition to the British. Anticonscription agitation strengthened the Republican forces in Ireland and the London Government turned again to repressive measures. Scores of Sinn Feiners were deported and others, like de Valera, were sent to prison on the pretext of their complicity in an alleged "German plot." The war ended, however, before Britain could initiate the draft in Ireland.[3]

Another act in the drama opened after the Armistice on November 11, 1918, when it became evident how completely the nationalist movement had been seized by the extremists. In the British election of December 1918, the Sinn Fein party scored an overwhelming victory by winning every Irish seat outside Ulster except four. Seventy-three Sinn Feiners, thirty-six of whom were in prison, were elected to the Westminster Parliament; the Unionists elected twenty-six; and the now discredited Home Rulers won a mere six seats. Triumphant Sinn Feiners viewed the election as a plebiscite and hailed the outcome as a mandate from the Irish people for an independent republic. Refusing to take their seats

---

[3] *Ibid.,* pp. 168–69.

at Westminster, the victors instead gathered at Dublin's stately Mansion House where they formed a self-constituted Irish Parliament known thereafter as Dail Eireann. On January 21, 1919, in proceedings which were partly conducted in the Irish language, the Dail [pronounced "Doyle"] issued a declaration of independence and ratified the establishment of Soarstat Eireann, the Irish Republic, proclaimed on Easter, 1916. The Dail proceeded to assume the task of administering the country; there emerged courts to supercede the British legal system, boards to settle industrial disputes, and a land bank to make loans to people wishing to purchase farms. The Dail Government even sent delegates to the Versailles Peace Conference to plead the case for an independent Irish Republic and issued an appeal to the nations of the world for diplomatic recognition.

Warfare began in January 1919 as the Irish Republican Army (the new name of the Irish Volunteers) adopted guerrilla tactics in their attacks on British authorities in Ireland. Young men in civilian clothing ambushed army motorcades, assassinated "spies" and "informers," and shot soldiers and policemen. As the violence spread, the London Government began in March 1920 recruiting ex-servicemen in England and sent them to Ireland as reinforcements for the Royal Irish Constabulary. These notorious Black and Tans, so named because in the absence of sufficient Royal Irish Constabulary uniforms they were given surplus khaki uniforms with black belts, were joined in June 1920 by the Auxiliary Division of the R.I.C. The "Auxis," as they became known in Ireland, were recruited among ex-officers in England. I.R.A. guerrillas were hopelessly outnumbered but they had one telling advantage: their anonymity. Dressed in street clothes, they would appear suddenly and attack Tans and Auxis and, almost as quickly, would merge back into the civilian population which sheltered them and refused to inform on them. British forces met terror with terror and resorted once again to reprisals. They burned, looted, and murdered. But rather than breaking the spirit of Irish radicals, the atrocities only stiffened their determination.

Ulster Unionists by this date had broken with the southern Unionists since the latter were inclined to view a semiautonomous Irish Parliament as inevitable. Ulster Unionists were also alienated from English Unionists who were now reconciled to some form of home rule for Ireland. Sir Edward Carson and other Ulster leaders were strongly opposed to any form of Irish self-government but recognized their own inability to prevent one. They were resolved, however, that Ulster would remain the responsibility of Westminster no matter what might happen to the rest of Ireland. I.R.A. terrorism and British reprisals caused deep-seated bitterness on both sides throughout Ireland during the struggle for independence; and in Ulster the existing tensions between the Unionist majority and nationalist minority were considerably intensified.

In February 1919, Eamon de Valera was freed in a prison break which was planned and executed by Michael Collins. After his escape from Lincoln jail in England, de Valera secretly returned to Ireland and, in April, was elected president of the Dail. He then appointed Arthur Griffith as acting president of that body and left for the United States in June 1919 where he remained until December 1920. De Valera's dual purpose in going to America was to raise funds for the Republican cause and to procure United States recognition for the Irish Republic.

During his eighteen-month absence, the Dail Government was given full responsibility for the prosecution of the war. Besides Griffith, other important Cabinet ministers were Cathal Brugha, minister of defense and Volunteer (Irish Republican Army) chief of staff; and Michael Collins, minister of finance. Collins was the chief architect of the Volunteer organization and he coordinated the work of brigades formed in every county with a network of friendly railwaymen and post-office employees, thus providing a vital communications network. Moreover, Collins' famed intelligence service was in part a product of his friendships with the Dublin police "G" squad, some of whom would advise Collins as to the time and place of raids planned by the authorities. Other contacts in the post office, customs service, and even in government offices in London, provided Collins with useful intelligence.

Violence in Ireland intensified in 1920. There were no front lines and, on the Irish side, no uniforms or formal warfare. "Flying squads" of the I.R.A. would ambush police or army convoys on narrow country roads, shoot selected officials from roof tops or from behind garden walls, and sometimes conduct mass executions. The most infamous such occasion was on the morning of November 20, 1920, "Bloody Sunday," when the I.R.A. broke into fourteen houses and hotels scattered throughout Dublin and shot, in some instances in the presence of their families, a total of fourteen British officers and civilians. A week later, a party of seventeen Auxis, driving along the Dunmanway-Macroom road, was decoyed by an I.R.A. man dressed as a British soldier. Lying in ambush were twenty-seven members of the Cork Number 3 Brigade and all seventeen were left for dead, though one survived to tell the tale.

Guerrilla warfare produced a reign of terror. General Sir Nevil Macready put the total of British forces in Ireland in 1920, military and police, at about forty thousand. By contrast, the I.R.A. numbered no more than fifteen thousand and there were never more than five thousand on active service at any one time. Many of the Auxis and Black and Tans were poorly disciplined and, in Macready's own words, sometimes became "a danger to their friends and a disgrace to the uniform." Numerical superiority offered little advantage in battles fought by anonymous terrorists, and the Tans and Auxis vented their frustrations with reprisals. On the afternoon of "Bloody Sunday," a confrontation between Irish football fans and British soldiers led to the "massacre" at Croke Park where twelve civilians were killed and sixty wounded after someone allegedly fired at a soldier. Towns were sacked, the center of Cork City was burned, and Irish prisoners were treated brutally and were, in some instances, shot while "trying to escape." The British Government was as unable to contain the atrocities and excesses of its own forces as it was incapable of winning a military victory over the I.R.A. guerrillas and restoring some semblance of normalcy to Ireland. As the death toll mounted from the atrocities and reprisals, the deplorable conditions in Ireland evoked responses beyond the borders of that country. British public opinion became passionately divided over the Government's handling of the Irish disorders; several of the Dominion governments reminded London that injustices in Ireland might compromise the integrity of the Empire; and millions of Irish Americans demonstrated militantly on behalf of their kinsmen.

Eamon de Valera faced both success and failure during his eighteen-month campaign in America. He did succeed in gaining widespread sympathy for the Irish cause and he was able to raise several million dollars for the prosecution of the war effort at home. Among Irish Americans, de Valera enjoyed enormous popularity and he was accorded enthusiastic receptions in the major cities and small towns from coast to coast across the United States. He failed to secure official recognition for the republic, however, and was unable, during the American presidential campaign of 1920, to gain the endorsement of either the Democratic or Republican conventions for the according of self-determination for Ireland. Even with the united and unqualified support of Irish American leaders, these latter objectives would have been difficult, if not impossible, to attain in the increasingly isolationist atmosphere in postwar America. But the sharp controversies which raged between de Valera and his native Irish entourage on the one side, and immigrant Fenian John Devoy and Judge Daniel Cohalan's Friends of Irish Freedom organization on the other, doubtlessly weakened the political bargaining power of the Irish movement in America. Indeed, Irish American groups were divided over whether they should endorse an Irish republic, or simply Irish self-determination, and there was also little agreement about administering monies collected for the "Victory Fund." De Valera found that some Irish American spokesmen were more concerned with advancing their own political ends than aiding the fight for Irish freedom and his departure from America in December 1920 was not unwelcome to some American Hibernians.

Part of the reason for de Valera's secret return to Ireland was the length and severity of the Anglo-Irish war. In many respects, 1920 was the year of military decision and while the I.R.A. continued to harry British forces in Ireland, the war of attrition was taking its toll among the war-weary population of that country. De Valera was sufficiently impressed by the alarming costs of the war that he shocked some of his comrades by suggesting partial disengagement through a calculated diminishing of aggressive activities. Although de Valera suggested this move as a temporary expedient so that the burden of the people could be somewhat relieved, the proposed tactic also revealed a willingness among at least some Irish leaders to consider methods other than sustained conflict in achieving their objectives. A negotiated settlement of the war became the leading objective of the London Government. Within England the pressures for ending the war and all its savagery were applied by leading politicians of the different parties, eminent churchmen, newspapers of various political complexions, and the influential Labour party commission of inquiry which was active in Ireland in the autumn of 1920.

THE PARTITION BILL OF 1920

Even as the war raged, London attempted to provide a constitutional solution to the most critical problem in any Irish settlement: a political arrangement which would allow the Catholic and Protestant communities of Ireland hegemony in their respective spheres while proceeding toward an ultimate fulfillment of their common destiny. By the end of 1919, Prime Minister Lloyd George had begun toying with the idea of combining a form of Irish self-government with partition of the country. He devised a plan for the creation of *two* parliaments in Ireland, an idea which was different from any previous British proposal and certainly not in accord with the demands which had been made by either the Nationalist or Unionist camps. Under this scheme, each parliament would have very limited powers on the understanding that both would subsequently amalgamate into a single parliament and government for the whole of Ireland. The conservative provisions of the plan provided for an eventual national parliament in Dublin with powers substantially less than those which had been accorded Ireland in the Home Rule Bill and placed in the Statute Book in 1914. The proposals were scarcely calculated to appeal to the Nationalist element whose representatives in the Dail had overwhelmingly decided upon the establishment of an independent Irish republic and whose partisan forces were already conducting a guerrilla war against the British authorities for that cause. Unionist reaction in Ulster, however, was cautiously receptive.

Lloyd George introduced a bill in February 1920 which generally embraced the proposals he had offered earlier for consideration. The British strategy in seeking to enact the bill was probably twofold: to shelve temporarily an awkward legislative problem and to persuade the United States that London had some Irish policy besides calculated violence. As such, the bill was a palliative and a subterfuge because the British Government was aware that a modified form of home rule would never satisfy republicans, nor the majority of the Irish population. And London was equally convinced that Irish independence would have to be resisted by whatever means necessary. Once again the British resorted to a carrot and stick approach to the Irish problem as the Government simultaneously intensified the military effort against Sinn Fein while attempting to mediate differences with that foe through a variety of third parties.

Nationalists viewed with contempt the formal proceedings at Westminster pertaining to the Irish bill proposed by Prime Minister Lloyd George. Ulster Unionists were suspicious of the suggested Council of Ireland which was to be representative of both the Northern and Southern parliaments. The Council was intended to provide a measure of unity from which stronger bonds might be forged. Although the Council's authority was restricted to railways, fisheries, contagious diseases and only those additional powers which the two parliaments agreed to confer upon it, the Unionists were as hostile as the Nationalists to this arrangement. Northern Protestants were particularly dismayed by the part of the proposal which accorded counties Donegal, Monaghan, and Cavan to the southern parliament since these areas, together with the counties of Armagh, Antrim Down, Derry, Fermanagh, and Tyrone, were all a part of the historic province of Ulster. The Ulster Unionist Council met on March 4 in Belfast and reluctantly consented to the planned division. Ulster leader Sir Edward Carson bitterly observed that Northern Ireland had little other choice since it was calculated that Nationalists would outnumber Unionists if all of Ulster were to be administered by a Northern parliament. With six counties, a Unionist and Protestant majority in parliament could be assured even though a large Nationalist minority was unavoidable. It was also reasoned that the economy and resources of the six-county region were sufficiently varied to render it economically capable of subsisting as a separate political entity. Amidst much soul-searching and deep misgivings, therefore, Ulster Unionists made a pragmatic decision to desert their fellow Unionists in Donegal, Cavan, and Monaghan as they had earlier parted company with the Unionists of Southern Ireland.

Fighting in the north and south of Ireland became, if anything, even more intense following Lloyd George's proposed partition scheme. I.R.A. gunmen made attacks, frequently fatal, upon Protestant workmen and the police throughout Ulster. In May and

June of 1920, riots broke out in Londonderry between Catholic and Protestant groups which left twenty persons killed. Civil disorders spread to Belfast during July and August where four thousand people were left destitute and homeless. Orange Clubs were revived and armed Ulster Volunteers engaged in illegal drills without interference from the Government. Another response to Sinn Fein was the organization of the Protestant Workman's Union which began to terrorize Roman Catholics in the Belfast shipyards. Catholics in isolated villages poured into Belfast where their coreligionists at relief centers attempted to serve the needs of both these refugees and the victims of mounting civil strife within the city. It was against this background that the London Government, against the recommendation of its military commander in Ireland, Sir Nevil Macready, agreed to authorize the formation of a special constabulary of loyal citizens for the purpose of preserving order. Organized and paid for by the British, these gestapo-like groups became the infamous "B specials" whose behavior was frequently indistinguishable from the fanatical terrorists of the I.R.A. except that the conduct of the former possessed a legitimacy which the latter did not.

By the summer of 1920, Sinn Fein had succeeded in destroying the British administrative apparatus throughout much of Ireland. Tax collectors' offices were systematically destroyed; Royal Irish Constabulary barracks were burned, forcing police and supporting military forces to find temporary quarters in the towns and villages; Republican courts, held in secret, dealt with civil and criminal cases while the British courts remained open but idle for lack of litigants. London virtually acknowledged in August 1920 that she had ceased to govern Ireland with the announcement of the Restoration of Order in Ireland Act. Under its provisions the powers of the military were extended to treason and felony cases. Terror and reprisals continued undiminished, however, and tensions were heightened by the death of Cork City Lord Mayor Terence MacSwiney following a seventy-four day hunger strike in an English prison. Throughout the period of "The Troubles," the heaviest fighting took place in the rugged terrain of the south and west of Ireland and it was principally in these areas that the British sought to contain the "flying columns" of the I.R.A. guerrillas. Accordingly, martial law was finally declared on December 10, 1920 in the counties of Cork, Kerry, Limerick, and Tipperary, extending a month later to counties Clare, Kilkenny, Waterford, and Wexford. A violent year was climaxed on December 11 when undisciplined Black and Tans and Auxis took revenge by setting Cork City afire. Even Englishmen who had winked at the Government's previous unofficial sanctioning of reprisals were shocked to learn that forces of the Crown had indulged in an orgy of arson and pillaging.

In the absence of other alternatives, the partition plan which had been the subject of debate and deliberations at Westminster for almost a year became British law after it received royal assent on December 22. Few were enthusiastic over the passage of the law and it came into being almost by default since the strongest argument the Government had made on its behalf was that "something" had to be done in Ireland. The law was in fact ignored by Southern Ireland and never did become effective for the twenty-six counties since it was superceded by the Treaty of 1921. But Northern Ireland's separate existence began with this act as the region became a distinct political entity within the United Kingdom, a status which the Treaty of 1921 recognized and accepted. It was also a status which was unique in the British system. The Six Counties became a part of the United Kingdom, ostensibly in the manner of England, Scotland, and Wales. But from its inception Northern Ireland was really a case apart. The region sent twelve members of Parliament to Westminster but was permitted to control its local affairs from its own parliament at Stormont, a prerogative enjoyed by no other part of the United Kingdom.

British Unionists who wished to guarantee Protestants of Northern Ireland protection against domination by a Dublin Parliament had proven the staunchest advocates of the Government of Ireland Act. A number of British Conservatives, together with some Liberals, supported the Act in the belief that it was necessary to prevent civil war between Catholics and Protestants in Ireland. But the Act ignored the reality of the Irish Nationalist opposition which regarded partition as anathema and rejected modified versions of home rule as unacceptable. Neither did the Act satisfy any desire for self-government in Northern Ireland for it was not a settlement desired by Ulster Protestants. They had resisted home rule for all of Ireland and had never sought it for themselves. What they desired most was to maintain the union of Britain and Ireland which had served the interests of the Protestant ascendancy in

Ireland so well for 120 years. Failing that, Ulster Unionists were reluctantly resigned to allowing most of the country to take the direction it liked as long as their own region remained a constituent part of the United Kingdom. Hence, no element of any political persuasion in Ireland wanted or welcomed the partition of the country into two separate entities. Its implementation was an expedient imposed on the nation by a British Government which was the object of increasing pressure both from within England and from America and the Dominions to end the bloodshed in Ireland. London sought nothing more than the immediate objective of holding two groups of Irishmen from each other's throats and providing them with an opportunity for living peaceably apart, since they seemed unable to live peaceably together.[4]

Elections for the parliaments of Northern and Southern Ireland were set for May 24, 1921, and the months preceding that date were marked by what was perhaps the most desperate fighting of the Anglo-Irish war. Exasperated British officials were helpless to prevent the violence on both sides as murders, kidnappings, execution of hostages, ambushes, raids and incendiarism continued to serve as effective weapons for the I.R.A. in keeping its vastly more powerful adversary off balance. Both the London Government and its military command in Ireland were frustrated and embarrassed by the apparent inability of a major world power to win a decisive military victory over the comparatively miniscule but tenacious guerrilla forces of Sinn Fein. And the British effort to defeat the nationalist army of liberation was further hampered by London's refusal to either recognize the Irish Republic or even to admit to the existence of a state of war. The English held to the fiction that they were involved in a police action to put down a rebellion in Ireland. To have conceded even a state of general belligerency would have compromised the international case because the British insisted Ireland was an internal problem and asked the cooperation of foreign governments in preventing arms shipments by I.R.A. sympathizers abroad. Moreover, London was hoping to fight a limited campaign against Sinn Fein without jeopardizing the prospects for a future peace with the Irish people if one could be negotiated without humiliation or dishonor.

---

[4]J. C. Beckett, "Northern Ireland" in *Journal of Contemporary History* (1971), vi, No. 1, 124.

Mounting casualties, both civilian and military, atrocity stories, and the worsening of unsolved social problems and unemployment throughout England combined to produce considerable antiwar sentiment in Britain. Disillusion grew after World War I and took a strong grip on the collective consciousness of the population, particularly the working classes. English war veterans did not find the golden age forecast by President Woodrow Wilson in the speech he had delivered at Manchester, England in December 1918; nor was there any evidence of "the world fit for heroes" that Prime Minister Lloyd George had promised. People were tired of violence and its waste, especially since the Irish war seemed to many a senseless and immoral war. Prominent Anglican clergymen, among them the Archbishop of Canterbury, the Asquith wing of the Liberal Party, and the Labour Party joined in condemning the Government's prosecution of the war in Ireland. A growing chorus of denunciations came from the pulpit, the Opposition benches in the House of Commons, and the editorial pages of the left-wing press. All argued that the terror tactics of the I.R.A. did not justify reprisals which seemed little different from genocide. They demanded an end to the war and a settlement which would accord a negotiated form of home rule and allow the Irish people to govern themselves.

In the May 24 balloting, Sinn Fein treated the election, held under British auspices, as a new election of the Dail. Sinn Fein won all but four of the 128 seats in uncontested elections held in the South. Once again the Republican Sinn Feiners refused to participate in any but their own assembly and the four members elected by Trinity College, Dublin, together with the senators nominated by the Lord Lieutenant, the official representative of the British Crown, met as the Parliament of Southern Ireland on June 28. Following a brief address from the throne of the Lord Chief Justice, the membership adjourned the charade and the Southern Parliament never emerged again.

Predictably, election patterns were different in the North where Unionists elected forty members, the Nationalists and Sinn Fein twelve, including Eamon de Valera, Michael Collins, and Arthur Griffith who were also elected for southern constituencies. Sir James Craig was elected Prime Minister of the new government of Northern Ireland and King George V arrived to open the parliament in Belfast on June 22. The king took advantage of the opportunity to express the acute concern of the British monarchy over the affairs in Ireland. In remarks published in part by the English and Irish press, George V declared to the assembled parliament of Northern Ireland:

> I speak from a full heart when I pray that my coming to Ireland today may prove to be the first step towards an end of strife amongst her peoples, whatever their race or creed. In that hope I appeal to all Irishmen to pause, to stretch out the hand of forbearance and conciliation, to forgive and forget and to join in making for the land which they love a new era of peace, contentment and goodwill.

George V's appeal doubtlessly contributed to the spirit which ultimately permitted both sides to enter into negotiations. But the passions generated by the war made the road to peace long and difficult. I.R.A. gunmen and Ulster patriots kept hatreds aflame in the North while in Dublin the Dail decided to boycott all trade between Southern Ireland and Ulster. Just as with the raids of southern Sinn Fein into the Six Counties, many Ulstermen who were hitherto indifferent to partition were converted by such policies into supporters of separatism. The southern Irish were treating the Ulstermen as foreigners, and the consequence was that spiritual partition supplemented the political.[5]

THE ANGLO-IRISH TREATY OF 1921

Prime Minister Lloyd George took the initiative following the King's speech at Belfast and invited Eamon de Valera to join in a tripartite conference between the British Government and representatives of Northern and Southern Ireland. Absent from his proposal were the terms Sinn Fein had previously found unacceptable, such as the surrender of arms or the barring of certain individuals from the conference table. After consulting with his chief ministers, de Valera replied that he would agree to negotia-

---

[5]Charles Loch Mowat, *Britain Between the Wars* (London, 1968), pp. 80–81 [new edition].

tions on two conditions: an actual truce would have to be declared *before* the President of the Dail Eireann traveled to London; and Northern Ireland Prime Minister Sir James Craig was to be excluded from discussions. Lloyd George agreed and the long-awaited truce came at noon on July 11, 1921. Eamon de Valera arrived in London on the following day, accompanied by four members of his Cabinet. In deference to his wishes, Lloyd George met with de Valera and Sir James Craig in separate meetings held at No. 10 Downing Street.

Although the truce seemed to come quite suddenly, there had been frequent unofficial contacts between the opposing sides. Lord Derby, General J. C. Smuts of South Africa, and Archbishop Clune of Australia were but a few of the mediators who held secret talks on behalf of the British Government with Sinn Fein representatives. There were also circumstances which inclined both parties toward a truce, if not a negotiated settlement. The British Government found itself besieged by appeals from its own citizenry, and many others in America, Europe, and from all parts of the Empire called for a cessation of hostilities in Ireland. Conservatives like Robert Cecil changed their position and joined critics of the war while others like Winston Churchill, Lord Birkenhead, and Austen Chamberlain warned Lloyd George that he would never gain national support for his Irish policies until he granted that country the widest possible measure of self-government. Even General Sir Henry Wilson, Chief of the Imperial General Staff and hawkish supporter of the war against Sinn Fein, told the Prime Minister quite bluntly that the choice was "to go all out or to get out."

The I.R.A. itself was facing critical shortages of men and materials. Its arsenals had never contained anything more than machine-guns, rifles, and home-made bombs and with the depletion of these the I.R.A. was scarcely able to engage in anything more than harassment. As Michael Collins would later admit, at the time of the truce Irish resistance could not have lasted more than a few more weeks. The people of the towns and countryside upon whose support, or at least indifference, the guerrillas depended, were growing increasingly weary of the long and costly war of attrition. Their physical and psychological endurance had reached the breaking point. People were becoming more anxious for an end to the violence and a return to normalcy than they were about possible political solutions. Like the British, Sinn Fein thought the moment propitious for an armistice since the conditions required to continue the war effort were growing decidedly worse rather than better.

Initial conversations between Lloyd George and de Valera were unproductive. The pragmatic Welsh politician pointed repeatedly to the restrictions under which he had to labor as prime minister of the United Kingdom; the doctrinaire Irish revolutionary responded by lecturing him on the history of English exploitation in Ireland. Lloyd George did offer Ireland virtual dominion status, which was more than any previous British Government had ever offered, but he also attached some rather vital qualifications. England would continue to maintain certain air and naval facilities in Ireland, besides reserving the right to recruit volunteers from that country for the British armed forces. A contribution to the British war debt would be stipulated and the Irish government in the south would be expected to recognize the legitimacy of the Northern Ireland Parliament. De Valera judged these terms to be unacceptable but agreed to return to Dublin and submit them for the Dail's consideration. That body's recently elected membership renounced the limited dominion status proffered by London, collectively took an oath to bear allegiance to the Irish Republic, and authorized de Valera, as President of that Republic, to form a new Cabinet with which to administer the country.

Neither side wished a total breakdown of negotiations, however, and de Valera made a conciliatory gesture when he announced that he was not "a doctrinaire Republican." He also declared that he would support a treaty which permitted Ireland to enter in a free association with the British Commonwealth of nations. Lloyd George pursued the opportunity for an agreement and, after a lengthy exchange of letters which were published by newspapers in both countries, the British prime minister offered to join de Valera in another conference. The purpose of the new meeting would be to ascertain how the association of Ireland with the British Empire could best be reconciled with Irish national aspirations. For reasons which neither de Valera nor his biographers have ever satisfactorily explained, the President of the Irish Republic excluded himself from the delegation which went to London to negotiate a treaty. Some have contended that de Valera did not wish to risk his political reputation by direct association with what he must have known would be a less than favorable agreement. Others have defended the decision claiming, as has de Valera himself, that the Irish President remained in Dublin to insure that extreme Republican colleagues like Cathal Brugha and Austen Stack did not torpedo any British proposal short of an outright republic. De Valera also felt his remaining in Ireland was the best guarantee for insuring that an Anglo-Irish treaty would be given careful consideration in Dublin before it was accepted.

Arthur Griffith, Michael Collins, E. J. Duggan, George Gavan Duffy, and Robert Barton comprised the five-man Irish delegation. Their counterparts at meetings held at the Prime Minister's residence on Downing Street were Lloyd George, Austen Chamberlain, Lord Birkenhead, and Winston Churchill, all men who were experienced in the skills and nuances of politics and diplomacy. Two questions dominated the conference sessions which extended from October 11 to December 6, 1921: would Ireland remain within the Empire as a dominion, or be in "external association" with it as a republic; and would Ulster be included or not. The Irish delegates were never unanimously agreed on the first question, but they conceded everything—first the republic, then external association—for the sake of winning the second question, a united Ireland, unpartitioned.[6]

In the course of the deliberations, the British consented to allow the Irish to design an oath of allegiance that would put primary allegiance to an Irish dominion or Free State rather than to the Crown. But de Valera was pressured by the same extreme republicans he allegedly remained in Dublin to hold in check, and the Irish President sent word to his delegates in London that neither the oath nor dominion status could be considered. Michael Collins and Arthur Griffith, however, were induced to accept dominion status in return for Lloyd George's promise that Ulster's boundaries would be so contracted by a Royal Boundary Commission that it would be forced to join Southern Ireland in order to survive. There was an element of deceit on both sides of this bargain. The prime minister could not predict the consequences should his or any other British Government provoke Ulster by any radical reshaping of its boundaries. Lloyd George knew this but he was seldom troubled by any sense of obligation to deliver on promises.

---

[6]*Ibid.,* pp. 86–91.

Michael Collins agreed to dominion status for Ireland so that the British would consent to end partition and to abandon Ulster. He too was insincere. Collins had no intention of renouncing forever the claim to a republic. Dominion status and membership in the community of nations known as the British Commonwealth were not desirable in themselves. But Collins saw them as stepping stones, a new posture from which Ireland could and would strike out again for the cherished Republic. As he later told the Dail when urging that assembly to accept dominion status, it was " . . . not the ultimate freedom that all nations desire and develop to, but the freedom to achieve it."

Lloyd George knew that the Irish delegates had promised the Dail Cabinet they would sign no treaty before submitting it to the Dail. He also knew that the compromises and concessions made by Collins and Griffith particularly would not be supported by the fanatical republicans in Ireland. Accordingly, on the afternoon of December 5 the prime minister brought the protracted negotiations to a sudden halt with the declaration of an ultimatum. Holding two sealed envelopes, one in each hand, he addressed the Irish delegates saying:

> Here are the alternative letters which I have prepared, one enclosing Articles of Agreement reached by His Majesty's Government and yourselves, and the other saying that Sinn Fein representatives refuse to come within the Empire. If I send this letter it is war, and war within three days. Which letter am I to send? Whichever letter you choose travels by special train to Holyhead and by destroyer to Belfast . . . we must know your answer by ten p.m. tonight. You can have until then, but no longer, to decide whether you will give peace or war to your country.[7]

The Irish delegates were told that each of their signatures would be necessary if orders to resume hostilities were not to be sent to the British military command in Ireland. Lloyd George may have been bluffing but the Irish could not afford to gamble on that

---

[7]Lord Longford, *Peace by Ordeal* (London, 1967), pp. 239–40 [new edition].

assumption and no one knew that better than Michael Collins. Peace had eroded the tight I.R.A. organization and its intelligence system had become far less effective during the idle months of the armistice. Collins and other leaders who had previously been unfamiliar to authorities were now widely recognized. The majority of the Irish population was content with the peace and could not be depended upon by the I.R.A. for future assistance if the war were resumed. By contrast, the British forces had been given a respite with the truce. They had not abandoned their entrenched positions at the time of the cease-fire and they had plenty of reserves to draw upon. The likely outcome of a renewed Anglo-Irish war was painfully apparent to reasonable men like Collins and Griffith. At 2:30 a.m. on December 6, 1921, the Irish delegates affixed their signatures to the agreement which ended 120 years of British rule in all but six counties of Ireland.

De Valera rejected the treaty and also led the opposition when it was subsequently debated in the Dail in January 1922. While it is generally believed that a majority of the population in Southern Ireland favored the treaty because they wanted peace, impassioned speeches for and against the treaty by scores of representatives in the Dail revealed a substantial division among the Irish leadership. When the tally was finally taken, the treaty was ratified by a margin of sixty-four votes to fifty-seven. De Valera promptly resigned as president of the Dail and Arthur Griffith was elected to succeed him. Some I.R.A. commanders refused to accept the verdict of their government and, with the support and encouragement of de Valera and other irreconcilable Republican politicians, they plunged the country into a bloody civil war which lasted until May 1923. It was left to the Provisional Government of the Irish Free State to suppress such internal insurrection since the British Parliament, which transferred official powers to the Free State in March 1922, evacuated all of its forces from Southern Ireland by December of that year. Civil wars are nearly always more vicious than those fought against an alien people, and in this respect the violent internecine struggle among Irishmen was no exception. Rebels who had once fought the state were now themselves the state and they fought their former comrades with more viciousness and brutality than had been witnessed in the Anglo-Irish war. The Irish Free State executed seventy-seven rebels, as compared to twenty-four military executions by the British in 1920-21, and

11,000 men were in internment camps by the end of the civil war. Free State casualties included Arthur Griffith, who died of a heart attack under the strain of leadership in those difficult days, and Michael Collins, who was assassinated in his native County Cork by gunmen from the I.R.A. force he once controlled. This fratricidal conflict has left residual scars upon the Irish community.

On December 6, 1922, the establishment of a Free State Government was proclaimed and the Provisional Government came to an end. In accordance with the provisions of the Anglo-Irish treaty, Northern Ireland was allowed to vote on its own future and it promptly exercised its option not to join the Free State in a decision announced on December 7. Discussions between representatives of Northern and Southern Ireland on the boundary question proved completely fruitless and the new British Prime Minister, Andrew Bonar Law, a longtime Unionist and Ulster ally, opposed any redistricting scheme which threatened the existence of Northern Ireland. Several years of unsuccessful bargaining for the annexation of Ulster's Roman Catholic areas finally led Irish Free State representatives, in an agreement signed in London in 1925, to recognize the boundary of Northern Ireland. In return the English Government relieved the Irish Free State of its obligation to contribute to the British War debt, a concession which scarcely compensated for the perpetuated partition. There was reason for disappointment—none of Ireland's dreams were fulfilled.

> Not the Gaelic League's Irish speaking nation, nor Yeats' literary-conscious people, nor the republic of the I.R.B., nor the worker's republic of Connolly, nor Griffith's economically self-sufficient dual monarchy, nor Redmond's home rule within an empire which the Irish had helped to build, nor Carson's United Kingdom.[8]

The Anglo-Irish treaty provided no solution to Ireland's most critical problem, it merely postponed it once more. The expedient of partition left two Irelands to face an uncertain future.

---

[8]Donal McCartney, "From Parnell to Pearse" in *The Course of Irish History*, ed. T. W. Moody and F. X. Martin (Cork, 1967), p. 312.

IRELAND SINCE PARTITION

The South. Ireland, except for the larger part of Ulster, was after nearly eight hundred years finally free of direct English control. But there was little reason or opportunity to celebrate during the civil war which convulsed the country from June 1922 until May 1923. The conflict left more than six hundred killed, three thousand wounded, and more than £30 million in property destroyed. Out of a population of 2,750,000 in the Free State, about 130,000 were unemployed in 1923. There were also twelve thousand anti-treaty sympathizers, including de Valera, in jails or in internment camps. William T. Cosgrave and Kevin O'Higgins, president and vice-president of the Executive Council of the Dail, provided the strong leadership which the Free State so desperately needed after the deaths of Griffith and Collins. When the Irish Army mutiny of 1924 resulted from the Government's attempt to demobilize its troops following the civil war, political control over the military and the very survival of the state were imperiled. In these circumstances, the Free State Government was at a decided disadvantage in contesting the decisions of the Royal Boundary Commission. Cosgrave's acceptance of the tripartite agreement signed in London, in which Britain, the Irish Free State and Northern Ireland agreed to allow the boundary of the 1920 partition to stand unchanged, was inspired by the recognition that Northern Ireland was an accomplished fact which the Free State could scarcely alter. The South's internal turmoil made a resolution of the problem in the North appear all the more attractive to Dublin.

Cosgrave and O'Higgins were no more reconciled to either limited dominion status or to the partition of their country than were de Valera and his supporters. The former, however, believed as Michael Collins had that while the treaty had not given Ireland the freedom which all nations desire, it did give them "the freedom to achieve it." In 1923 the Irish Free State entered the League of Nations, and in the following year appointed its own minister to Washington, a step which no other dominion had yet attempted. The Irish Free State struck a blow for the principle that dominions were the full equals of Great Britain in the international community by its bid for election to the League of Nations Council in 1926. Furthermore, Cosgrave's representatives assumed leadership roles in the Imperial Conferences of 1926 and 1930, and their views found expression in the British Parliament's Statute of Westminster in 1931 which empowered any dominion to repeal unilaterally United Kingdom legislation hitherto binding in its territory.

In 1924, Eamon de Valera broke his ties with both the Irish Republican Army and with the more militant antitreaty republicans. Neither group wished to seek change through constitutional means, especially since entering the Dail would require taking the hated Oath of Allegiance to the British Crown. De Valera resigned from Sinn Fein in 1926 after failing to reach any agreement on this issue and founded the Fianna Fail (Warriors of Ireland) party. In the general election of June 1927, Fianna Fail won forty-four seats in the Dail—only three fewer than the party in power. Cosgrave followed with an electoral amendment bill designed to vacate the seats of deputies who failed to take the Oath, a parliamentary tactic which forced de Valera and his deputies to capitulate and take the Oath. "The bill had important consequences for Irish democracy in that it compelled the second party in the state to accept a fully responsible role in the parliamentary system and made the change of administration possible in the future."[9] Once the stability of democratic procedures was firmly established within the Irish Free State, its leaders were able to turn their attention to the quest for greater independence and to an end to partition.

When the Fianna Fail party succeeded in winning seventy seats in the general election of March 1932, Eamon de Valera formed his first government with the support of the Labour Party in the Dail. The triumph of the antitreaty Fianna Fail party and de Valera's return from the political wilderness did not reflect any popular endorsement of a republic or the end of partition. De Valera had come to power by calling for larger and more comprehensive doles, protection for Irish industry and repudiation of the debts owed to Britain. He naturally felt no compunction to preserve a treaty he had never supported, and he continued the work Cosgrave had begun with the campaign to achieve greater independence for dominion governments. De Valera proceeded to remove from the Free State Constitution the Oath of Allegiance

---

[9]Timothy Patrick Coogan, *Ireland Since the Rising* (London, 1966), p. 65.

to the Crown, the right of appeal to the British Privy Council from Irish judicial decisions, and British citizenship for Irish citizens. London protested that these unilateral repeals were illegal in that they violated the treaty which was ratified by both governments in 1922. Unmoved, de Valera replied that he regarded the treaty to be illegal and continued his assault by actually deleting all reference to the king from the Irish constitution.

In May 1937, de Valera introduced a new constitution to replace the one which had been imposed upon Ireland sixteen years earlier. It declared the right of the "Irish nation" to choose its own form of government and its relations with other nations. The new constitution also claimed as "national territory" the whole of Ireland but acknowledged that "pending the reintegration of the national territory" the laws of its parliament would apply only to the area of the Irish Free State, an implicit admission that the partition of Ireland was a fact which the Dublin Government remained unable to change. De Valera's proposals were nonetheless sufficiently radical to make the twenty-six counties of the South a republic in everything but name. The new state would be called Eire (Gaelic for Ireland) and would be headed by a president elected by popular vote. Actual power would be exercised by a prime minister and his cabinet, together with a parliament consisting of the Dail and a Senate. In a plebiscite held on July 1, the Irish people approved the new constitution, but not by any significant margin. Uncompromising republicans rejected it because it did not establish the "Republic of Ireland," while other Irishmen seemed unconvinced that any change was necessary. Despite this opposition, the new constitution superseded the Irish Free State on December 29, 1937 and both the British Government and the Dominions declared their acceptance of the country's new name without admitting to any fundamental change in the nature of its government.

Encouraged by his success, de Valera next led a delegation to London in January 1938 where he met with a British delegation headed by Prime Minister Neville Chamberlain. When Northern Ireland Prime Minister Lord Craigavon (the former Sir James Craig) learned that de Valera was making a strong bid for the termination of partition, or at least for the British government's benevolent neutrality in the matter, the Ulster leader called for an election on November 9 on the issue of "no surrender." Unionists in Northern Ireland responded with a strong vote which increased Craigavon's already secure majority in the Stormont Parliament. Craigavon's intention, of course, was to forewarn London and the message was duly received. The British refused to yield on the partition question but sought instead to appease de Valera with other concessions. In place of land annuities and other payments due her, Britain agreed to accept a single, lump sum of £10 million and simultaneously renounced other claims amounting to more than £100 million. Another agreement provided for freedom of trade, subject to specific quotas and preferential duties. Much to the displeasure of Winston Churchill, then a member of Parliament, Prime Minister Chamberlain also consented to abandon the treaty ports. Churchill rejected Chamberlain's reasoning that the removal of this affront to Irish sovereignty would improve relations and he correctly predicted that the concession would prove costly since Ireland would remain neutral if England became involved in any future European war.

Ending partition remained de Valera's major unfinished task. He was opposed to the formal declaration of an Irish Republic precisely because he feared such a step might only serve to perpetuate the division. When World War II began, de Valera resolutely committed his country to neutrality and in taking that action he enjoyed the support of the vast majority of his countrymen. As long as Ireland remained divided by a partition that was supported by Britain, de Valera had no intention of joining Britain in a campaign for democratic freedom and national self-determination. Ireland's neutrality was partly responsible for the country's increased unemployment and rising emigration, but the people endured these and other hardships willingly. Appeals from both Prime Minister Churchill and President Franklin Roosevelt had no effect upon the Irish determination to remain out of the war although morally the Irish people supported the Allied cause. Irish neutrality was, moreover, frequently one-sided. British airmen who parachuted from disabled planes into Ireland were returned safely to England. German airmen were interned in Ireland for the remainder of the war. Thirty thousand Irish recruits voluntarily served in the British armed forces. Germany accepted Ireland's partisan neutrality since the Irish at least denied the use of their ports to the British Navy.

Ireland's first postwar general election was held in 1948 and, after sixteen consecutive years in power, Fianna Fail was defeated. De Valera's party remained the largest party in the Dail but a coalition of opposition parties combined to form a governing majority. There was no consensus evident in the national vote other than a general desire for change for its own sake. John A. Costello of the Fine Gael (Tribe of Gaels) party became the new taoiseach (prime minister). One of the more bizarre developments in modern Irish history followed when Fine Gael, the old protreaty party which had fought the republican antitreaty forces in 1922, passed the Republic of Ireland Bill in the Dail over the opposition of de Valera and other life-long republicans. Costello recommended the formal establishment of an Irish Republic as a means of removing the ambiguities in the constitutional position and of taking "the gun out of politics" in the twenty-six counties.[10] The latter reference was to the nefarious activities of the illegal I.R.A. which operated on both sides of the border. The British Government responded with the Ireland Act of 1949 and fortunately left the new Republic all of the advantages of the old relationship. The Irish would continue to be invested with the same rights and obligations as citizens of the United Kingdom. But the same act also guaranteed Ulster Unionists that Northern Ireland should never leave the United Kingdom unless she did so voluntarily and on her own initiative.

Welfare services, industrialization, and I.R.A. violence constituted some of the major political issues during the 1950s. Southern Irish politicians continued to urge an end to partition but debate on the subject incited fewer passions each year. Eamon de Valera again became head of government from 1951 to 1954, and his tenure was followed by another Fine Gael administration under John Costello from 1954 to 1957; de Valera was returned as taoiseach for the last time in 1957. Two years later he was elected President of the Irish Republic and Sean Lemass succeeded him both as taoiseach and as leader of the Fianna Fail party.

The 1960s seemed to herald the beginning of a new era of greater harmony and understanding in Ireland. Tensions between

---

[10]Patrick Lynch, "Ireland Since the Treaty" in *The Course of Irish History*, ed. T. W. Moody and F. X. Martin (Cork, 1967), p. 331.

North and South were visibly reduced and in 1964 the Northern Ireland Government recognized the all-Ireland Irish Congress of Trade Unions as a negotiating body. The Anglo-Irish free trade agreement of the following year removed economic barriers which had hampered trade between the Republic and the Six Counties. The agreement was highlighted by a dramatic meeting between Sean Lemass, the taoiseach of the Irish Republic, and Captain Terence O'Neill, Prime Minister of Northern Ireland, which held out the promise of closer and more constructive relations between the two parts of Ireland. Eamon de Valera was reelected President of the Republic of Ireland in June 1966 and optimists speculated that the unification of the nation might be achieved during his term of office. But that was before the Civil Rights Association in Ulster (a nonpolitical, nondenominational organization which principally reflected the aspirations and frustrations of Northern Ireland's Catholic middle class) marched in August 1968 as part of a demonstration protesting poor housing in Dungannon. The movement spread and ugly confrontations ensued, leading to the battlegrounds of Londonderry and Belfast where British troops attempted to restrain both Catholic and Protestant militants from engaging in civil war.

Throughout the troubled months of 1971 and early 1972 Jack Lynch, Irish Republic taoiseach since 1966, was increasingly pressured to attack and denounce the Northern Ireland Government in order to mollify outraged Catholics in the South. The abolition of the Stormont Parliament and the extension of direct British rule over Northern Ireland were welcome developments to the Dublin Government which hoped to bring justice and equal rights to Ulster Catholics, and also to isolate and suppress the I.R.A. A reduction of tensions in the North would also permit Dublin itself to act more decisively against the I.R.A. in the South where it is gaining increased influence. In many respects, British intervention and establishment of direct rule over Ulster was a deliverance for the Catholic Republic of Ireland too. No matter how critical conditions might have become in the North, the Dublin Government had neither the military nor material means to alter the situation in the Six Counties.

The North.   Three counties in the historic province of Ulster were surrendered by the Unionists in the Government of Ireland Act,

1920, because their inclusion would have given the region a Catholic nationalist majority. The six remaining counties comprised slightly less than one-fifth of the island but contained about one-third of the island's inhabitants. London never intended to include only those counties with unionist majorities. Tyrone and Fermanagh were made a part of the new state of Northern Ireland despite their nationalist majorities for two reasons: it was hoped that an area large enough to make the North economically and politically viable would pacify the Protestant unionists; and that the security provided by the latter's two-to-one majority over the Catholic nationalists would produce a tolerant northern government which would seek to conciliate and integrate the minority. But it did not. The mood of Ulster unionists was reflected by Sir James Craig, the first Prime Minister of Northern Ireland, who announced that the Six Counties would be a Protestant nation for a Protestant people.

Northern Ireland's inception as a separate state within the United Kingdom in 1920 was accompanied by the most serious outbreak of sectarian violence since the religious riots in Belfast during 1886. Northern Ireland greeted the news of the Anglo-Irish treaty with sullenness in 1921, and responded to the continued civil strife in Ulster by passing the Civil Authorities (Special Powers) Act in 1922 which, after several renewals, was made permanent in 1933. By its terms, the Northern Ireland Minister for Home Affairs and the police were given sweeping powers of search, arrest and imprisonment without trial. Through this and similar means order was restored in the North and Protestant unionist rule perpetuated among the 1,250,000 population, about one-third of whom were Catholic and largely nationalist. The subsequent gerrymandering of constituencies and the large number of Class B special police (11,514 of them supplemented 2,867 regular police in 1936) severely checked nationalist ambitions.

A resurgence of sectarian strife followed the persistent depression and unemployment which gripped Northern Ireland in the 1930s. The two great Ulster industries, linen and ship building, were in decline and agriculture suffered locally and in Britain from the industrial depression. An attack on an Orange demonstration in 1931 set off a wave of reprisals culminating in 1935 with widespread rioting in Belfast which claimed a number of lives. The incidents of violence continued intermittently into the 1940s, and justified, in Unionist eyes, the retention of the Special Powers Act.

Events in the rest of Ireland during this period also helped to sustain old antagonisms in the North. The Irish Free State's dismantling of the Anglo-Irish treaty after 1932, and the new Irish constitution of 1937, gave encouragement to Ulster's nationalists and correspondingly renewed Unionist determination to remain within the United Kingdom and the Empire. Relations between northern and southern Ireland began to improve only after the termination of I.R.A. violence which plagued the border regions during the period between 1956 and 1962. But the apparent lessening of tensions was deceptive and the grievances of the Catholic minority were again manifest in the civil rights movement which began in the late 1960s.

Fear and suspicion kept alive old hatreds between Northern Ireland's Catholics and Protestants. Despite the poverty and unemployment which they shared with Catholics, Ulster workers and farmers followed the political leadership of the ultraright Unionist party. And the leadership of that party used no-popery to control Six County politics and to avoid seriously confronting that region's severe social and economic problems, a burden which was eased by the generosity of the British welfare state. Northern Irish politicians exploited the bigotry of the Protestant masses whose religious zeal is expressed in racist rhetoric. They believe Catholics to be an inferior species: lazy, superstitious, improvident, irresponsible ("they breed like rabbits") and treacherous. Northern Irish Unionists accept as an article of faith that Catholics must be excluded from positions of power lest they destroy the existence of the Six Counties. There is, of course, justification for some of their apprehensions. Most Ulster Catholics are nationalists and they have traditionally regarded the partition of their country as an unholy bargain struck between Orangemen and British politicians.

Catholic ghetto life in the Six Counties has produced a nationalism and cultural alienation much more intense than that in Southern Ireland. Catholics attend parochial schools which emphasize Irish history, culture and language; they play Gaelic football; and their Sunday night socials are frequently traditional folk-type dances. Protestants attend schools emphasizing British history and culture; they play soccer and rugby; and they dance to the rock music popular in Britain. The result has been the growth of two entirely alien and antagonistic culture groups existing side by side in a State made all the more precarious by economic depression and growing unemployment.

Although Irish Protestant alarmists interpreted the civil rights movements of the late 1960s as another subversive attempt by Catholics to achieve union with the Republic, the agitators were actually "more unionist than the Unionists" in that they sought "British standards" of administration. Some Catholic moderates, inspired by the civil rights movement in America, came to appreciate the potential for a better life in a Northern Ireland supported by the British welfare state. A few Unionist politicians also reevaluated the situation and noted that the increasing Catholic population would someday mean a Catholic majority. Apartheid and oppression did not strike them as either attractive or viable permanent policies. Catholic moderates were joined by Protestant liberals in the Northern Ireland Civil Rights Association, a coalition organized in 1967 which included socialists, republicans and university students. They asked the Government to provide jobs, housing, better education, and greater suffrage for the Catholic minority, and marched and demonstrated to rally support for their cause. Northern Ireland Prime Minister Terence O'Neill, partly at the urging of British Prime Minister Harold Wilson, made a few modest concessions which brought an immediate response from the fanatics of the Orange Lodges. Ian Paisley, the archenemy of popery, and William Craig, the leader of the backlash Protestant Vanguard, led the counterattack. Caught between civil rights agitation and Orange fanaticism, O'Neill resigned. His successor, James Chichester-Clark also promised changes but moved too slowly for Catholics and much too quickly for militant Orangemen. He too resigned and was succeeded by yet another moderate, Brian Faulkner. By this time, the days of moderation had passed. Orange extremists, the timidity of politicans, and the impatience of Catholic radicals—socialist and republican—combined to destroy the spirit and influence of the 1967 civil rights movement.[11] But they also destroyed the parliament at Stormont as Brian Faulkner's Northern Ireland Government was displaced by

---

[11]McCaffrey, "The Catholic Minority in the North" in *Divided Ireland,* pp. 52–55.

the extension of British rule over Ulster after civil disorders threatened to plunge the Six Counties into a state of anarchy.

Direct rule from Westminster has provoked the extremists in both parts of Northern Ireland's polarized society. The I.R.A., mindless of life or property, continues its campaign of terror while the Protestant Vanguard organization conducts military drills and speaks darkly of impending civil war. Violence in Ulster is likely to continue until the populations, both Catholic and Protestant, weary of the shootings and the bombings and resolve to conciliate their differences. Only then will there be no sanctuary for the arsonist, and no anonymity for the assassin. Only then will there be any hope for real peace.

Final unity between North and South, Catholic and Protestant, could promote greater liberty in Ireland. If the myths perpetuating religious and regional bigotry were discarded, a common effort could be made to solve the problems of poverty, unemployment, low agricultural production and emigration in all of Ireland. Unity of North and South would help Catholics and Protestants emancipate each other; Protestants from their fears and bigotry, Catholics from their parochialism. Indeed, the influx of a large Protestant minority would diminish the unwholesome influence of the Catholic Church on the Government in the South, leading to a desirable separation of organized religion from the functions of the state. It would also expedite the demise of the Irish Republic's traditional role in enforcing the dictates of Catholic morality, particularly with respect to legislation in the areas of divorce, abortion, birth control and censorship.

The recent course of events in Ireland has introduced new frictions between the North and the South and the prospects for unification, never an imminent likelihood, are dimmer today than at any time since the effecting of partition in 1920. Following the I.R.A. bombing attack in downtown Belfast on "Bloody Friday," July 21, 1972, which left nine persons dead and 130 injured, British administrator for Ulster William Whitelaw abandoned his effort to negotiate a peaceful understanding with I.R.A. militants. He authorized Lieutenant General Sir Harry Tuzo, commander of Britain's twenty-one thousand troops in Northern Ireland, to destroy the barricades which the I.R.A. had retained for nearly three years in Catholic strongholds throughout Belfast and Londonderry. Accompanied by armored convoys and bulldozers, British troops launched an assault at 4 A.M. on July 31 and quickly destroyed the controversial barricades. Mr. Whitelaw subsequently declared Ulster to be completely free, a curious choice of words to describe a community under a virtual state of seige.

BIBLIOGRAPHY

General background reading for the historic roots of the Irish problem

F. S. L. Lyons, *Ireland Since the Famine* (New York, 1971) is the most comprehensive history of modern Ireland available; Lawrence J. McCaffrey's *The Irish Question* (Lexington, Kentucky, 1968) treats with Ireland during the period of union with Britain, 1800–1922, and is decidedly the best short history of this era yet published. Other useful works on the historic background of the Irish problem are: T. W. Moody and F. X. Martin (editors), *The Course of Irish History* (Cork, 1967); Oliver MacDonagh, *Ireland* (Englewood Cliffs, New Jersey, 1968); J. C. Beckett, *The Making of Modern Ireland* (London, 1966); P. S. O'Hegarty, *A History of Ireland Under the Union* (London, 1952); Edmund Curtis, *A History of Ireland* (London, 1936); Brian Inglis, *The Story of Ireland* (London, 1956); Nicholas Mansergh, *Ireland in the Age of Reform and Revolution* (London, 1940).

Ireland during the period of "The Troubles"

Tom Barry, *Guerrilla Days In Ireland* (Dublin, 1949); Piaras Beaslai, *Michael Collins and the Making of a New Ireland,* 2 vols. (Dublin, 1926); Dan Breen, *My Fight for Irish Freedom* (Dublin, 1924); Mary Bromage, *De Valera and the March of a Nation* (London, 1956); Max Caufield, *The Easter Rebellion* (London, 1963); Frank Gallagher, *The Anglo-Irish Treaty* (London, 1965); Edgar Holt, *Protest in Arms* (London, 1960); Dorothy Macardle, *The Irish Republic* (Dublin, 1951); P. S. O'Hegarty, *The Victory of Sinn Fein* (Dublin, 1924); Frank Pakenham, *Peace by Ordeal* (London, 1935); Desmond Ryan, *James Connolly,* (Dublin, 1924).

The North since partition

W. S. Armour, *Ulster, Ireland, Britain* (London, 1938); Dennis Barrit and Charles Carter, *The Northern Ireland Problem* (London, 1962); Frank

Gallagher, *The Indivisible Ireland* (London, 1959); Denis Gwynn, *History of Partition 1912–1925* (Dublin, 1950); Nicholas Mansergh, *The Government of Northern Ireland* (London, 1936); Thomas Wilson, *Ulster Under Home Rule* (London, 1955); Francis W. O'Brien, ed., *Divided Ireland: The Roots of the Conflict* (Rockford, Illinois, 1971); see especially the excellent chapters on the Ulster problem by Donal McCartney and Lawrence J. McCaffrey. The latter's article actually anticipated the extension of direct rule by Britain over Northern Ireland.

The South since partition

Denis Gwynn, *The Irish Free State, 1922–27* (London, 1928); T. D. Williams, ed., *The Irish Struggle* (London, 1966); Nicholas Marsergh, *The Irish Free State: its government and politics* (London, 1934); J. L. McCracken, *Representative government in Ireland: a study of Dail Eireann, 1919–48* (London, 1958); Donal O'Sullivan, *The Irish Free State and its Senate* (London, 1940); Francis Mac Manus, ed., *The Years of the Great Test, 1926–1939* (Cork, 1967); Cornelius O'Leary, *The Irish Republic* (Notre Dame, 1961); Timothy Pat Coogan, *Ireland Since the Rising* (London, 1966); Timothy Pat Coogan, *The I.R.A.* (London, 1970).

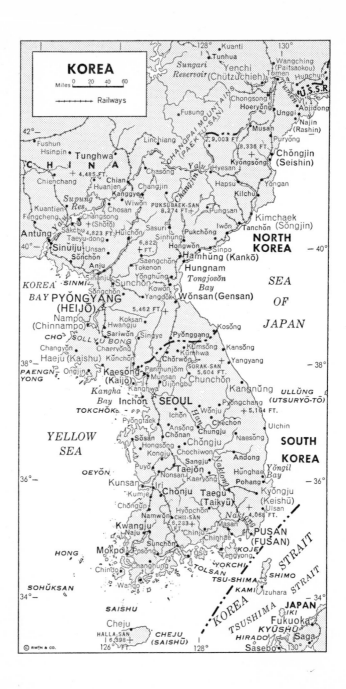

Chapter 2.

The Partition of Korea: Cold War Casualty

Hilary Conroy
and
Wayne Patterson
University of Pennsylvania

INTRODUCTION AND BACKGROUND

Korea's partition in 1945 was an especially traumatic experience for the Korean nation. As in several other divided countries, Korea's partition was consummated against the will of the people, following no natural ethnic or linguistic dividing lines. The act of division also flew in the face of the historic unity of the Korean nation, a nation which had been a single national unit since the seventh century, and which had exhibited a strikingly high degree of homogeneity.

Korea, occupying a peninsula attached to the Chinese mainland, first came to the attention of the Han Dynasty in the second century. In order to secure its flanks against the Hsiung-nu invaders from the Northwest, China quickly restructured the primarily tribal organization of the peninsula into military commanderies controlled by Chinese generals. With the fall of the Han Dynasty in the third century and the subsequent weakening of these Chinese organizations in Korea, the indigenous tribal clans drove out the Chinese and reasserted their control by the end of the fourth century. From this loose confederation of tribes, three "states" emerged: Koguryŏ, Paekche, and Silla, each intent upon establishing hegemony over the entire peninsula. After three centuries of fighting among the three, Silla, with the aid of the newly-installed T'ang Dynasty in China, was able to bring the country under its rule in 675.

From this time forward, Korea's politics and culture became intertwined with China's as Korea assumed a position in international relations of a Chinese "tributary" or dependent state. Korea not only modeled many of its institutions after the Chinese, but also benefited from the protective stance assumed by its nominal overlord. The historical Chinese protective instinct toward Korea manifested itself in three key events: the Hideyoshi invasions from Japan in the 1590s, the opening of the "hermit kingdom" by the West in the second half of the nineteenth century, and, most important for our topic, the Korean War of 1950.

With Chinese protection assured, centralized dynasties were established. In 918, the Koryo Dynasty (from which we get the term "Korea") established itself upon the foundations of the Silla state. However, the twin evils of foreign invasion—embodied by the thirteenth century Mongol attacks and the depredations of Japanese pirates in the fourteenth century—and internal factionalism, combined to bring about the demise of Koryo and the creation of the Yi Dynasty in 1392.

The Yi Dynasty proved to be susceptible to foreign invasion as well when Hideyoshi attempted to conquer Korea as a stepping stone to the conquest of Ming China. Forty years later, Korea was invaded by the Manchus who subsequently became the Ch'ing Dynasty in China.

By now it should be clear that Korea, occupying a strategic position on the Asian continent, had become a bone of contention, a pawn for the larger powers surrounding it. This was to remain the case even though the Chinese and Japanese were replaced by the Russians and the Americans. Korea could remain independent only by possessing a strong and powerful regime, but by the middle of the nineteenth century this did not seem possible, as factionalism, corruption, agricultural stagnation, institutional rigidity, and other aspects of dynastic decline set in.

This perspective became more clear as Japan, upon "opening" Korea in 1876, rapidly became involved in the internal politics of Korea. The increasing influence of liberal Japanese aroused sentiments in the Korean court for progressive reform, but also caused a reaction by China, Korea's "elder brother," which suppressed this reformist movement in 1884. From 1884 to 1894, China had the upper hand in Korean affairs, but the antiforeign Tonghak Rebellion provided an opportunity for the Japanese to challenge the Chinese position. This resulted in a war in 1894–95 in which the Japanese were easily victorious. The Japanese, having eliminated China from its predominant position of influence, now faced increasing Russian influence there. Fearing a threat to their security, the Japanese leaders tried to negotiate Russia out of Korea. In these negotiations, Japan, having just made an alliance with England in 1902, tried to persuade Russia to accept Japan's predominant position in Korea in exchange for Japanese recognition of Russia's predominant position in Manchuria. Russia would have no part of this and countered with a proposal to divide Korea at the 39th parallel. Here was the first mention of the feasibility of dividing Korea to assuage two big powers. This proposal was to recur forty years later, and, as before, the wishes of the Korean people were not considered. Naturally, the Japanese wanted a Korea entirely free of Russian influence and so the negotiations broke down and in the next year, 1904, war broke out.

The Russian defeat at the hands of the modernized Japanese army allowed Japan a free hand in Korea, which became a protectorate. Japanese influence gradually increased when foreign acquiescence and annexation, which had been discussed for several years, occurred in 1910, marking the downfall of the Yi Dynasty.

Korean appeals to Western nations (particularly America) were to no avail as the military rule of the Japanese Governor-General Terauchi remained. The death of the last Yi emperor in 1919 became the occasion for a mass movement protesting Japanese rule. Known as the March First Movement and similar in scope to the Chinese May Fourth Movement, voices were raised asserting the aspirations for Korean independence. Although Japan subsequently relaxed its rule, changing to a "cultural policy," Japanese rule remained nevertheless, stifling any effective independence movement on the part of the Korean nation.

Korean nationalists were not quiescent during the annexation period. Some went to the United States, Syngman Rhee being the most prominent, to appeal to the conscience of the American government which was morally committed to the Wilsonian ideal of national self-determination. But the United States could hardly criticize Japan's rule in Korea without undermining its own colonial policy in the Philippine Islands. So, Rhee's effort to have the United States declare its support for Korean independence, far from being successful, earned him the status of a nuisance to the United States government in the interwar years. Rhee was more successful with the many overseas Koreans in Hawaii and the United States who were sympathetic to his cause and who supported the nationalist movement financially during these years.

In China, the Korean nationalist movement became organized as the Korean Provisional Government (KPG) with which Rhee was aligned, in 1919. Centered in Shanghai, the KPG was a government in exile to take over the reins of leadership upon the advent of Korean independence. Leadership was in the hands of the rightists Kim Kyu-sik and Kim Ku while Rhee, himself a rightist, was in America. The existence of the KPG was a shaky one due to factionalism, policy differences, the meager funds available, and the seeming unshakeable Japanese hold on Korea. The dormant KPG organization was split into left and right wings by 1924 and from 1927 to 1931 it was allied with the Communists. After 1931, as the Japanese pressed on into China, the KPG came increasingly to rely upon the Nationalist government in Nanking under Chiang Kai-shek in the common fight against Japanese aggression. Following the China Incident of 1937, the KPG followed the Kuomintang government to the wartime capital of Chungking to wait out the war.

A third strand of the nationalist movement was the communist one. This group began among the immigrants who had fled from Japanese control to Siberia from 1910-20 and who came into contact with Bolshevism following the October (1917) Revolution. By allying themselves with the Comintern, the Korean Communists had access to a ready supply of funds. Another advantage was ideological. The Korean Communists could explain Japanese action as capitalistic exploitation; but socialism, as well as independence, was their goal. However, as with the KPG, factionalism and policy conflicts cut the effectiveness of the movement, a weakness that could not be eliminated even by an alliance with the Nationalists from 1927 to 1931.

In Korea proper, the efficient Japanese police worked with amazing effectiveness to prevent any nationalist successes. In addition, the inability to organize an effective underground operation greatly hampered the activities of nationalists and communists alike. Outside of Korea, in Manchuria, small guerrilla bands operating either independently or in connection with the Chinese Communists initiated small-scale harassing activities and terroristic attacks against the famed Kwantung Army. It was from these groups that Kim Il-sŏng, the present ruler of North Korea, rose to prominence.

With the outbreak of war in 1937, Korea was transformed into a supply base for the Japanese military effort, providing food, clothing, material, and later, manpower. With the entire population mobilized, the economy was transformed from a completely agricultural one to a partially industrial one oriented toward Japan's economic system.

Politically, the harsh rule of Japan permitted no efficient organization or leadership to emerge during the colonial experience. There was no consensus among Korean intellectuals about the road Korea should take and the lack of institutionalization permitted little or no political experience.

OCCUPATION AND COLD WAR POLITICS

As the war progressed and an Allied victory became more and more certain, thought began to turn to the ordering of the postwar world. In this vein, the Atlantic Charter of 1941 asserted the right of self-determination of all peoples and planning for the United Nations was begun. Korea was first mentioned specifically by the Allied Powers at the Cairo Conference in 1943. Here it was stated that " . . . *in due course* Korea shall become free and independent." Koreans translated this as meaning independence immediately or within a few days.

President Franklin D. Roosevelt's plans for Korea were for a trusteeship lasting perhaps for forty years, after the model of the Philippines. Although he later reduced the time length, he was able to persuade Joseph Stalin at the Teheran Conference to support a four-power trusteeship, run by a multipower centralized military government. Harry Hopkins later obtained Stalin's reaffirmation of his trusteeship stand.

More immediate concerns involved the successful ending of the war. Although the United States developed the atomic bomb, it still wanted the Soviet Union to enter the war against Japan as agreed upon at the Yalta Conference because American planners overestimated the size of the Kwantung Army. Consequently, after the first bomb at Hiroshima on August 6, the Soviet Union attacked Japanese forces in Manchuria and Korea, advancing rapidly. As their advance continued and even though there was no need for American troops, the War Department did not want the Soviets to occupy the entire peninsula. So, sometime between August 9 and August 10, the Operations Division of the War Department proposed a *temporary* division of Korea at the 38th parallel (rejecting the 39th parallel as unfeasible) north of which Russian troops and south of which American troops would disarm the Japanese. This plan was quickly approved by the Joint Chiefs of Staff (JCS), the State, War, Navy Coordinating Committee (SWNCC), and the new President, Harry S. Truman, who obtained Stalin's agreement on August 13. On the next day the Japanese surrendered unconditionally and the decision was communicated to General MacArthur.

Just as in Vietnam and Germany, the division of Korea was supposed to be temporary, after which joint control would extend throughout Korea. It never occurred to Truman, who relied on military thinking, that the division would be permanent. Others in the State Department took a different view. Among these, Averill Harriman recommended airlifts of U.S. soldiers to the north. Nevertheless, the primary objective was to prevent Soviet occupation of the entire peninsula, an event which was considered inevitable without an agreement of some kind.

In Korea after the Japanese surrender, General Abe Nobuyuki, the governor-general, sought to create a transition government run by Koreans which would safeguard Japanese lives and property. Assuming that the Soviet Union would occupy the entire peninsula and ignorant of the division plans, he sought out a left-wing leader. Accordingly, he found Lyuh Woon-hyung, former publisher of *Chung-ang Ilbo* and leader of the Alliance for Korean Independence, an underground organization formed in 1944. Lyuh formed a leftist government, the Korean People's Republic, on August 15, 1945. The ranks of the new government, which had Japanese backing, were swelled by many communists and nationalists who were released from jail. Local branches, known as People's Committees, soon proliferated. This interim government soon gained the allegiance of much of the Korean population as it extended its control and legitimacy, taking over most of the functions of a national government.

This was the situation when General John R. Hodge, Commander of the 24th Division in Okinawa, was ordered to proceed to Korea to administer the surrender and disarming of Japanese troops south of the 38th parallel, to establish an effective government, and to train Koreans for self-government.

How well-equipped was Hodge for this task? In the twenty months that had elapsed from the Cairo Conference, where Korea was first mentioned, to the Japanese surrender, there was no planning at all for Korea. Admittedly, the development of the A-bomb ended the war sooner than most planners had expected, but when Hodge arrived on September 8, he had only a few men trained in civil affairs and one Japanese expert. He had no one who was an expert on Korea assisting him. In addition, his instructions were meager and ambiguous. So, upon arrival, Hodge, having no knowledge of the existence of the People's Republic nor any indication of its great degree of support and lacking specific instructions, viewed the government as a communist front because rightists were excluded and ordered it dissolved. Hodge thus asserted that his military government was the only legal government, retained the Japanese temporarily in their offices, and threatened death to anyone who disobeyed his directives. As such, Korea was administered as an occupied, rather than a liberated, area which did little to engender friendly feelings toward the United States.

The disintegration of the People's Republic meant that a power vacuum existed. Factions multiplied as dozens of parties on the left and right emerged, some with only a handful of followers. Among the more prominent individuals were: the rightist Syngman Rhee (Yi Sŭng-man), Kim Ku, and Kim Kyu-sik, all members of the KPG who returned to Korea as individuals and not at the head of an exile government. Amidst the flurry, the military government tacitly aided the rightist parties on the advice of American missionaries and because, for the most part, they were English-speaking.

John Carter Vincent, Chief of Far Eastern Affairs in the State Department, announced that United States policy was a four-power trusteeship of short duration. Trusteeship plans were based on the assumption of Allied harmony and this harmony prevailed at the Moscow Conference which was held on December 15, 1945. At this meeting Secretary of State Byrnes agreed with Molotov and Stalin on a trusteeship of short duration. However, even here strains began to appear. The Russians wanted to set up a provisional Korean government while the United States pushed for trusteeship and even tried to extend it to ten years to prevent Russian domination of Korea.

Koreans right and left opposed the trusteeship and United States prestige fell to a low ebb as the people feared an indefinite trusteeship. Paradoxically, as antitrusteeship demonstrations broke out in South Korea, General Hodge called for immediate independence and denounced trusteeship as a communist plot. As he was belatedly informed by the State Department that trusteeship was official United States policy, his change of posture not only infuriated Koreans, but his initial pronouncement aroused Soviet suspicions of United States intentions which were later to be exacerbated. Thus, an incoherent and fluctuating policy operated in the American zone.

Whereas the American occupation took the form of a military government which refused to allow Koreans to share in the administration and which possessed meager information and instructions, the Soviet occupying forces seemed a little better prepared. While their plans were the same as the United States, that is, to form a government not hostile to them, they gained a tactical advantage by ruling through the already-existing People's Committees, the local branches of the People's Republic, and did not erect a military government.

Accompanying the Red Army was a Korean of relatively unknown origin, Kim Il-sŏng. Kim had not belonged to the "old" Korean Communist Party but had fought under the Chinese guerrillas in Manchuria, commanding the Sixth Division of the First

Route Army of the Northeast Anti-Japanese Allied Army under the Communist General Yang Ching-yu. Born in 1912 in south Pyongan Province, he traveled to Manchuria in 1925 to attend Chinese schools. He soon became a leading figure in the East Kirin Area Communist Youth Association, an organ of the Chinese Communist Party. From 1931 to 1941, he fought the Japanese in Manchuria, never commanding more than two or three hundred guerrillas. By 1941, increasing Japanese pressure caused him to flee to Siberia where, apparently, he made contacts with the Russian Army. Rumored to have fought in the battle of Leningrad, Kim, with a rank of major, appeared in the Soviet occupying army led by General Chistiakov.

Kim's candidacy for leadership of the North Korean government was promoted by the Russians. Initially, a coalition government headed by Kim and Kim Tu-bong was used as a facade for Soviet control. In this government many nationalists served but real power resided in the hands of Kim and his "new" communists, as members of the North Korean Workers' Party.

How were Kim and his "new" communists able to supplant the indigenous or "old" communists? Aside from Russian help, the ruthless effectiveness of the Japanese police had severely weakened the indigenous communists. Secondly, most were located at Seoul, the capital, which was located in the American zone, where they engaged in terrorism, strikes, and demonstrations against American rule, leaving the North with few communists. Third, they failed to appraise accurately the semipermanent nature of the occupation and the Cold War situation. It should have been obvious that more fertile ground for their activities could have been found in the North, but led by Pak Hŏn-yŏng, they futilely continued agitation in the South. Soon, the covert suppression of communists in the American zone became active and overt, beginning with the Chŏngp 'an-sa counterfeiting incident in 1946. After this, the "old" communists began to migrate North where they found Kim and the "new" communists firmly entrenched with Russian aid. Failing to unite with Kim or work with the Russians, the unorganized "old" communists became easy marks for Kim's purges. Pak himself was executed in 1955 as an American spy.

As mentioned earlier, in South Korea, people of all political persuasions, including the communists, denounced the trusteeship decision as an abridgement of sovereignty. But halfway through the antitrusteeship demonstrations, the communists, apparently on instructions from Moscow, changed their stand and supported trusteeship. This seemingly inconsequential event subsequently took on great importance. A U.S.-U.S.S.R. Joint Commission was established to negotiate a unification of the two sides with Korean participation. Presumably, the Koreans who would work with the Joint Commission were to be the new Korean government. During the negotiations, however, the Soviet Union wanted to exclude from consultation any Korean who opposed the Moscow Decision. This would mean that anyone who opposed the trusteeship proposal could not share in the formation of the new government and since only the leftist elements had come out in favor of trusteeship, this meant that rightists and moderates would be excluded, making the new government a leftist one. This was clearly unacceptable to the U.S. and the first Joint Commission ended in failure on May 8, 1946.

The failure of the U.S. and the U.S.S.R. to agree in Korea was mirrored in other similar imbroglios in the Far East. The virtual monopoly of the U.S. in the occupation of Japan by MacArthur was bitterly resented by the Soviet Union. Consequently, the Far Eastern Commission (FEC) was chosen to direct MacArthur with the Allies participation. The U.S., unwilling to allow Russian influence in its occupation, allowed MacArthur to operate on an "interim" basis in case of a Soviet veto in the FEC, thus forestalling any Russian initiatives.

The building Russo-American antagonism caused hope to fade in Korea for an end to their division. The Americans began to suppress the communists more harshly now. At this point, U.S. policy made another shift. Having courted rightists like Rhee, who was causing the U.S. considerable embarrassment by advocating a separate state in the South, and Kim Ku, head of the old KPG, the military government was now ordered to build up the moderate elements in South Korean society. In vain, Hodge tried to effect a coalition between Lyuh Woon-hyung and Kim Kyu-sik as a third force between the leftists and the rightists. This is an example of the vacillating policy of the U.S. in Korea.

The Joint Commission was finally reconvened in May 1947. But Rhee and Kim Ku were still opposed to trusteeship and the Soviet

Union again refused to consult with them. Thus a stalemate was reached. A severe anticommunist witchhunt in the South, which certainly must have damaged Russian estimates of American good faith caused the Commission to adjourn on August 28, 1947. It failed because both the U.S. and the U.S.S.R. wanted to set up a nation to serve their own national interests.

Acting Secretary of State Lovett proposed a substitute to the Moscow plan, calling for a meeting of the four powers and the holding of general elections under the supervision of the United Nations. When this was not accepted by the Soviet Union, the U.S. took the Korean problem to the UN in September 1947, feeling that no "satisfactory" solution could come at the bilateral level. This decision to wash their hands of the Korean problem and throw it to the UN may also have come from a Joint Chiefs of Staff judgment that Korea was not worth stationing U.S. soldiers (45,000 in 1947) due to the financial drain on the U.S. and the restiveness of the Korean people. By handing the problem to the UN, the U.S. would have a good chance of having things come out more satisfactorily than in the Joint Commission.

In the UN, the Soviet Union objected to the consideration of Korea by that body, pointing to an already existing agreement (the Moscow Conference). The United States rejected this argument and formed the United Nations Temporary Commission on Korea (UNTCOK), an ad hoc committee of eleven nations, to circumvent a Soviet veto in the Security Council. UNTCOK called for nation-wide elections in Korea. The Russians retaliated by demanding the withdrawal of all occupation troops (the Russian Army had left by December 24, 1948). In general though, the United Nations was reluctant to engage in activities which would perpetuate the division in Korea. This became a distinct possibility when the Soviet Union indicated that it would not allow elections to be held in its zone. Since two-thirds of Korea's population was located in the South, a nationwide election would have been unfavorable to the North. But pressured by the United States, UNTCOK prepared to hold elections in South Korea only.

Turning the Korean question over to the UN was the first step in the American attempt to get out of Korea. But domestic matters still had to be resolved. If the U.S. Army were to be withdrawn, a Korean army had to be formed. Originally Rhee and Hodge had clamored for the establishment of an army but MacArthur vetoed the proposal because he knew that the Russians would call it perfidious.

Nevertheless, the military government secretly sponsored anticommunist youth groups which could be used as an army if talks with the Russians failed. A more important element was the police. The police, the military government's chief instrument of rule and riddled by factionalism and corruption, included many Japanese collaborators. The police were used against liberals, left-wingers, and anyone opposed to the government. For the general populace, this meant searches and harassment which, when resisted, evoked charges of communism by the military government.

These two groups, then, the police and the youth groups plus former troops and officers in the Japanese Army, were to be used as a nucleus for an army when the time arrived. The issue of building an army was given further definition by General Albert C. Wedemeyer who, having just returned from China, advocated an independent army. As Russo-American relations deteriorated, a Constabulary Training Center was established to train officers in a country which had no strong military tradition. Most of the Koreans who entered had served in the Japanese Army.

On the political scene in South Korea, preparations got under way for the coming UN-sponsored elections. Rhee's group, the National Society for the Acceleration of Korean Independence began activities with U.S. support. Many other right-wing groups proliferated as factionalism was prevalent. U.S. policy, which had first supported the rightists, and had then switched to support the moderates, again supported the rightists who would set up an anticommunist administration.

The political scene was chaotic. Political parties took on the aspect of fluid associations made up of opportunistic individuals formed for access to power. Groups, *per se,* were perceived to be unworthy of loyalty as men would always place personal power desires above the value of remaining with the group and helping it to gain power. Thus, most candidates were independents, affiliated with no party and there were many defections from one party to another. Long range interests were ill-defined, condemning political parties to transiency.

Moderates as well as leftists and communists (South Korean Workers Party) were opposed to the UNTCOK election because they foresaw that elections in South Korea alone would probably result in a permanent partition of their homeland. In a last-ditch attempt to stave off this "half-election", Kim Kyu-sik and Kim Ku, former Rhee supporters-turned-liberals, went to Pyongyang on the invitation of Northern leaders to negotiate a unification devoid of big power and UN interference. Even though this North-South conference was a failure, Kim Ku returned south and became one of Rhee's most formidable opponents.

The elections were held on May 10, 1948 with many moderates and liberals refusing to participate. The remaining communists attempted to sabotage the elections. Thus, mostly rightists ran for office and Rhee's slate won the majority of the votes for the National Assembly, with seventy-five percent of the population participating in the first election ever held in Korea. On May 31, Rhee was elected chairman of the Assembly. On July 20, he was elected President of the Republic of Korea with Yi Si-yŏng as Vice-President. He was inaugurated on July 24th and on August 15th, the Rhee government formally took over from the U.S. military government.

With the establishment of a separate and independent South Korean government which the UN regarded as the legitimate *de jure* government of all Korea, many avenues of unification were closed. In retaliation, North Korea ratified a constitution on September 3, 1948 and on the following day Kim Il-sŏng was elected premier by a Supreme People's Assembly which had been elected earlier. Kim had obtained nearly complete control by using Stalinist-type tactics. Internally, North Korea quickly undertook reforms such as equality of the sexes, an eight-hour day, confiscation of land held by Japanese and Korean landlords and its redistribution (to the peasants) in a land reform program, a drive against collaborators with the Japanese, and the nationalization of industry. In international affairs, the North Korean regime leaned heavily on the Soviet Union for military and economic assistance as their attitude toward South Korea hardened and guerrilla warfare in South Korea was encouraged.

In the South, the constitution which bore Rhee's stamp created arbitrary rule with a democratic facade. Article 28 included "restrictions" when necessary for public order. Article 57 provided for "emergency measures." Although on paper the system looked like a strong legislative government, it was conducive to a predominantly executive government and thus a tendency to autocracy. Only Rhee's personality could determine the path that Korea would take, as his role as a precedent-setter was crucial if democracy were to succeed. In a constitution in which people's rights were only nominally guaranteed, and in which separation of powers was rejected, Rhee had free rein. Rhee, however, had an egocentric personality. His administration was dominated by personalism as he kept the bureaucracy mobile and dependent upon him by frequent turnovers, dismissing those ministers who did not follow his lead. Obviously, he did not appoint any adherents of Kim Ku and Kim Kyu-sik to important posts.

The regime turned further away from democracy when an army mutiny at Yosu in October 1948 gave Rhee the excuse to pass a National Security Law which suspended civil liberties. Many political arrests were made as "communists" were jailed. Press regulations went into effect, newspapers were closed, and "leftist" teachers were fired. When members of the National Assembly protested these acts, they were arrested and convicted in farcical judicial proceedings. Finally, with the 1950 elections approaching, Kim Ku was assassinated under mysterious circumstances, removing Rhee's foremost antagonist. The convicted assassin, An, was sentenced to life imprisonment, but served only three years of his sentence, was released, and rose to high rank in the South Korean Army during the Korean War.

The South Korean economy was also in a state of chaos. Having been geared to the Japanese economy for thirty-five years, the Korean economy was far from self-sufficient for its own domestic needs. Secondly, there was no exchange of goods between the North, with an abundance of industry and electricity, and the agricultural South. Third, the exodus of trained Japanese personnel after the war represented a "brain drain." Fourth, a heavy influx of refugees from North Korea added even more burdens to an economy that was operating at only ten percent of prewar levels.

In spite of these problems in politics and the economy, despite increasing tension along the border with North Korea, and despite $181.2 million of American aid between 1946 and 1948, the

United States continued to withdraw, giving only economic aid. Notwithstanding appeals by the Korean National Assembly to remain with troops, the U.S., sensitive to the fact that Soviet troops had already been withdrawn in the north removed all American troops by July 1, 1949, leaving behind only UN observers to monitor North Korean military actions against the South, and a small military advisory group under U.S. Ambassador Muccio. Requests for military assistance were given little consideration, perhaps because Rhee was constantly threatening to invade the North, and the Korean Aid Bill received bad treatment in Congress. By March, 1949, Republic of Korea security forces numbered only 114,000 ill-equipped men.

South Korea was certainly unprepared to wage war and the U.S. seemed to be indicating that it would not support the Republic of Korea. The Joint Chiefs of Staff and General Wedemeyer, stressing a manpower shortage, stated that Korea was of no strategic interest to U.S. security. On January 12, 1950, Secretary of State Dean Acheson, in a speech to the National Press Club, excluded Korea and Taiwan from the U.S. Pacific defense perimeter. General MacArthur publicly reiterated Acheson's defense perimeter view. Seven weeks before the outbreak of the Korean War, Senator Tom Connally, Democratic Chairman of the Senate Foreign Relations Committee, declared that Korea would have to be abandoned. Republicans were later to charge that the Democratic administration had given an open invitation to North Korean and Soviet aggression in South Korea.

But this policy was only one part of a two-part paradoxical policy. On the one hand, the U.S. was withdrawing from the Far East because of a severe manpower shortage in which men were needed in Europe and, on the other hand, the U.S. was becoming more intent on stopping communist aggression. This second aspect of U.S. Far Eastern policy on the eve of the Korean War had been evolving since the end of World War II.

Our relations with the Soviet Union had been cordial during the war, but began to shift immediately afterwards. Based on a series of events and perceptions, this new ideological outlook was best expressed by George Kennan in 1947. He stated, "... it [the United States] must continue to regard the Soviet Union as a rival, not a partner, in the political arena, . . . [this rivalry was] in essence a test of the overall worth of the U.S. as a nation among nations

... by providing the American people with this implacable challenge."[1] Kennan's answer to this challenge was the famous "containment" policy against the spread of International Communism.

Struggles against communism in Iran, Greece, and Turkey (1946–47) gave rise to the Truman Doctrine which was offered to prevent communist expansion and which was consonant with containment. The Berlin Crisis of 1948 and the subsequent formation of NATO in 1949 hardened the already existing Cold War lines. The French were losing to the Vietminh in Indochina and the Soviet Union exploded its first atomic bomb in 1949. Perhaps the most serious jolt was the victory of Mao Tse-tung and the Chinese Communists in October, 1949, the signing of the Sino-Soviet Friendly Alliance Pact, and the retreat of the U.S.-backed Nationalist regime of Chiang Kai-shek to northern Burma and the island of Formosa.

Thus, the United States, by 1949, while apprehensive about war, saw the world as bipolar, threatening and requiring the use of force. This thinking is best exemplified by Dean Acheson, Secretary of State, who viewed the Soviet Union as the wellspring of international communism bent on world aggression. In such a situation, he reasoned, negotiation was futile. Instead, we should pump up our allies militarily and economically to meet the threat.

Given this situation and these attitudes, several things occurred. Irrational anticommunism in the form of McCarthyism was born. The National Security Council declared that an increase in military spending was necessary to counter Russian advances. The decision was made to rearm Japan in the fight against communism. Finally, a strong commitment to collective security, as embodied in the UN, was made.

Nevertheless, the policies in force on the eve of the Korean War indicated that the U.S. was prepared to lose Korea and would not intervene in the Chinese civil war.

South Korea on the eve of the Korean War was plagued by armed insurrection which gave Rhee an additional excuse to use the emergency powers given him in the constitution. As the elections for the legislature loomed in May 1950, inflation and severe repression made Rhee very unpopular. Under a pretext, Rhee announced that these elections might be postponed. Only when

---

[1]"X," "The Source of Soviet Conduct," *Foreign Affairs,* Vol. 26 (July, 1947), 580.

Acheson advised him that U.S. aid would be reviewed were measures against inflation undertaken and elections held. The result of these May 30, 1950, elections was defeat for Rhee's supporters and, had the Korean War not intervened, Rhee would most likely have been forced out. Finally, half-hearted attempts at unification continued as many private meetings between the two sides took place without success.

THE KOREAN WAR

Meanwhile, throughout the spring of 1950, intelligence reports indicated a North Korean buildup and an accompanying move toward the South, but General MacArthur predicted only continuing guerrilla warfare for the remainder of the summer. Washington apparently agreed with his assessment and even went so far as to transfer men out of the Korean Military Advisory Group (KMAG).

The North Korean attack began at 4 a.m. on June 25, 1950. The United Nations Security Council voted 9-0 (the Soviet Union being absent) to condemn the aggression. By June 30, President Truman had committed U.S. ground troops in Korea and by interposing the Seventh Fleet in the Formosa Straits and interfering with the Chinese civil war, created another divided country. Truman also began massive aid to the French effort in Indochina and a third country, Vietnam, was on its way to partition as the Domino Theory came to complement containment.

It is clear then, that there was something lacking in our policy toward Korea. In the first place, the personal diplomacy of Roosevelt and the early policy of Truman were founded on military considerations which were based on Russo-American cooperation in the joint war effort. The State Department, which had doubts about Soviet intentions, was not consulted. Later, the 38th parallel scheme was a disaster. It would have been preferable to have a unified administration of the entire country. Third, the idea of trusteeship in which Korea would receive forty years of political tutelage like the Philippines completely ignored the will of the Korean people and aroused their ire against the U.S. Fourth, there was a lack of coordination between the occupation authorities and the policy planners in Washington which often caused conflicting and contradictory policies. Finally, the ineffectiveness of our policy was largely due to Korea's assumed remoteness from American national interest since the U.S. was Europe-oriented.

Two questions immediately arise: why was there a sudden change in U.S. policy? and who started the war? The answers to both are still far from satisfactory.

Reasons often given for the shift in U.S. policy mention that the attack represented a challenge to collective security, to the security of Japan, and to the "Free World" in general. Others mention the necessity of standing up to the Soviet Union for the benefit of NATO. Still others note the rising tide of McCarthyism at home which necessitated a militant response to communist aggression anywhere in the world.

The question of placing responsibility for the war has also seen much speculation. The official U.S. version is that North Korea, with Russian aid and encouragement, tried to unify the country by force of arms. This action was viewed as a Soviet effort to divert Western pressures from Europe. Others, particularly the Republicans, attribute Soviet motivation to the scant interest shown by the U.S. in Korea. A third view of Soviet motives notes the possibility of counteracting the separate U.S. peace treaty being negotiated with Japan. A fourth idea suggests that Stalin wanted to bring war between the United States and China. However, all these explanations are subject to reservation. For example, if the Russians were behind the attack, why did they boycott a Security Council meeting at which they could have vetoed branding North Korea an aggressor? The U.S.S.R. had been protesting the inclusion of the Nationalist, rather than the Communist Chinese, regime in the Security Council. Furthermore, the Russians had withdrawn their forces much earlier than the U.S. had. Yet, it could be argued that the Russians thought the UN an ineffective body and expected North Korea to win the war quickly.

A second body of opinion on the cause of the war attributes guilt to North Korea which hoped to force the U.S.S.R. to back it in a scheme to unify the Korean nation by force.

The third theory states that Syngman Rhee deliberately provoked the North Koreans in the hope that they would retaliate by crossing the border in force, necessitating U.S. aid and intervention. This view cannot be entirely ruled out because of the known bellicosity of Rhee's attitudes toward the North.

This view also implicates the U.S., charging that the covert diplomacy of General MacArthur and John Foster Dulles counteracted Acheson's defense perimeter notion by providing the South Korean leadership with inside knowledge that the U.S. would in fact support them. This may have emboldened the South Korean leadership to take action. Also, according to I. F. Stone, high-ranking Chinese Nationalists in the U.S. made a thirty million dollar killing on the soybean futures market due to the war-caused disruption. Aside from pure luck, only advance inside information could have resulted in such a windfall. Secretary of State Acheson refused to discuss the soybean affair when asked about it by reporters.[2]

To meet the North Korean attack, the U.S. organized a defense by UN forces under the rubric of collective security and based their action on the Uniting for Peace Resolution in the General Assembly. General MacArthur was placed in charge of the UN troops which battled the North Koreans back across the 38th parallel and into North Korea toward the Yalu River, the border between North Korea and China. Carrying the war into North Korea by UN forces represented a breach in the spirit of collective security, for collective security requires that the united forces return the situation to the *status quo ante bellum,* and not make war on the aggressor after his initial breach of the peace has been rectified. This action caused the heretofore "limited war" to assume larger dimensions as Chinese "volunteers" entered to turn the tide and MacArthur, in turn, advocated atomic bombing to decimate major Chinese cities which were serving as "sanctuaries" for the Chinese and North Korean war effort.

After two years of back and forth fighting, a cease fire, suggested by the U.S.S.R., was implemented by Prime Minister Nehru of India and truce talks were initiated in the small town of Panmunjom. Finally, in July 1953 a truce was signed with Korea remaining divided essentially along the same line as before the war. Two months later, South Korea signed a mutual defense treaty with the

---

[2]I. F. Stone, *The Hidden History of the Korean War* (New York, 1952) pp. xi–xii.

United States. The war took a toll of four million lives and cost three billion dollars, and Korea was devastated economically.

SOUTH KOREA SINCE THE KOREAN WAR

In South Korea, the war worked to the advantage of Rhee. When the war began, utilizing martial law, he acted to silence his opponents. After creating the Liberal Party in 1951 to organize his forces for the 1952 elections, he introduced a constitutional amendment which would allow the direct election of the President, instead of indirect election by members of the National Assembly. This was necessary if Rhee were to remain President in the face of a legislature hostile to him. The amendment was soundly defeated in the National Assembly so Rhee turned to sponsoring "spontaneous" mass demonstrations by young hooligans to intimidate recalcitrant assembly members. When this was ineffective, he arrested some assemblymen under the guise of martial law, releasing them when they had "changed their minds." In conjunction with this, Rhee trumped up a plot by Chang Myŏn, leader of the opposition, to have him assassinated. Finally, aided by bribery, Rhee's amendment passed.

In view of the tactics just described, Rhee and his Liberal Party won handily (by seventy-two percent) in the 1952 elections, helped out by wartime conditions and the rampant corruption which had infiltrated the government, the bureaucracy, and all aspects of society. Two years later, in 1954, Rhee's Liberal Party won overwhelmingly because of the divided opposition. With Rhee's party now commanding a majority for the first time in the National Assembly, constitutional amendments abolishing the office of prime minister, which had been a thorn in Rhee's side, and abolishing the two term limit for president, which would allow Rhee lifetime rule, were easily passed early in 1956.

In the 1956 elections, in spite of the death of his Democratic Party opponent, Shin ik-hi, and the "irregularities" of rigged elections, Rhee received only fifty-six percent of the vote and Chang Myŏn of the Democratic Party won the Vice-Presidency. This feat established the Democratic Party as a major contender for power and demonstrated the ebbing popularity of Rhee's Liberal Party and administration. This trend continued in the 1958 elections for the legislature as the Liberal Party was barely able to retain its majority as the rise of a liberal urban bloc led the opposition to Rhee and the police. The latter had an especially nefarious role to play as Rhee had the police arrest Democratic legislators to insure passage of the National Security Law. Ostensibly aimed at communists, the bill allowed the arrest of anyone spreading "false rumors," a provision which would be quite useful to Rhee in the coming 1960 elections.

The elections in 1960 were perhaps the most rigged in the nation's history. Cho Pyŏng-ŏk and Chang Myŏn were nominated by the Democratic Party to run against Rhee. Cho, the Presidential candidate died, leaving Rhee unopposed for President. But, even more than in 1956, the vice-presidential position was of extreme importance because of Rhee's advanced age. But the election returns showed a ninety-two percent majority for Rhee and his vice-presidential candidate, an incredible figure in light of the steady deterioration of the position of the Liberal Party. The election results were immediately protested by the National Assembly and thousands of students. Even U.S. Secretary of State Christian Herter questioned the validity of the elections. As protests continued, heavy police retaliation followed and several students were killed as the police opened up on the unarmed students. The floodgates of protest were thrown open wide when, on April 19, the body of a high school student was found with a tear gas canister embedded in his eye socket.

Thousands upon thousands of students and professors poured into the streets as Rhee declared martial law. But it was too late to save the regime as the Student Uprising (now called the April Uprising) caused the entire cabinet to offer its resignation if Vice-President Yi Ki-bung would. When Yi resigned, the cabinet resigned *in toto* and Rhee saw fit to resign. The students did not direct their wrath at Rhee himself, but at his underlings, the most prominent of whom was Yi, who had organized the rigged elections. Other targets included police and Liberal Party officials, the major complaints being police brutality, corruption, and election rigging. It was a spontaneous revolution without any political intent or leadership.

Thus, the Rhee administration was marked by a gap between the idealistic aspirations of democracy and the realistic capabilities of traditional authoritarianism. As such the regime was marked by the growth of personalism, the lack of institutionalization, a suspicion of liberals, no separation of the executive, legislative, and judicial functions, and the erection of communism as a bugaboo to form an extreme rightist autocracy.

The April Uprising succeeded because the military had remained neutral in the whole affair. Why was this so? It seems that the students had preempted a coup which the military themselves had been planning. Younger officers, frustrated by the slowness of postwar promotions, were also disgusted by the corruption of their superior officers. A military academy which resisted corruption had been established earlier. Furthermore, with modernization, the army had become skilled and professionalized, stressing specialization and managerial techniques new to Korean society. It was just the next small step to politics, as the military became "development-minded," thinking in "save-the-society" terms. So, the army waited in the wings to see if a new pattern would emerge following the Student Uprising.

Chang Myŏn and the Democratic Party now became the head of government in the Second Republic. This party had been born in opposition to Rhee's Liberal Party and, consisting of various coalitions, drew its support from the urban and middle classes. When it came into power in 1960, the familiar patterns of factionalism dominated the scene, as the party was split into Old and New Factions. These factions had to be dealt with when appointments were to be made.

The Second Republic got off to an auspicious start by abandoning the Presidential System in favor of a Cabinet System with a Prime Minister. A Central Election Committee was established to insure fair elections, civil liberties were guaranteed with no escape clauses, and the government was completely purged of Rhee supporters as the discredited Liberal Party simply disintegrated.

The elections of July 29, 1960 saw the split in the Democratic Party widen as Kim To-yŏn of the New Faction dropped out to form the New Democratic Party. Many other factions existed as well. In addition, many left-wing and socialist parties appeared or reappeared in the liberal atmosphere.

Many problems also burdened the fledgling government. The police were stripped of their powers, producing a wave of lawlessness and demonstrations. The unemployment rate remained high. The press, freed from its restrictions, criticized the Chang Myŏn government unmercifully, undermining public confidence. Factional deadlock in the legislature paralyzed government action and the resulting immobilism created a crisis of authority. However, reunification, the most pressing problem in this period of instability, caused the downfall of the government.

The desire for a neutralist unification, high among many students and professors in South Korea, was encouraged by the North Korean government. The formation of the National Students Federation for National Unification and the Northern plan for confederation by a Supreme National Council alarmed rightist groups and high military officers. The military officers of what was now the fourth largest standing army in the world translated the purification movement to eliminate corrupt generals to elimination of corrupt politicians. These men had little commitment to the political system and disparaged democracy. On May 16, 1961, as an anticommunist reaction to loose controls, corruption, and lack of progress in the Second Republic, the military carried out a bloodless coup d'état.

The United States, which was supporting the government, initially opposed the military coup. Since the South Korean Army was technically under the command of the UN and General MacGruder, he and the American Minister, Marshal Green, defending the ideal of democratic and freely-elected governments, urged President Yun Po-sŏn to crush the revolt. He refused, and the U.S. had no choice but to accept the coup and express the hope for an early return to civilian rule.

The military junta was controlled by the Supreme Council for National Reconstruction (SCNR) and consisted of younger officers headed by General Chung-hee Park. Yun Po-sŏn remained as President to prevent a crisis in diplomacy and foreign relations. The new government started by rooting out corruption, outlawing parties, and promulgating censorship and anticommunist laws. A rather efficient police state thus began operations.

Park, the mastermind of the revolt and the present ruler of South Korea, was born in 1917. After having been a teacher, Park entered a Japanese military academy in Manchukuo in 1940. He graduated from the military academy in Tokyo in 1944, and served as an officer in the Kwantung Army. Upon liberation he became a policeman, but resigned to enter the Korean military.

By 1953, at the age of 36, he was a Brigadier-General and, after attending the Fort Sill artillery school in Oklahoma, became a Major General and Chief of Staff of the First Army in 1958.

Park saw himself as a doctor who had to perform an operation to save the patient (South Korea). Seeing little foundation for democracy in Korea, he stressed moral reform and martial law. His ideas were translated into action when he issued political blacklists on three thousand Koreans.

Even though Koreans placidly accepted the military regime, it lacked legitimacy for the majority of the people. The Junta's prestige was hurt even more by a corruption scandal involving Japanese automobile imports, the proceeds of which were earmarked for the financing of a political party for the military once the ban on political activity was lifted. Furthermore, the constitution once again was amended to have a Presidential system.

As corruption again spread and as pressures mounted from the United States and the United Nations for a return to civilian rule, Park acknowledged that the revolution had indeed failed and promised an end to military rule. General Park announced that he would become a civilian to run in the elections on January 1, 1963, and the ban on political activity was lifted. At this time, the Democratic-Republican Party, the party of the military, emerged from hiding. Directed by Kim Chong-p'il, it had been formed a year earlier by the Korean Central Intelligence Agency. Its composition soon revealed that factional strife had existed even among the military leaders.

A last-minute attempt by Park to extend military rule for four years met with such negative reaction from the United States that he was forced to carry out the elections as scheduled on October 15, 1963. Park ran against five opponents, chief of whom was President Yun Po-sŏn. The combined vote of the five opposition candidates was fifty-seven percent with Yun polling forty-one percent, but they were unable to form a united front to defeat Park who got only forty-three percent of the vote, attesting to the dislike of the military regime on the part of the Korean people. In the contest for seats in the National Assembly the next month, the military's Democratic-Republican Party received almost two-thirds of the seats. Thus, the Third Republic was dominated by younger, military personnel directed by President Park. Park presided over a unicameral legislature, appointed the judiciary, and had many "emergency powers" making him a stronger President than Syngman Rhee.

Park's main program has been termed "national modernization." Under this program, which has involved three five-year plans, Korean society has been marked by internal stability and a high growth rate. Korea has also benefited in her modernization by American aid which has accounted for seventy-five percent of the military budget and fifty percent of the civilian budget, receiving the largest amount of military assistance of any country except South Vietnam. Business and war-related industry got a rapid boost as South Korean troops were sent to fight in South Vietnam in January 1965. This has also kept the army busy and out of politics and the U.S. has footed the bill for the entire operation since then ($927.5 million during 1965–69).[3]

Nonetheless, in the 1967 election Yun Po-sŏn again opposed Park. The campaign was issue-oriented and this time it was almost a two-man race. It showed that the South Korean masses have become politically sophisticated, ignoring splinter parties and turning out for the vote. In an election remarkably free of rigging, Park won with forty-nine percent of the vote and extended his political base. However, in the June 1967 elections for the legislature, widespread "irregularities" propagated by the rich Democratic-Republican Party occurred, and riots and protests by students, press, business, and the New Democratic Party followed.

On April 27, 1971, President Park, benefiting from a 1969 constitutional revision, ran for a third term against Kim Dae-jung of the New Democratic Party and polled fifty-one percent of the votes. His opponent had charged him with aspirations to lifetime dictatorship, corruption, and inequitable representation in favor of rural voters in the electoral districts. After two decades of massive U.S. aid, the ROK is moving toward self-reliance. With a literacy rate of ninety percent and a third five-year plan which is scheduled to expire in 1976, South Korea continues to have a high growth rate. Critics wondered, if South Korea was strong enough to send forces to Vietnam, why were U.S. troops still needed? Perhaps taking note of this, President Nixon announced in 1970 a 20,000 man troop reduction to reduce U.S. troop strength to 44,000 in the belief that Korea should shoulder more of the bur-

---

[3]"Money For Men in the Draft," *New Republic*, Vol. 164 (October 9, 1971), 7.

den of its defense. Similarly, U.S. aid, which amounted to $378 million in 1971 and which was scheduled to be trimmed to $294.3 million in 1972,[4] was completely terminated by the Senate in the fall of 1971. It remains to be seen whether aid is to be renewed. Finally, the imposition of textile quotas by the U.S. in 1971 has damaged Korea's export industry severely.

Thus, in South Korea, a government has been formed which except in nationality is not unlike that formerly imposed by Japan. It is bureaucratic, economy-oriented, militarily sufficient, anticommunist, and authoritarian. Economically, a high rate of inflation and unfair income distribution remain. Socially, there is an increasing rate of urbanization. Politically, there is a great deal of stability as charges of corruption continue to be censored from the press and Korea's "CIA" and police remain strong.

NORTH KOREA SINCE THE KOREAN WAR

The Korean War devastated the North Korean economy, creating limited human resources and food shortages. Since one of North Korea's goals is an independent national economy, many reforms were initiated. In 1946, land reform gave peasants individual ownership of the land they had been tilling. After the 1953 truce, the second stage, "cooperativization," began. By the next year, however, the peasants were resisting and after intimidation, in August, 1958, all land was collectivized. Two months later, in the third stage, larger units were formed remarkably similar to the communes created by the Great Leap Forward in China. Like Mao, Kim expressed belief in the infinite capacity of the masses but also clearly values expertise.

On balance, collectivization has been an economic success. Since a major goal was industrialization, savings had to come from agriculture. This means that living standards are kept at a low level and, therefore, peasants do not reap the benefits of their increased production.

After a successful five-year plan, North Korea launched a seven-year plan in 1961. This sort of development planning in their drive

---

[4] *Ibid.*, p. 8.

for modernization has been aided by the sizeable industrial base left by Japan, economic assistance from the Communist Bloc, and a totalitarian government which is able to mobilize effectively and impose sacrifices for modernization.

Two events caused a slowdown in development, however. First, many resources had to be drained off to the military when the military coup in South Korea occurred in 1961 and militantly anticommunist leaders assumed power there. Second, in a squabble with the Soviet Union in 1962, all Soviet technicians were withdrawn. The economy improved slightly as differences were patched up in 1965. Thus the seven-year plan, which was extended for three years until 1970, did not live up to expectations. North Korea is now embarking on decentralization of its economy, but with a priority given to heavy industry and thirty-one percent of the budget for defense, agriculture is still receiving the short end of the stick.

Politically, Kim Il-sŏng, who is Premier of the Democratic People's Republic (DPRK), General Secretary of the Korean Workers Party (KWP), and Commander-in-Chief of the Korean People's Army, is the head of the government. Ruling ostensibly on the principle of collective leadership through a Political Committee, Kim has steadily consolidated himself and his partisan group in power. In doing so he has relied on the symbols and rhetoric of nationalism, pursuing what has been called a cult of personality in which Kim emerges as the only true revolutionary in modern Korean history. His rule has not gone unchallenged.

In 1953, the domestic faction (the Old Communists) allegedly attempted to overthrow Kim, but failed. Three years later, in 1956, a more serious challenge arose as a coalition of Yenan and Soviet Korean factions accused Kim of cult of personality in the wake of the anti-Stalinist mood of the Twentieth Congress of the CPSU. One of them, Pak Ch'ang-ok, secretly asked Khrushchev's aid in their efforts. (A similar pattern in China emerged three years later when Marshall P'eng Teh-huai asked Khrushchev to help him in his campaign against Maoist excesses in the Great Leap Forward.) Kim quashed this threat also. In 1958, Kim ousted Kim Tu-bŏng to complete the purges. In subsequent maneuvers, Kim's partisan group became stronger in the reorganization of the Fourth Party Congress in 1961. In 1966 a further reorganization lifted Kim's partisan group, which has close personal connections with Kim, to the Presidium and the Secretariat, giving the regime a military overtone.

North Korea, which took a blow to its national pride when the Chinese Peoples Liberation Army had to come to the rescue during the Korean War, has dictated a more or less independent line in the Communist world while culling the favor of both the U.S.S.R. and China. Not able to afford to alienate either China or the Soviet Union, North Korea, while vilifying U.S. imperialism, remained neutral in the issues of de-Stalinization, peaceful coexistence, and communes.

After 1961, North Korea seemed to lean toward China. This was a reaction to the feeling that the Russians, in collaboration with some Korean leaders (notably Ch'oe Ch'ang-sik and Pak Ch'ang-ok) were trying to overthrow Kim. It also resulted from disagreements in the international arena, notably the Cuban Missile crisis, the Soviet unwillingness to commit itself fully during the Korean War, the solidarity felt with China because both countries' revolutions are incomplete because of American imperialism, and hatred of big-power chauvinism. North Korea began praising Albania's independent stand, took China's side against India in 1962, and began to attack "revisionism."

Between 1964 and 1968, North Korea swung back to the U.S.S.R. especially when Kim came under Red Guard criticism during China's Cultural Revolution in 1966. The new Soviet leaders Brezhnev and Kosygin renewed their suspended aid, and denounced the Pueblo incident as U.S. imperialism.

However, as the U.S.S.R. moved increasingly toward détente with the West, North Korea again favored Peking. Mutual fear of a hostile U.S.-Japanese alliance may have been one factor. Furthermore, when North Korea shot down a U.S. Navy EC-121 reconnaissance plane in April 1969, the Chinese supported the action while the U.S.S.R. helped the Americans search for survivors. In general then, the status-quo orientation of the Soviet Union did not agree with the North Korean view.

In its relations with the South after the attempt to unify the entire country by force of arms from 1950 to 1953, the North Korean regime turned to psychological warfare and underground infiltration and subversion. The attitude of the North toward the South was conciliatory after the 1960 April Uprising, but became militant after the establishment of the anticommunist military junta a year later. North Korea became even more bellicose toward the South after the conclusion of a normalization treaty with Japan in late 1965 and the growing financial ties between the two nations. South Korea was also perceived as a threat as its GNP rose quite rapidly.

The increase in the number of agents in the South and their more bellicose stance was made possible by aid from China and the Soviet Union. The peak of violence came in the 1966–69 period and was highlighted by a commando assassination attempt on President Park in January 1968. Two days later, the Pueblo spy ship was seized (it was not released until December 23). Since 1969, there have been fewer border incidents and less violence in general. It seems safe to say that communist activity in South Korea will occur on a large scale only when there is a strong and influential Communist Party in the South, when the regime is weak, when international intervention is improbable, when violence will raise communist prestige, and when violence will stiffen popular resistance.

EPILOGUE

In spite of the hostility of the two regimes toward each other, national unification is a major goal of both sides. Undoubtedly, partition has been disastrous as seen in terms of Korea as a nation. Consequences such as war, a bifurcated economy, differing political systems, psychological strain, and the threat of a new war attest to the fact that partition as a solution is self-defeating.

In seeking to discover the prospects of unification, it is pointless to assess relative guilt or innocence on either side. We must also admit the existence of certain factors which tend to increase the likelihood of division. Increasing differences in socioeconomic and political environments, the long absence of communication, the almost complete ignorance of the people regarding conditions in the opposite region, and memories of a bitter war certainly militate against unification.

North Korea charges that only U.S. imperialism stands in the way of unification. So, in 1960, Premier Kim proposed that a Supreme National Council be selected by the Supreme People's

Assembly of North Korea and the National Assembly of South Korea to develop a confederation plan on the basis of unanimity, followed by an election supervised by neutral nations. With conditions of removal of U.S. troops and abrogation of all South Korean defense treaties, the North used the nationalistic theme of Koreans to solve Korean problems.

But their stance hardened in 1961 after the military coup in the South. Statements abounded that North Korea had the responsibility of liberating the South; in 1961, North Korea signed a Treaty of Mutual Defense with both the Peoples Republic of China and the U.S.S.R. Propaganda efforts during the 1960s emphasized that North Korea was the homeland of true patriots. Additional propaganda efforts were made, trying to alienate the South Korean masses from the U.S.-backed regime, and trying to organize communist sympathizers. Finally, to attract loyalty and effect unification, North Korea sought to make itself strong militarily, economically, and culturally, setting up a strong "democratic" and industrial base.

This basic policy remained for several years. Then in June 1970, North Korea announced its willingness to limit troops to 100,000 on each side after the removal of U.S. troops and the Park regime. It also proposed commercial and cultural exchanges. This program was reaffirmed at the Fifth Party Congress held in November, 1970. It was rejected by South Korea.

South Korean unification policy basically supports the UN strategy of free elections in all of Korea. In 1960–61, there was a public clamor for unification in the South. Since the military coup in 1961, however, no discussion of unification has been permitted and the government has stressed economic development as a precondition for unification. The North Koreans rejected the UN as an agency of unification because, having fought a war against North Korea, it was to them far from being an impartial body. Similarly, free elections in all of Korea, with two-thirds of the population in South Korea, would not be in their interest.

So it would seem that the more eagerly each side pursued unification, because of their divergent policies, the less the prospect for unification. Recently, however, the prospects seem to be improving. In August 1969, President Park issued a major statement on unification and in the same year created a cabinet-level organization devoted to unification which discovered that nearly ninety-one percent of the people wanted unification. An International Conference on Reunification was held in the following year at Seoul from August 24–29. For the first time, the ban on the discussion of unification was temporarily lifted to permit an airing of ideas and opinions from academia. Simultaneously, Washington encouraged dialogues between Seoul and Pyongyang on the subject. Just prior to the conference, on August 15, President Chunghee Park offered to discuss unification if the North would accept conditions of UN authority. The proposal was rejected by the North for reasons given above, but it was significant because it was the first time that Park had addressed himself to the problem. A further prod of South Korea came when President Richard Nixon announced his support for a seat for China in the UN and his intention of visiting Peking. It might, then, be foreseen that the same could happen with North Korea.

The most promising news came at the end of the summer of 1971 when Red Cross officials of both North and South Korea met at Panmunjom in a preliminary meeting to negotiate the reuniting of families divided by the war. A second meeting was held on October 14, 1971. These events represent an important beginning since they were the first bilateral talks since the war and more importantly, since the spill-over may result in steps toward mutual reconciliation.

This may seem to be an overly optimistic view. One way to reconciliation, of course, is a four-power agreement, involving the U.S., U.S.S.R., China, and Japan. For reasons of proximity, the last three nations must be considered. Although Japan was not directly involved in the Korean War, a unified Korean government hostile to Japan would make it difficult to remain neutral and/or unarmed. Similarly the U.S. and China must be considered because they have fought a war there. Thus, given the divergence of the separate national interests of these countries, the prospect of a four-power agreement should not be exaggerated.

Putting aside for the moment the problems of mutual hostility and the necessity of a four-power agreement, what are the factors in favor of unification? One factor is the educational policies of the two regimes, which stress the idea of one Korea. A second factor is that, with the passage of time, a new generation of leaders, unschooled in the tactics and rhetoric of the Cold War, may exert an ameliorative effect on the process of unification.

A third and very complicated factor in favor of unification is residual Korean nationalism. Even though each side has become tied to differing international systems and has become isolated from one another, these phenomena have *not* been accompanied by a decline in identification with the old national unit, as the cutting of ties would suggest.

This phenomenon is at variance with certain theories of community integration held by political scientists. First, the ties were cut forcibly, against the will of the people, and the division did not occur along natural, ethnic, or linguistic lines. Second, national identification is an important part of the process of self-identification. The existence of a basic national identity is necessary to prevent anomie. In fact, ideological identification with an international system will tend to aggravate the national identity crisis— a crisis that cannot be resolved until the nation is again one unit. So national identities do not decline or disappear with the abolition of social communication, but remain strong.[5]

The Korean unification problem should be approached with caution. Without abandoning the realistic notion that attitudes do not change overnight, it is likely that Korea will not remain divided in the long run. Although it is unlikely that we will see a settlement in the foreseeable future (one futurologist has predicted Korean unification in the 1990s),[6] we should not be overly pessimistic either. A limited amount of nonpolitical exchanges similar to those now taking place would seem to be in order. Also mail flow, cultural and sporting exchanges, and economic exchanges may be cultivated. So, while we must remain pessimistic regarding the prospects of reunification in the short run, there is every reason to believe that the barriers which now exist to prevent unification can be broken down and that the emotion-laden desire of the Korean people for national unification will be realized.

Editor's note: Developments subsequent to the writing of this essay serve to underscore the wisdom of the authors' cautious

---

[5]Bruce R. Sievers, "The Divided Nations: International Integration and National Identity—Patterns in Germany, China, Vietnam, and Korea," in *Communist Party States,* ed. Jan F. Triska (New York and Indianapolis, 1969), pp. 160–188.

[6]Yung-hwan Jo, "Political Futuristics for the Divided Nations in Asia: A Pre-Theory," *Proceedings of American Philosophical Society* (October, 1970), p. 387.

optimism. On July 4, 1972 North and South Korea, in a dramatic joint announcement, revealed that representatives of their respective governments had signed a seven-point agreement whose ultimate goal was to end the twenty-seven year partition of their homeland. The agreement pledges both sides to refrain from armed provocation and propaganda defamation of each other, encourages various exchanges of personnel and equipment, and provides for the establishment of a "hot line" between the two capitals.

Preceded by a series of preliminary talks between Red Cross representatives of North and South Korea on the problem of reuniting families separated by the armistice line, the first meeting between government officials from both sides was held in May at Pyongyang, North Korea. Hu Rak Lee, director of South Korea's Central Intelligence Agency, conferred at length with North Korean Premier Kim Il-sŏng and Kim's younger brother and heir apparent, Politburo member Kim Young Ju. Three weeks later North Korea sent its second Vice Premier, Pak Sung Chul, to Seoul for secret talks with South Korean officials.

Contacts between North and South Korea are continuing. On August 5, 1972 the first full session of Red Cross talks was scheduled to begin in Seoul with a future session planned for Pyongyang. It is expected that the Red Cross negotiations will result eventually in an accord which will permit travel and an exchange of mail and monetary remittances between relatives in the North and South. Discussions pertaining to other kinds of travel, cultural exchanges, and possible air, sea, land and telecommunication links will be conducted later at higher levels.

Unification of the two Koreas still faces formidable obstacles. Indeed, neither side seriously has suggested how a Communist North can be united with a non-Communist South in the predictable future. But both regimes seem sensibly agreed that the future of Korea should be the exclusive concern of Koreans and that, at least, could be a beginning.

BIBLIOGRAPHY

Caridi, Ronald J. *The Korean War and American Politics: The Republican Party as a Case Study.* Philadelphia, 1968.

Cho, Soon-sung. *Korea in World Politics, 1940–1950: An Evaluation of American Responsibility.* Berkeley, 1967.

Conroy, F. Hilary. *The Japanese Seizure of Korea: A Study of Realism and Idealism in International Relations, 1868–1910.* Philadelphia, 1960.

———. "Chosen Mondai: The Korean Problem in Meiji Japan," *Proceedings of the American Philosophical Society,* (October 1956).

Hatada, Takashi. *A History of Korea.* Translated and edited by Warren W. Smith, Jr., and Benjamin H. Hazard. Santa Barbara, 1969.

Henderson, Gregory. *Korea: The Politics of the Vortex.* Cambridge, 1968.

Kim, C. I. Eugene and Han-kyo Kim. *Korea and the Politics of Imperialism, 1876–1910.* Berkeley, 1967.

Kim, C. I. Eugene and Ke-soo Kim. "The April 1960 Korean Student Movement," *The Western Political Quarterly,* (March 1964).

Kim, Joungwon Alexander. "The Republic of Korea: A Quest for New Directions," *Asian Survey,* (January 1971).

Kim, Se-jin. "South Korea's Involvement in Vietnam and its Economic and Political Impact," *Asian Survey,* (June 1971).

Koh, Byung-chul. "Dilemmas of Korean Unification," *Asian Survey,* (May 1971).

———. "North Korea: Profile of a Garrison State," *Problems of Communism,* (January–February 1969).

Lee, Chong-sik. *The Politics of Korean Nationalism.* Berkeley and Los Angeles, 1965.

———. "Korean Partition and Unification," *Journal of International Affairs,* Volume XVIII, No. 2., (1964).

———. "Land Reform, Collectivization, and the Peasants in North Korea," *China Quarterly,* (April–June 1963).

———. "Stalinism in the East: Communism in North Korea." Robert A. Scalapino, editor. *The Communist Revolution in Asia: Tactics, Goals, and Achievements.* Englewood Cliffs, N.J., 1969.

———. "The Socialist Revolution in the North Korean Countryside," *Asian Survey,* (October 1962).

Lee, Hahn-been. *Korea: Time, Change, and Administration.* Honolulu, 1968.

Lee, Yur-bok. *Diplomatic Relations Between the United States and Korea, 1866–1887.* New York, 1970.

Morley, James W. *Japan and Korea, America's Allies in the Pacific.* New York, 1965.

Oh, John Kie-chiang. *Korea: Democracy on Trial.* Ithaca, 1968.

Paige, Glenn D. *The Korean Decision, June 24–30, 1950.* New York, 1968.

———. "Korea." Cyril E. Black and Thomas P. Thornton, editors. *Communism and Revolution: The Strategic Uses of Political Violence.* Princeton, 1964.

Simmons, Robert R. "North Korea: Silver Anniversary," *Asian Survey,* (January 1971).

———. "China's Cautious Relations with North Korea and Indochina," *Asian Survey,* (July 1971).

Stone, I. F. *The Hidden History of the Korean War.* New York, 1952.

Suh, Dae-sook. *The Korean Communist Movement, 1918–1948.* Princeton, 1967.

Wright, Mary C. "Adaptability of Ch'ing Diplomacy: The Case of Korea," *Journal of Asian Studies,* (May 1958).

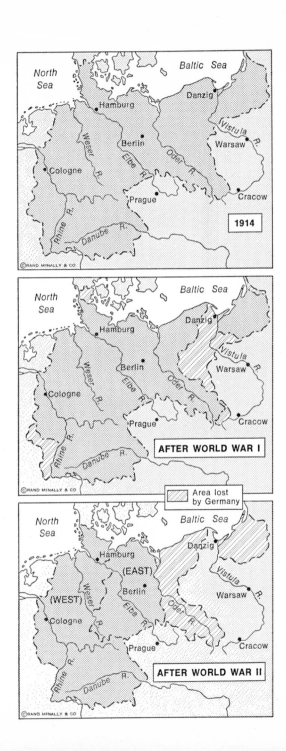

Chapter 3.

The Partition of Germany: Cold War Compromise

Berenice Carroll
University of Illinois - Urbana

The division of Germany has been at once the most dangerous and the most stable of the partitions which came about in the wake of World War II. It has stood in the center of the Cold War confrontations of the great powers; on occasion it threatened to draw them across the threshold of nuclear war. Yet the division of Germany may also be seen as a key to the peace which has prevailed in Europe for over twenty-five years.

GERMANY

Viewed from the perspective of 1971, the unification of Germany one century earlier has the appearance of an experiment which failed: disastrously for the world, ignominiously for the Germans. The idea of "Germany" as a cultural and ethnic region, a "geographical expression" to cover the patchwork of small states and imperial domains of central Europe in medieval and early modern times, is old. But Germany as a modern nation-state was short-lived, and doubtful from the start in its character and territorial extent.

In its foundation, the German Empire was the artificial creation of an aristocratic Prussian nationalist, Otto von Bismarck. Its borders were established to suit the requirements of Prussian supremacy: excluding Austria and other Hapsburg lands, including Alsace and Lorraine. These borders, established between 1864 and 1871 by a series of military victories (over Denmark, Austria, and France) were stable for less than forty-five years. In 1914, impelled by expansionist ambitions and paranoid fantasies, the German Empire plunged willingly, even joyously, into World War I. Thereafter, the boundaries of "Germany" changed in every decade until the close of World War II.

Unquestionably there had developed, in the seventy-five years between the formation of the German Empire and the destruction of the Third Reich, a sense of German unity and even a fierce patriotic loyalty to the idea of a German nation. The National Socialists, under Adolf Hitler, were especially determined to abolish the particularist loyalties which had been preserved in Bismarck's Germany through the *Länder* (the state governments) and their prerogatives.

Nevertheless, Hitler was no more a simple German nationalist than was Bismarck. For Hitler's vision was that of a Germany extending to the Urals or further: ". . . the new Reich must again set itself on the march along the road of the Teutonic Knights of old, to obtain by the German sword sod for the German plow and daily bread for the nation."[1]   And in accord with this vision, the Third Reich became the truest embodiment of the charge that "no one can understand Germans who does not appreciate their determination to exterminate the East."[2] If Germany were to acquire what Hitler dreamed of, "the Urals, with their incalculable wealth of raw materials, and the forests of Siberia, and . . . the unending wheatfields of the Ukraine," it was not to be by merely subjugating the Slavs who inhabited those territories, but by eliminating them,

---

[1] Adolf Hitler, *Mein Kampf* (Munich, 1930), pp. 153–54.
[2] A. J. P. Taylor, *The Course of German History* (New York, 1962), p. 14.

through deliberate policies of mass depopulation, by starvation, deportation, slave labor and extermination.

That there is a Germany has seemed intuitively certain, to Germans and non-Germans alike, but to the question: "What is Germany?" there have been manifold answers. Today the question may still have many theoretical answers, but the political reality is that of two German states, both of which have given up the claim to Empire.

DISMEMBERMENT

Germany, within her frontiers as they were on the 31st December, 1937, will, for the purposes of occupation, be divided into three zones, one of which will be allotted to each of the three Powers, and a special Berlin area, which will be under joint occupation by the Three Powers.[3]

With these words, representatives of the three great powers allied against Germany in World War II initiated the gradual division of the country into the two Germanies of the present day. Yet it was at no time the declared policy of these powers to bring about that result.

"Dismemberment" of Germany had indeed been mentioned repeatedly in wartime Allied policy conferences as a serious postwar goal. Thus the Yalta Conference Protocol of February 11, 1945, authorized the three powers to "take such steps, including the complete disarmament, demilitarization *and dismemberment* of Germany as they deem requisite for future peace and security" (DG, p. 8). Nevertheless, the Allied Powers were so little able to agree on the character and terms of "dismemberment," that this goal was dropped six months later from the objectives specified in the Potsdam Conference Protocol.

---

[3]"Protocol on Zones of Occupation," September 12, 1944, *Documents on Germany, 1944–1970,* prepared for the Committee on Foreign Relations of the United States Senate, Washington, D.C.: U.S. Government Printing Office, 1971. This collection of documents is cited in the text following quotations from the documents, as "DG."

The Potsdam Protocol called upon the occupying powers instead to provide "uniformity of treatment of the German population throughout Germany," and specified as one of the principles guiding occupation policy: "To prepare for the eventual reconstruction of German political life on a democratic basis and for eventual peaceful cooperation in international life by Germany" (DG, p. 34). At Potsdam, then, it appeared that the zonal division of Germany was to be temporary and to serve administrative, not political purposes; eventually, it seemed, *a* reconstructed Germany was expected to rejoin the international community.

The idea of dismembering Germany had grown out of the concern of all three powers to insure that they would not again have to contend with the militarist, expansionist power in central Europe which had twice in this century been their enemy in wars of cataclysmic proportions. U.S. President Franklin D. Roosevelt particularly favored the policy of dismemberment, though he had in mind not an East-West split, but a division of the country into several parts, perhaps along lines of preunification states. Later the French, admitted to equal status as a fourth occupying power in Germany and Berlin, became the strongest advocates of a policy of multiple dismemberment (having in mind partly their traditional diplomatic objective of a weak Germany, partly their more immediate interest in consolidating the Saar with French territory).

Neither Roosevelt while he lived, nor the French in the postwar years, were able to secure Allied agreement on an avowed policy of dismemberment. The Anglo-Allied counsels were severely divided on this point, and there was strong opposition to dismemberment on a variety of grounds, ranging from fear of reviving traditional nationalist forces, to the desire to preserve a strong Germany as a bulwark against Bolshevism. As for the Russians, their primary interest was to insure Germany's demilitarization, neutralization, and commitment to making reparations on a massive scale for the injuries and destruction inflicted upon Europe, especially Russia, during World War II. For these purposes, they preferred a unified Germany in which the Soviet Union could exercise its influence.

Despite these preferences for a united Germany, the Allied agreements at the close of World War II divided the prewar territory of the German Reich into not merely two, but rather eight parts. In addition to the four main zones of occupation, the city of Berlin was given separate status, also under quadripartite control; the city of Königsberg and its surrounding area was given outright to the Soviet Union; the territory east of a line formed by the Oder and western Neisse rivers was placed "under Polish administration"; and the Saar was given a special status under the control of France.

Viewed from this angle, it appears that the multiple dismemberment of Germany discussed in the wartime conferences was in fact accomplished. Though the four occupation zones were later reduced to two states, and France was, most reluctantly, obliged to turn over the Saar to the Federal Republic of Germany in 1956, the loss of the eastern territories to Russia and Poland is now acknowledged by both German states, and Berlin still retains its separate status, formally under quadripartite rule. Above all, the two states which now occupy the bulk of the territory of the former German Reich are today firmly established as separate sovereign entities, of widely disparate character.

How did this come about?

THE ZONAL DIVISION

The circumstances surrounding the initial Allied agreement on zones of occupation were symptomatic of the problems which brought about ultimate partition. The text of the agreement was prepared by the European Advisory Commission (EAC) and signed by its members, on behalf of the Allied governments, on September 12, 1944. The EAC had been established to serve as a high-level inter-Allied commission to deal with major issues of postwar policy. But the agreements on zonal division and administration of occupied Germany were among very few acts of importance permitted to the EAC. Situated in London, it was viewed with suspicion by Roosevelt as a British tool. In any case, both western Allies wanted to keep their postwar options open and were unwilling to commit themselves to decisions formulated under wartime conditions, especially by a body proposed originally by the Russians.

The EAC's success in the zonal agreement was largely a result of pressure from the military leaders of the Allied governments, who regarded it as imperative that agreements be reached on the administration of occupied areas as the Allied armies moved into Germany. In fact, the Anglo-American military leaders had already agreed upon the zonal division over a year earlier, at the Quebec Conference of August 1943, basing their allocation of occupation zones upon their strategic planning for the invasion of western Europe, and their expectations concerning the pace of the Soviet advance from the east. Soviet adherence to the proposal was secured as early as February 1944, but agreement was held up by differences between England and the United States. President Roosevelt, in particular, had sought a much larger zone of occupation for the United States, and preferred the northwestern zone, with its port facilities and heavy industrial concentrations, to the landlocked, largely pastoral southwestern zone. But Roosevelt was not supported by the State and War departments, and ultimately it was the design of the Quebec Conference of 1943 which prevailed.

The zonal division outlined by the EAC agreement of September 1944 was later amended to confirm allocation of the northwestern zone to the British (on condition the latter would grant U.S. control of the ports of Bremen and Bremerhaven, and guarantee transit facilities for U.S. forces), and to provide occupation zones for the French out of the Anglo-American zones in western Germany and west Berlin. An agreement on control machinery was also reached and signed on November 14, 1944.

The agreement on control machinery, confirmed by the military commanders and issued publicly on June 5, 1945, gave the Commanders-in-Chief of the Allied armed forces the supreme governing authority, each separately in his own zone of occupation, and jointly, in a Control Council, in "matters affecting Germany as a whole." This arrangement was intended to be temporary, to "operate during the initial period of the occupation of Germany immediately following the surrender" (DG, pp. 7, 19). Provisions for control and administration of Germany in a later period were to be established by a separate agreement—one which never materialized.

CONFLICTING OCCUPATION POLICIES AND THE REPARATIONS ISSUE

Failure to reach a more detailed and permanent agreement for uniform political and economic administration of occupied Germany was closely bound up with failure to reach agreement on the issue of reparations; both were consequences of the ambivalent and conflicting attitudes of the occupying powers toward the future of Germany and central Europe.

None of the Allied powers wanted to resurrect the Germany which had been their prime rival and sometimes enemy in economic, military, or political power. But neither was England or the United States willing to see Soviet power extend deep into central Europe, without a strong Germany to confront and oppose it. Nor was the Soviet Union willing to relinquish its claim to a victor's say in the future of the western zones of Germany, or to see the economic resources of that area turned to the use of an anti-Bolshevik alliance. Thus while the postwar aims declared at Yalta, for the "disarmament, demilitarization and dismemberment" of Germany, reflected the desire of all three Allies for the destruction of Germany as a power capable of challenging them for a third time, it was already clear at Potsdam that other aims and objectives, in which the Allies were sharply at odds, were to take precedence in the postwar era.

The critical differences emerged most clearly in acrimonious debate on the question of reparations at Potsdam. As Gabriel Kolko has written:

> ... for the United States the German question was essentially whether Germany should be weak or strong in the postwar period—or a balance between the two—a barrier to the expansion of Communism and Russia toward the Atlantic. A harsh peace, with heavy reparations, would require that the Germans, rather than the battered Russians, pay for a substantial part of postwar Soviet reconstruction.[4]

---

[4]Gabriel Kolko, *The Politics of War: The World and United States Foreign Policy, 1943–1945* (New York, 1968), p. 569.

What the western Allies granted was extremely ambiguous, and in any case more in the nature of an exchange of goods than of outright reparations. No definite reparations figure was set. The principle agreed upon at Yalta, for "annual deliveries of goods from current production for a period to be fixed," disappeared from the wording of the Potsdam terms.

What was agreed, in essence, was that each of the occupying powers was to draw reparations from its own zone, and from "appropriate German external assets." In addition, in recognition of the exceptionally high Soviet losses during the war, and of the industrial wealth of the western zones, the Soviet Union was to receive twenty-five percent of

> ... such usable and complete industrial capital equipment, in the first place from the metallurgical, chemical and machine manufacturing industries as is unnecessary for the German peace economy ... (DG, p. 37).

Of this twenty-five percent, only ten percent was to be provided to the Soviet Union "without payment or exchange of any kind in return"; the remaining fifteen percent was to be "in exchange for an equivalent value of food, coal, potash, zinc, timber, clay products, petroleum products, and such other commodities as may be agreed upon."

This left undetermined both the standard for judging what was "unnecessary for the German peace economy" and the total figure from which twenty-five percent was to be allocated to the Soviet Union. To deal with this problem, the Potsdam Protocol provided that "the amount of equipment to be removed from the Western Zones on account of reparations must be determined within six months from now at the latest," according to a determination of "the amount and character of the industrial equipment unnecessary for the German peace economy" by the Allied Control Council, "under policies fixed by the Allied Commission on Reparations, ... *subject to the final approval of the Zone Commander in the Zone from which the equipment is to be removed*" (DG, p. 37; italics added).

In effect, then, the military commanders of the western zones were given veto power over reparations payments from their zones to the Soviet Union. This was one of a number of serious contradictions in the Potsdam Protocol which gave rise to endless recriminations in subsequent years. For it was hardly possible to insist upon "uniformity of treatment of the German population throughout Germany" and, at the same time, upon the supreme authority of each military commander in his own zone, extending even to a veto power in decisions of the Allied Control Council. Nor was it only in reparations questions that the zonal commanders held such veto power but in all other matters as well, according to the terms of the agreement on control machinery, which provided that decisions of the Allied Control Council had to be unanimous.

Thus while the United States complained that the Soviet Union was violating its obligation to "uniform treatment" of the German population, for example in beginning at once to nationalize industry and introduce land reform in the Soviet zone, the United States did not hesitate to rely equally upon the independence of the zonal commanders to call a unilateral halt to payment of reparations from the American zone to the U.S.S.R. The veto power over such payments accorded to the zonal commanders at Potsdam was invoked by General Clay, commander of the American zone, within eight months. On May 3, 1946, Clay ordered the suspension of all reparations shipments from the American zone to the east. They were never resumed.

While reparations payments from the west, and exchange shipments from the east, ceased to flow between the zones in Germany, polemics continued between the occupying powers. The dispute centered increasingly upon interpretation of the Potsdam Protocol, particularly on the point of whether payments to the U.S.S.R. from the western zones were to have been made out of current production or only out of removals of plant existing at the end of the war.

In any case, the western Allies continuously denied any commitment to pay reparations out of current production in their zones. Secretary of State Byrnes maintained in September 1946 that the levels-of-industry agreement, arrived at with difficulty pursuant to the terms described above, had made no allowance for reparations from current production, and that higher levels of industry would have to be fixed if such reparations were to be made:

The levels of industry fixed are only sufficient to enable the German people to become self-supporting and to maintain living standards approximating the average European living conditions (DG, p. 61).

Actually, what the Potsdam Protocol specified was a subsistence level for Germany, not "average European living standards": payment of reparations, it stated, "should leave enough resources to enable the German people to subsist without external assistance" (DG, p. 36).

In December of 1947, the new U.S. Secretary of State, George Marshall, made clear not only that the United States repudiated any obligation to make reparations payments out of current production from the western zones, but that he fully understood the significance of this point for the division of Germany:

We will not agree to the program of reparations from current production which under existing conditions could only be met in one of two ways. The first would be that the United States would pay for such reparations. This the United States will not do. The only other method of obtaining reparations from current production from Germany at the present time and for the foreseeable future would be to depress the German standard of living to such a point that Germany would become not only a center of unrest in the heart of Europe but this would indefinitely, if not permanently, retard the rehabilitation of German peace-time economy and hence the recovery of Europe.

And Marshall concluded:

I wish it to be clearly understood that the United States is not prepared to agree to any program of reparations from current production as a price for the unification of Germany.[5]

---

[5]Speech of December 10, 1947, in: *Documents on American Foreign Relations,* (1947), p. 65. Published for the World Peace Foundation by Princeton University Press from 1944–45 through 1951; later volumes in this series (the 1959 and 1961 volumes cited herein) were published by Harper and Bros. for the Council on Foreign Relations. This series is cited in the text below, following quotations from the documents, as "DAFR."

On Marshall's suggestion, the Council of Foreign Ministers, which had been established by the Potsdam Conference to formulate the peace settlement, and which had met fruitlessly five times in the preceding two years, adjourned indefinitely, acknowledging its inability to reach agreement on the issues still outstanding between the powers.

THE COLD WAR AND THE PARTITION

As the Cold War took shape and intensified, the partition of Germany kept pace. The two seemed increasingly enmeshed: German rearmament and East-West intransigence, German reunification and European disarmament, Berlin and nuclear brinksmanship—all were intricately entwined. And in the twenty-five years since the end of World War II, divided Germany often seemed the most dangerous of the arenas of international crisis. Here the nuclear superpowers have confronted each other most directly, their troops stationed continuously in direct contact— sometimes in subtle forms of hostile contact.

Berlin, divided into miniature occupation zones and situated 110 miles into the territory of the Soviet zone—now the German Democratic Republic—has been the focus of the most threatening of these crises.

The basis of the quadripartite occupation of Berlin was laid in the same EAC agreement of September 12, 1944, which provided for the zonal division of Germany. The agreement on control machinery of November 14, 1944, which called for the administration of Germany by a "supreme organ of control called the Control Council," provided also for an Inter-Allied Governing Authority for Berlin (the "Kommandantura") consisting of the Commandants of each of the sectors, serving in rotation as head of the Kommandantura. A subsequent agreement of July 7, 1945, specified that the period of rotation of the Chief Military Commandant would be fifteen days, and that all sectors of the city would be administered under the Chief Commandant:

> ... utilizing for this purpose conferences of the Allied Military Commandants to solve questions of principle and problems common to all zones. The resolutions of such conferences are to be passed unanimously (DG, p. 22).

The Commandants were to "organize the administration in their respective zones in conformity with the orders of the Chief Military commandant, taking into account local conditions."

Quadripartite rule by unanimous decision worked better than one might have supposed, both for Germany as a whole and for Berlin. Many practical aspects of administering the four zones and the former capital city were managed with ready agreement of all four powers, as were also policies and procedures on which the four powers were already in accord such as the trials of major German leaders as war criminals, and the denazification, demilitarization, and decartelization programs in their early stages. As differences between the powers grew sharper and more acrimonious, however, it became increasingly difficult to operate with the rule of unanimity.

The agreements on zonal division and quadripartite administration of Berlin made no mention of access from the British, French, and American zones of Germany to Berlin. The western powers have always maintained that their rights of access were inherent in their rights of occupation. Nevertheless, that their rights of access were not wholly unrestricted was clear from the outset, for between September and December 1945, a number of administrative recommendations regulating the means of access were proposed by the Transport Directorate and the Air Directorate, and confirmed by the Allied Control Council. These agreements provided for air corridors which could be used freely by the western occupying authorities, for a limited amount of rail traffic, for military maintenance, and for shipment of coal and food to the western sectors of Berlin. Specifically, the western occupying powers were allowed a total of 16 freight trains per day, "under Russian control and supervision," to pass through the Soviet zone by a specified route.

Beyond these minimal arrangements, customary procedures gradually developed to regulate the flow of traffic between West Berlin and the western occupation zones and in some respects these were improvements for the western powers, for example in the addition of alternative railroad routes. But given the hostility and suspicion between the governments and armed forces involved, it was hardly surprising that Soviet control of western military and civilian traffic to and from Berlin led repeatedly to heated and potentially explosive confrontations.

The first and still most vividly remembered of these was the Berlin blockade and airlift of 1948–49. The blockade was imposed by the Soviet Military Administration as a retaliatory measure, when the western powers introduced into West Berlin the new uniform currency of the western zones. Behind this act stood the repeated failure of the powers to reach agreement on a European peace settlement, set in the mounting hostility of the Cold War.

On December 2, 1946, the United States and Great Britain had agreed to an economic fusion of their two zones of occupation "as the first step towards the achievement of the economic unity of Germany as a whole," purportedly in accordance with the Potsdam agreement. The union of the two zones, now known as Bi-Zonia, went into effect on January 1, 1947.

Shortly afterward the Allied Foreign Ministers, meeting for the fourth time in the spring of 1947 in Moscow, found themselves still unable to agree on major issues of policy relating to Germany: on reparations, on "uniform treatment" of the German economy, on the powers of the projected central German government, on acceptance of the Oder-Neisse line as the permanent boundary between Germany and Poland, on control of the Ruhr (a matter related to the reparations issue), and on other matters as well, the Allied governments were still committed to sharply differing positions. But when the conference broke up without advancing at all toward a peace settlement, the Americans at least wasted no tears; W. Bedell Smith, then Ambassador to the U.S.S.R., called it "a very successful failure."

On June 5, 1947, Secretary of State George C. Marshall announced, on the occasion of an address delivered at Harvard University, that the United States would be willing to extend economic aid to "any government that is willing to assist in the task of recovery" in Europe. But he added a warning which made clear at the outset the political character of the offer:

> Any government which maneuvers to block the recovery of other countries cannot expect help from us. Furthermore, governments, political parties or groups which seek to perpetuate human misery in order to profit therefrom politically or otherwise will encounter the opposition of the United States (DAFR, 1947, p. 10).

The response to this offer hardened the lines of division in Europe as nothing else had yet done. Western European governments—with some like France facing the opposition of mass-based left-wing parties—welcomed the offer and immediately set about "the drafting of a European program" such as Marshall called for. But the Soviet Union repudiated the offer as it certainly was intended to do, and the eastern European governments which stood in the shadow of Soviet power did likewise, though in some cases only under severe pressure.

In July, there appeared in *Foreign Affairs* "Mr. X's" influential exposition of the "containment" doctrine which was to shape much of U.S. foreign policy in the succeeding years, ultimately taking on a military character which "Mr. X" himself later repudiated.[6] In September, the sixteen-nation conference which met to devise plans for the European Recovery Program recommended, in its final report, that the western zones of occupation in Germany be included under the program.

How far the Western Powers, and indeed western European countries in general, now stood from any expectation or genuine desire for German unity was made clear early the following spring in the Communiqué issued at the conclusion of an "informal discussion of the German problem" held by France, the U.K., the U.S., and the Benelux countries in London, in February-March 1948. According to the Communiqué, issued on March 6:

> It was agreed that for the political and economic well-being of the countries of western Europe and of a democratic Germany there must be a close association of their economic life. Since it has not proved possible to achieve economic unity in Germany, and since the eastern zone has been prevented from playing its part in the European Recovery Programme, the three western powers have agreed that close cooperation should be established among themselves and among the occupation authorities in western Germany in all matters arising out of the European Recovery Programme in relation to western

---

[6]George F. Kennan, a member of the State Department Policy Planning Staff when in 1947 he signed himself "Mr. X," denied in January, 1959, in the midst of a revived Berlin crisis, that the intention had been "to contain militarily, in permanence, a Soviet Empire extending from the Elbe to the Pacific." "Berlin: Disengagement Revisited," *Foreign Affairs* (January, 1959).

Germany. Such cooperation is essential if western Germany is to make its full and proper contribution to European recovery (DG, p. 92).

When shortly thereafter Marshal Sokolovsky, Commander-in-Chief of Soviet occupation forces, demanded in the Control Council to have a full report on the details of the London discussions as they related to Germany, the western Commanders declined to give the information requested without first consulting their governments. On March 20, 1948, Sokolovsky announced the definitive withdrawal of the Soviet representatives from the Allied Control Council for Germany stating, quite correctly, that at the London conference:

> Official representatives of the United States, Britain and France discussed and decided such questions regarding Germany which come directly within the competence of the Control Council and can be decided only on the basis of agreement among the Four Powers occupying Germany. . . . By their actions these three delegations once again confirm that the Control Council virtually no longer exists as the supreme body of authority in Germany exercising quadripartite administration of that country (DG, pp. 92–93).

It was the last meeting of the Allied Control Council.

In these circumstances it is hardly surprising that General Clay "felt instinctively that a definite change in the attitude of the Russians in Berlin had occurred and that something was about to happen." What happened was that regulations and checks on military and civilian transit from the western zones to Berlin were gradually tightened and restricted or, as western accounts put it, the traffic was increasingly "harassed."

In June 1948, the crisis was brought to a head by the decision of the western powers to introduce a currency reform in the western zones, a move they regarded as essential to the economic recovery of Germany, and hence of western Europe. On June 18, the currency reform was announced, but introduction of the new currency into Berlin was postponed "for the time being," in view of the continuing four-power status of the city. The western announcement made clear, however, that Berlin was to remain tied to the west economically:

> The three Military Governments [of western Berlin] will, however, take all measures in order to maintain and strengthen Berlin's economic ties with the west which are vital to the welfare of the city. Berlin, too, is to share the benefits of the European Recovery Plan, which stands behind the new currency (DG, p. 99).

In any case, it was only a few days later that the new "Deutsche Mark" was in fact introduced into West Berlin. The Soviet Military Administration had insisted that, since Berlin was situated in the Eastern occupation zone, the city as a whole should use the same currency as that of the zone. At a meeting on June 22, representatives of the four military administrations failed to reach agreement on control of the currency to be used in Berlin, and immediately following the meeting, the Soviet Military Administration announced its own currency reform for the Soviet zone and the whole of Berlin. The western powers, declaring themselves unable to "submit to such arbitrary action which is in violation and total disregard of the actual quadripartite status of Berlin," then announced the introduction of the "Deutsche Mark" into the three western sectors of Berlin effective June 24, 1948. Soon afterward, the Soviet government announced the withdrawal of the Soviet Commandant of Berlin from the Berlin Kommandantura, thus putting an end to all vestiges of effective quadripartite rule in Germany, and marking the political as well as the economic division of the city of Berlin.

On June 23, following announcement of the extension of the western currency into Berlin, the Soviet authorities began to institute a series of measures which were ultimately to constitute a complete land blockade of Berlin. Railroad passenger and freight service, road traffic, mail and parcel post between the western zones and Berlin were almost completely cut off, as were deliveries of electricity, coal, and other supplies from the eastern sector of the city to the western sectors.

The western response to the blockade was the massive airlift operation by which the western sectors of the city of Berlin were supplied for nearly a year. While the Soviet and Western powers

negotiated, failed to agree, and negotiated again, the airlift continued and expanded, at enormous cost to the west, at considerable
sacrifice on the part of West Berliners, and at the price of hardening the division of Germany and Berlin. General Clay, who
thought the Russians had been showing "a new attitude" as early
as March 1948, "from Sokolovsky on down, . . . faintly contemptu-
ous, slightly arrogant, and certainly assured," now formulated an
early version of the domino theory: "When Berlin falls, western
Germany will be next. . . . If we withdraw, our position in Europe
is threatened. If America does not understand this now, does not
know that the issue is cast, then it never will and communism will
run rampant."[7]

When the blockade was lifted, after a year in which West Berlin
was supplied primarily by airlift, a great deal had changed in the
European political scene. In the atmosphere of open hostility, the
western powers had succeeded in consolidating the North Atlantic
Treaty Organization, which they viewed as an important bulwark
of their "defense" and "security." They had also taken advantage
of the conflict to press ahead with their plans to amalgamate the
western zones of Germany and integrate the reconstructed unit
into their program for western European economic recovery. In
short, they proceeded rapidly to the establishment of a West German state.

Thus it came about that a "Parliamentary Council," comprised
of representatives of the provincial governments (the *Länder*) of
the western zones, drafted a "Basic Law" to serve as the constitution of a new state, the Federal Republic of Germany. On May 12,
1949, the Allied Military Governors of the western zones approved the draft law, and it was submitted for ratification by the
Land governments. Upon ratification by all except Bavaria (which
agreed to be bound by the will of the majority), the Basic Law was
adopted on May 23, 1949. The three western powers then instituted a complete trizonal fusion of their residual occupation
functions under a new office, the Allied High Commission for
Germany.

The initial reactions of the Soviet Union were conciliatory, and
apparently bent on preventing the permanent division of Ger-

---

[7]Quoted by Wilfrid Knapp in *A History of War and Peace, 1939–1965* (London,
1967), pp. 129, 134.

many implied in the establishment of a separate west German state. Early in 1949, the Soviet Union gave it to be understood that it would lift the blockade of Berlin in return for an agreement to reconvene the Council of Foreign Ministers, "to review the whole German problem." This led to the New York agreement of May 4, 1949, by which all restrictions on communications, transportation, and trade between the zones would be mutually lifted as of May 12, and a meeting of the Foreign Ministers would be held in Paris beginning May 23, 1949. Whether by accident or design, May 23 was also the date on which the adoption of the "Basic Law" of the Federal Republic was proclaimed. In June the Foreign Ministers again adjourned without agreement on substantive issues, though they did agree to "consult together in Berlin on a quadripartite basis" for the purpose of achieving a "restoration of the economic and political unity of Germany" (DG, p. 164).

Nevertheless, the machinery for establishing a separate West German state continued in motion. Elections were held in August, producing a Christian Democratic majority in the *Bundestag* (139 out of 402 seats), with Social Democrats running a close second (131 seats). The Communist Party, still legal at this time, won about five percent of the vote (fifteen seats). On September 12, Theodor Heuss was elected first Federal President, and on September 15, Konrad Adenauer, former Lord Mayor of Cologne, was elected by a doubtful majority of one vote to be Federal Chancellor.

On October 1, 1949, the Soviet Union directed to the United States a long note of protest concerning the establishment of a separate "puppet" government for western Germany, asserting that it violated the Potsdam obligations "of treating Germany as one single whole and of facilitating her transformation into a democratic and peace-loving state." Moreover, the note pointed out, it was in violation of the decisions of the recent Foreign Ministers' Conference, which committed the four powers to "continue their efforts to achieve the restoration of the economic and political unity of Germany." The western powers were accused of "abandoning the Potsdam decisions" and following a policy "of splitting Germany and restoring the dominant position of reactionary, militaristic and revanchist elements in Western Germany" (DG, p. 169).

Despite the plaintive and indignant tone of this note, which, taken as a whole, has a ring of sincerely felt injury about it, the Soviet Union was not to be outdone in the contest for the partition of Germany. The constitution for an east German state had already been prepared, and a provisional government of the German Democratic Republic was proclaimed on October 7, 1949. To this new government the Soviet Union transferred most of the functions previously performed by the Soviet Military Administration, and created a Soviet Control Commission to carry on the residual occupation functions.

The response to this move from the Allied High Commission was short and disdainful. It blamed exclusively the "Soviet refusal to cooperate" for the failure to reach agreement on a uniform policy for Germany. It asserted the democratic basis of the Federal Republic claiming that it "springs from the German people," and denied the legitimacy of the Democratic Republic, which it called the "artificial creation" of an assembly which had "no mandate":

> This so-called government, which is devoid of any legal basis, and has determined to evade an appeal to the electorate, has no title to represent Eastern Germany (DG, p. 173).

This exchange of hostile notes set the tone for the polemics of the succeeding years. The United States and the Federal Republic denied the legitimacy of the Democratic Republic, refused to allow it any form of recognition as a state or as a member of the international community, did all they could to prevent other nations from giving it recognition, and claimed for the Federal Republic the right to speak for all Germans as the only "freely elected" government in Germany. The Soviet Union and the Democratic Republic, for their part, held the United States and the other western powers responsible for the partition of Germany, called the Federal Republic a "puppet" of "imperialist circles," and accused the Federal Republic and its western sponsors of reviving militarism, Nazism, reactionary elites, and "revanchist" sentiment in West Germany.

By the year 1955, the Soviet Union and the German Democratic Republic had reason to feel that their worst suspicions were justified, when the Federal Republic of Germany was admitted to full membership in NATO. According to the terms of the Paris Treaties of October 23, 1954, the Federal Republic bound itself "not to manufacture in its territory any atomic weapons, chemical weapons or biological weapons . . . " (DG, p. 245), a step which was a unique instance of declared unilateral arms control. Nevertheless the Federal Republic was in no way prohibited from having under its control any weapons, including tactical nuclear weapons, which might fall under the command of NATO forces. In fact, plans had already been made

> to deploy tactical nuclear weapons on NATO's forward line in Germany . . . , the new strategy assigned new and crucial functions to the proposed German contingents. . . . Bonn renounced not a nuclear strategy but rather the independent production of nuclear weapons on German territory.[8]

When the Paris Treaties went into effect on May 5, 1955, the western powers terminated the occupation regime in the Federal Republic and abolished the Allied High Commission, reserving only "the rights and responsibilities . . . relating to Berlin and to Germany as a whole, including the reunification of Germany and a peace settlement," as well as certain rights to station their troops on German territory.

The Soviet response to these developments was the formation of the Warsaw Pact alliance by which the U.S.S.R. and a number of Eastern European countries bound themselves to "collective self-defense" in the event of armed attack, and for that purpose, to the establishment of a "Unified Command, to which certain elements of their armed forces shall be allocated" (DG, p. 263). The German Democratic Republic was accepted into the alliance on May 24, 1955, but at first no German troops were assigned to the Unified Command. The occasion was taken, however, to transform the "People's Police Forces" into a standing National Army, from which contingents entered the Warsaw Pact forces in January 1956.

The U.S.S.R. also followed suit with the western powers in abolishing the occupation regime in East Germany. On September 20, the U.S.S.R. and the German Democratic Republic signed a treaty recognizing the latter's sovereignty and terminating the functions

---

[8]Wolfram F. Hanrieder, *The Stable Crisis: Two Decades of German Foreign Policy* (New York, 1970), p. 8.

of the Soviet High Commissioner. This act, however, had unpleasant implications and consequences for the Federal Republic and the western powers.

In the first place, the Soviet Union proceeded immediately to establish diplomatic relations with the Federal Republic as well as with the Democratic Republic, calling attention explicitly to

> the actual situation which has come about at the present time, when on the territory of Germany there exist two independent sovereign states . . . (DG, p. 278).

The Federal Republic, finding that diplomatic relations with the Soviet Union would be advantageous, agreed to the exchange of diplomatic missions, but vigorously rejected the position that there existed "two independent sovereign states" in Germany. To discourage other countries from following the precedent now set by the Soviet Union the Federal Republic instituted—informally but nonetheless rigidly—the so-called "Hallstein doctrine," by which it refused to maintain diplomatic relations with any country except the U.S.S.R. which recognized the Democratic Republic. This doctrine was first applied in the case of Yugoslavia in 1957; though unwritten, it remained the firm policy of the Federal Republic for many years.

But the termination of the Soviet occupation regime had a still more unpleasant consequence for the west: namely, the transfer to the Democratic Republic of control over transport and communications on its territory. The Soviet Union did stipulate that control over the movements of military personnel and freight of the armed forces of the United States, Great Britain and France would remain in Russian hands, but only "temporarily until the achievement of a suitable agreement" (DG, p. 278). Eventually, this implied, military traffic would also be turned over to the German Democratic Republic.

BERLIN AND BRINKSMANSHIP

It was the prospect of just such a move which made Berlin a crisis center again in the years 1958 to 1961, all the more dangerous in the setting of the nuclear arms race.

The initiative in the crisis came this time from the East. Why the Soviet Union chose to press the issue of Berlin in 1958 remains matter for speculation. Possibly it was a manifestation of the expansive self-confidence of Soviet policy under Nikita Khrushchev, resting partly on the progress in weapons and missile technology which the Soviet Union had demonstrated spectacularly in 1957 by launching the first "Sputnik." Or perhaps it was instead a reaction of genuine alarm both at the rapid rearmament of the Federal Republic of Germany as a member of NATO, and above all, at steps pointing toward the acquisition of nuclear weapons by West German armed forces.

This was certainly the concern emphasized by Khrushchev in his speech of November 10, 1958, which marked the opening of the crisis. As Khrushchev pointed out, the United States had already begun to provide West Germany with rockets fitted with nuclear warheads. These weapons were still under American control, but the Bonn government was pressing for nuclear sharing arrangements, which would give the Federal Republic at least a joint voice in the deployment and use of such weapons. In any case, the Soviet Union now acceded to the desire of the German Democratic Republic to seek a "normalization" of the status of Berlin. That status was certainly anomalous. East Berlin had been established as the capital of the German Democratic Republic when it was founded in 1949. But West Berlin could not be given comparable status in the Federal Republic of Germany.

To begin with, the only legal basis for denying the claim of the Democratic Republic that the whole of Berlin lay on or in its territory was the wartime agreements providing for quadripartite rule of the occupying powers in Berlin. Quadripartite rule had long since ceased in practice, but the western powers clung to the fiction of "quadripartite responsibility" and "occupation rights" in order to maintain this basis. By its constitution of 1950, West Berlin became a *Land* of the Federal Republic. The western Allied Kommandantura declared this provision "suspended," but in practice West Berlin is represented in the Bundestag though by nonvoting members; adheres to legislation, administrative statutes and judicial practices of the Federal Republic; and is represented by the Federal Republic abroad and in international organizations. These ties with the Federal Republic are all confirmed in the landmark Quadripartite Agreement on Berlin concluded in 1971, yet the western powers continue to insist that their "sectors" of Berlin are not "a constituent part of the Federal Republic and not to be governed by it."

Moreover, the Soviet Union had clearly demonstrated in the Berlin blockade of 1948–49 that, at very little expense to itself, it could insure that running a West German government from Berlin would be prohibitively expensive, if not simply impossible. Thus it was necessary for the Federal Republic, despite its claim to be the sole legitimate representative of the German people, to establish its capital in Bonn, a provincial Rhineland town, rather than in the symbolic center of the German nation. While East Berlin was progressively integrated into the life of the German Democratic Republic, West Berlin remained isolated in its peculiar status as an "occupied territory."

In 1958, the Soviet Union and the German Democratic Republic were not willing to live with this anomaly. What the Soviet Union proposed was to transform West Berlin into a "free city," entirely independent, and to arrange for guarantees of its free and neutral status, whether by Four-Power action or through the United Nations.

The motivation behind this proposal is rather obscure. For the Soviet Union, the most "correct and natural way" to solve the problem of Berlin would have been to recognize the claims of the Democratic Republic to sovereignty over the whole city. Since that was impossible to achieve, as they recognized, they were searching for some way to insure that West Berlin would at least be less of a thorn in the flesh. On the face of it, what they hoped to gain was, first: neutralization and demilitarization of the western part of the city; second: a commitment on the part of the "free city" that it would undertake "not to permit on its territory any hostile subversive activity directed against the GDR [German Democratic Republic] or any other state"; third: a degree of international recognition for the German Democratic Republic, since the free city was to deal directly with it to arrange "guarantees of unhindered communications between the free city and the outside world—both to the East and to the West" (DG, pp. 364–65); and fourth: a definitive separation of West Berlin from the Federal Republic. Of these aims, one suspects that the last, which was nowhere made explicit, was the most serious and fundamental, at least to the German parties; the others all seem relatively unreal, or unenforceable.

But there was one thing in the Soviet note of November 27 on the status of Berlin which was neither unreal nor unenforceable: it was the long-dreaded threat, that the U.S.S.R. would turn over control of military traffic on access routes to and from Berlin to the German Democratic Republic.

The western response to this note was hardly persuasive. In a declaration of December 16, 1958, the North Atlantic Council reminded the Soviet Union that no state "has the right to withdraw unilaterally from its international engagements." Ignoring their own independent actions in regard to reparations, currency reform, Bi-Zonia, creation of the Federal Republic, its admission into NATO, and its rearmament, the western powers insisted that Soviet denunciation of the obsolete agreements on Berlin could "in no way deprive the other parties of their rights or relieve the Soviet Union of its obligations." Moreover, the Council asserted, "the Berlin question can only be settled in the framework of an agreement . . . on Germany as a whole" (DG, p. 367).

To this, the Soviet Union responded obligingly with the draft of a general peace treaty, transmitted to the United States on January 10, 1959. This was met with a surprisingly conciliatory answer on February 16, in which the United States proposed a Foreign Ministers' conference, to consider the problem of Germany "in all its aspects," while reminding the Soviet Union that the western powers "reserve the right to uphold by all appropriate means their communications with their sectors of Berlin" (DG, p. 412). This led to the Soviet proposal for a summit meeting, or for a Foreign Ministers' meeting as preparation for a summit meeting, which was accepted by the West, and resulted, in fact, in a Foreign Ministers' Conference which met in two sessions between May and August, 1959. As in the past, the meetings proved fruitless with respect to reaching a peace settlement. On the other hand, the six-months' deadline suggested in the Soviet note of November 1958 passed, unnoted, and was not revived. The great powers moved into a period of "détente," marked by Khrushchev's visit to the United States, and plans for the summit conference of May 1960.

But while the United States and the Soviet Union were dancing this diplomatic minuet, there was a discordant rattling of sabers in the background. The high point of this discordance was President Dwight D. Eisenhower's address to the nation of March 16, 1959. In retrospect, it seems likely that Eisenhower's hard line on this occasion had more to do with the arms budget request he had recently sent to Congress than with developments relating to Berlin. Nevertheless, the emphasis lay on Berlin and its significance for the world struggle between communism and the "free world":

> Ten years ago Senator John Foster Dulles, now our great Secretary of State, described the basic purpose of the Soviet Government. He said that purpose was: "... no less than world domination, to be achieved by gaining political power successively in each of the many areas which had been afflicted by war, so that in the end the United States, which was openly called the main enemy, would be isolated and closely encircled."
>
> The current Berlin effort of the Soviets falls within this pattern of basic purpose ... (DAFR, 1959, p. 26).

Having established that the Soviet purpose in Berlin was to encircle the United States, Eisenhower went on to argue that there were two alternatives open to the United States: one was to "shirk our responsibilities"; the second was to "face the possibility of war." The first, said Eisenhower, was "obviously ... unacceptable to us." It would solve no problems, would end all hopes for "a Germany under a government of German choosing," and would "undermine the mutual confidence upon which our entire system of collective security is founded."

On the other hand, "to face the possibility of war" was *not* unacceptable, even though Eisenhower acknowledged: "Global conflict under modern conditions could mean the destruction of civilization." This was clearly a small price to pay for "a Germany under a government of German choosing" and for maintaining "the mutual confidence upon which our entire system of collective security is founded." But of course Eisenhower was not really facing the possibility of war at all; he was persuaded that the United States could have its way without war.

Eisenhower went on to describe the massive United States "defense" establishment of "deterrent" and "retaliatory" nuclear weapons and delivery systems, speaking proudly of the "world-wide deployment of Army divisions, including missile units," serving to increase the ability of U.S. armed forces to "rapidly apply necessary force to any area of trouble."

The abortive summit meeting of May 1960, the embarrassments of denying, then admitting, the reconnaissance mission of the U-2 flight shot down over Soviet territory, and increasing preoccupation with Cuba, culminating in the Bay of Pigs invasion in the spring of 1961, distracted attention from Berlin for a time. But the crisis atmosphere revived and reached its peak in the summer of 1961.

Early in June the new President of the United States, John F. Kennedy, met with Chairman Khrushchev in Vienna. Khrushchev gave Kennedy an aide-memoire renewing the proposals which had been put forward by the Soviet Union in 1958: that a peace settlement in Europe was long overdue, that a peace treaty with Germany should be concluded immediately, and that it should embody the transformation of West Berlin into a demilitarized free city. The note was moderate in tone and showed many signs of flexibility. It offered, as a guarantee of the free and neutral status of West Berlin, to allow "token troop contingents" of the four occupying powers to be stationed there, as well as "military contingents from neutral States under the aegis of the United Nations" (DG, p. 525). The note also promised consideration to any other measures the western powers might propose to guarantee the status of a free, demilitarized West Berlin.

On the other hand the note did embody, more emphatically than before, expressions of determination to conclude a peace treaty within six months, even if it had to be by unilateral action. If no general peace treaty could be achieved, the Soviet Union would sign a peace treaty with the German Democratic Republic, along the lines of the Soviet proposals already indicated.

> At the same time, [the note warned] this would mean putting an end to the occupation regime in West Berlin with all its implications. In particular, questions of using the means of communication by land, water or air within the territory of the GDR would have to be settled solely by appropriate agreements with the GDR. That is but natural, since control over such means of communication is an inalienable right of every sovereign State (DG, pp. 526–27).

Kennedy was more shaken by his conversations with Khrushchev than by the precise contents of the note. It was clear from Khrushchev's manner that the subjects of the German peace treaty and the problem of Berlin were, of all the issues under discussion between them, of the most intense concern to him. But it was Kennedy's approach which placed the discussion immediately upon a hostile basis. Ignoring the whole proposal for a treaty and for a free city of West Berlin, Kennedy focused exclusively upon the alternative of unilateral action. He spoke of the consequences if "we allowed ourselves to be expelled" from Berlin and declared that America would not accept an ultimatum. He perceived the Soviet proposal as a move "to upset the world balance of power" and "to bring about a basic change in the world situation overnight." He told Khrushchev that he had not assumed office to accept arrangements totally inimical to American interests.

Khrushchev remarked, perceptively, that he understood Kennedy to mean the United States did not want a treaty. As for Khrushchev:

> All he wanted to do was to tranquilize the situation in the most dangerous spot in the world. The Soviet Union wanted to perform an operation—to excise this thorn, this ulcer—without prejudicing interests on either side. The treaty would not change boundaries; it would formalize them. It would only impede those, like Hitler's generals now in NATO, who still wanted *Lebensraum* to the Urals. . . . [9]

Moreover, there was precedent for a separate peace treaty: the United States had signed a separate peace treaty with Japan. Confronted with Kennedy's insistence on the most extreme interpretation of the Soviet note, and his failure to show any interest in the positive content of the proposals, Khrushchev's tone grew more strident. Why did the United States want to stay in Berlin, he asked:

---

[9]Arthur M. Schlesinger, Jr., *A Thousand Days: John F. Kennedy in the White House* (Boston, 1965), pp. 371–72. The following two quotations in the text below were also taken from this source, pages 372–73 and 380–81 respectively.

To unleash a war? . . . If America wanted war over Berlin, there was nothing the Soviet Union could do about it. Maybe he should sign the treaty right away and get it over; that is what the Pentagon had wanted. . . . The Soviet Union was determined to go ahead, and responsibility for subsequent violations of East German sovereignty would be heavy.

Kennedy left the meeting with Khrushchev disturbed, but uncertain of what to do. The fact was that the west had no positive policy with respect to Berlin. At a meeting in Washington, Lord Home, British Foreign Secretary, pointed out that the west was failing to offer any alternative to Khrushchev's proposed peace treaty:

We were in Berlin because of the right of conquest, but the right of conquest was wearing thin. Acheson coolly replied that perhaps it was western power which was wearing thin. Home continued that he was never happy about entering a negotiation without a position. To this a State Department official observed that, since no acceptable agreement was possible, we should do everything we could to avoid negotiation. The President sat poker-faced, confining himself to questions about the adequacy of existing military plans and saying that, if Khrushchev could be deterred only by fear of direct encounter, the allies must consider how to convince him that such an encounter would be sufficiently costly.

The policy debate had been going on for months, but in the end Kennedy came back to the same place: his chief preoccupation was to demonstrate to the Russians that if they persisted in their intention, the encounter would be "sufficiently costly." He was aware of the danger of a purely military response, or of seeming "unnecessarily bellicose, perhaps even hysterical," as Henry Kissinger put it. But he seemed even more worried about the possibility that Khrushchev might interpret his reluctance to wage nuclear war as a symptom of an American loss of nerve.

On July 25, 1961, Kennedy made a national television address on the Berlin crisis. Ignoring again the proposals put forward for negotiation by the Soviet Union, Kennedy informed the nation that Khrushchev "intends to bring to an end, through a stroke of the pen, first, our legal rights to be in West Berlin, and, secondly, our ability to make good on our commitment to the 2 million free people of that city." Like Eisenhower in 1959, Kennedy declared this possibility unacceptable:

> For West Berlin, lying exposed 110 miles inside East Germany, surrounded by Soviet troops and close to Soviet supply lines, has many roles. It is more than a showcase of liberty, a symbol, an island of freedom in a Communist sea. It is even more than a link with the free world, a beacon of hope behind the Iron Curtain, an escape hatch for refugees.
>
> West Berlin is all of that. But above all it has now become, as never before, the great testing place of Western courage and will, a focal point where our solemn commitments, stretching back over the years since 1945, and Soviet ambitions now meet in basic confrontation (DAFR, 1961, p. 97).

Kennedy did not go so far as to declare a national emergency, which he had seriously considered doing. But he did call for an increase of over $3 billion for the defense budget and for manpower increases requiring that draft calls be doubled and tripled in the following months. He also called up a number of reserve units, air transport squadrons, and Air National Guard squadrons. Perhaps most ominous of all, Kennedy proposed a new Civil Defense program, to provide increased air raid shelter protection, at a cost of an additional $200 million:

> In the event of an attack, the lives of those families which are not hit in a nuclear blast and fire can still be saved—*if* they can be warned to take shelter and *if* that shelter is available. . . .In the coming months I hope to let every citizen know what steps he can take without delay to protect his family in case of attack (DAFR, 1961, p. 100).

Kennedy did offer some generalized assurances that the United States was ready to negotiate but, as Theodore Sorenson later observed, in the absence of any positive proposals these were the weakest parts of the address.

Khrushchev was not alone in seeing the speech as a sign of "military hysteria" in the United States. He told John J. McCloy that it showed the United States "clearly intended hostilities." Nevertheless he hoped that sanity would prevail. As in the Cuban crisis the following year, he found a way to insure that it would.

In this instance he was assisted by an element in the crisis which had been mentioned by Kennedy only in passing but now took center stage: the East German refugees using West Berlin as their "escape hatch" swelled in numbers, in July and early August, to about 80,000. The flight of skilled workers and professionals, many of them trained and educated at state expense, had long been a serious problem for the German Democratic Republic; now it rose to an imminent disaster. Something had to be done about it.

What was done was rather original, though crude. On August 13, the East German government closed most of the crossing points between East and West Berlin with barbed wire barricades; on August 17, construction was begun on a concrete, brick and barbed wire wall along the entire dividing line.

This move was so bizarre and unexpected that it caught the western powers unprepared with any response, except futile protest notes. Feelings ran high, but it was apparent that building a wall on the territory of East Berlin was not a violation of the rights of the western powers, not an interference in the internal affairs of the government of West Berlin, and not a threat to expel the west from West Berlin. In short, it was not an occasion for war—the only means by which the wall could have been prevented or torn down—and it even implied acceptance of the continued presence of the western powers in West Berlin.

The wall, ugly as it was in physical and human terms, eventually put an end to the Berlin crisis of 1961. For the German Democratic Republic, it was a much more effective solution than the free city proposal would have been to the immediate problems posed by West Berlin: not only the flight of refugees, but also the use of the city for a variety of hostile purposes, ranging from propaganda to espionage. The United States had succeeded in preserving the formal occupation status of West Berlin, but at the cost of destroying much of its usefulness to the West, and of rendering it even less viable economically than before.

Had the free city proposal been accepted as a basis for negotiation, with four-power and neutral troop contingents as guarantors, West Berlin might have remained all that Kennedy said it was in his speech of July 25. After the building of the wall, it was certainly no longer "a showcase of liberty" since none of the "unliberated" could see it any longer, nor "a link with the free world, a beacon of hope behind the Iron Curtain, an escape hatch for refugees." Kennedy had placed Berlin's symbolic role as "the great testing place of Western courage and will" explicitly "above all." What the West won in the test remains to be judged.

THE ODER-NEISSE LINE AND THE REFUGEES

Americans commonly speak of the division of Germany into "West Germany" and "East Germany." West Germans, however, are more likely to refer to the latter either as the "East *Zone*" (the Soviet occupation zone) or as "Mitteldeutschland" (*Central* Germany). For them there was a different "East Germany," namely, the "former German territories" lying east of the Oder-Neisse line.

The separation of these eastern portions of the former German Reich from Germany and their complete integration into the territory and society of Russia or Poland is an aspect of the partition of Germany which has been among the sorest points in the postwar European scene, as it was in the inter-Allied diplomacy of the war years.

The roots of the problem reach back into the ancient migrations and hatreds of Germans, Russians, and Poles, but stem more immediately from the absence of a firm settlement in Eastern Europe after World War I. The Versailles peacemakers, attempting to grapple with the boundary problems of the tier of Eastern European nations which they had set out to create, accepted for the eastern boundary of Poland the so-called Curzon line, drawn up by a five-nation commission according to the ethnic character of the population at that time. This line was proposed to the Soviet Government in 1920, at a time when Poland seemed to be losing the war then in progress against the newly established U.S.S.R. The following year, however, Poland won a larger territory by the Treaty of Riga. By the terms of the Nazi-Soviet Pact of 1939, Stalin avenged this loss by a new partition of Poland. Driven out again by the German attack and rapid advances in 1941–42, the Soviet Union renounced the territorial provisions of the pact with Hitler, but proposed to its new Allies, the western powers, that the Curzon line be revived and established as the eastern boundary of Poland.

The Polish government-in-exile in London (under General Sikorski and, later, Stanislaw Mikolajczyk) vehemently rejected this proposal. Accordingly, the Anglo-American Allies insisted that the settlement of this and all other territorial issues be deferred to the postwar peace settlement. But since the Poles were interested in acquiring territory in the west from Germany, the British, under Churchill and Eden, soon tried to persuade them to trade the Curzon line (modified according to current ethnic distribution) for substantial compensation from Germany. Stalin was in accord with this proposal, provided that the Soviet Union should also receive some German territory, in particular the port and city of Königsberg and the surrounding territory of East Prussia.

The Americans, however, seeing in Poland "the test of future relations with Russia throughout the world," were especially reluctant to pressure the Polish exile government to accept the formula "Curzon and compensation." In any case, the London Poles were adamant, and indeed remained so throughout the war, strengthened in their determination to resist Russian incursions on Polish territory by the murky circumstances of the Katyn massacre (revealed in 1943), the formation of a competing political center in the Polish Committee of National Liberation in Lublin in 1944, and the events of the Warsaw uprising of the same year.

But the London Poles were impotent to determine this question. On December 31, 1944, with the Soviet Army in control of Warsaw, the Lublin Poles announced the formation of a Polish Provisional Government, which was recognized by the U.S.S.R. on January 4, 1945.

At the Yalta Conference in February, the Allied Powers arrived at an agreement coupling territorial concessions to the Soviet Union with an understanding that the existing pro-Soviet Provisional Government of Poland would give way to a "Government of National Unity" including "democratic" elements from inside and outside Poland (that is, noncommunists, including representatives of the London-based government-in-exile). The final declaration of the Conference did recognize both the Curzon line and Poland's claim to compensation, but left all details on the latter open:

The three heads of Government consider that the eastern frontier of Poland should follow the Curzon line with digressions from it in some regions of five to eight kilometres in favor of Poland. They recognize that Poland must receive substantial accessions of territory in the North and West. They feel that the opinion of the new Polish Provisional Government of National Unity should be sought in due course on the extent of these accessions and that the final delimitation of the western frontier of Poland should thereafter await the Peace Conference.[10]

Talks on the formation of a Polish Government of National Unity rapidly reached a stalemate, but Russian control in Poland at this time was tolerant, and the Provisional Government gradually acquired signs of mass support, as well as adherents from the leadership of noncommunist parties, ultimately including even Mikolajczyk. When the latter appeared at the Potsdam Conference, urging the British and Americans to recognize the Polish claims to German territory, and arguing that the opportunity for democracy in Poland would otherwise be lost, the western powers agreed to a tentative transfer of territory, "pending the final determination of territorial questions at the peace settlement."

What they agreed to was, first, a division of East Prussia, allotting the city of Königsberg and the surrounding region to Russia, the rest to Poland; and, second, with respect to Polish acquisition of formerly German territories:

The three Heads of Government agree that, pending the final determination of Poland's western frontier, the former German territories east of a line running from the Baltic Sea immediately west of Swinemunde, and thence along the Oder River to the confluence of the western Neisse River. . .shall be under the administration of the Polish State and for such purposes should not be considered as part of the Soviet zone of occupation in Germany (DG, p. 40).

While this left the "final determination" of the Polish-German boundary open for the peace settlement which never took place,

---

[10]Jozef Kokot, *The Logic of the Oder-Neisse Frontier* (Poznan, 1959), p. 14.

it gave explicit recognition to the separation from occupied Germany of territories bounded by the Oder and western Neisse rivers and to their administration, at least temporarily, by the Polish government.

By the time this decision was arrived at in Potsdam, there was already under way that massive transfer of populations in Eastern and Central Europe which accompanied the advance of the Soviet armies, the establishment of new governments, and the transfer of territories. Millions of persons displaced from their homes in the course of the war were seeking to return, to find relatives long separated, to find a suitable place to settle down. Millions of Poles whose homes had been in the territories acquired by Russia moved into Polish territory, particularly that just acquired from Germany. Millions of Germans from all countries in Eastern Europe, above all from East Prussia and the territories transferred to Poland, fled before the Soviet advance or were expelled by the new governments.

This transfer of populations did not come as any surprise to the Allied powers. Stalin made use of the flight or expulsion of Germans from the eastern territories as an argument in favor of transferring the allegedly then-vacant territories of Poland. Churchill openly defended the expulsion of the Germans in a speech to the House of Commons on December 15, 1944:

> The transference of several millions of people would have to be effected from the east to the west or north, and the expulsion of the Germans (because that is what is proposed—the total expulsion of the Germans) from the area to be acquired by Poland in the west and north. For expulsion is the method which, so far as we have been able to see, will be the most satisfactory and lasting. There will be no mixture of populations to cause endless trouble as in Alsace-Lorraine. A clean sweep will be made. . . .
>
> Nor do I see why there should not be room in Germany for the German population of East Prussia and of the other territories I have mentioned. After all, 6,000,000 or 7,000,000 Germans have been killed already in this frightful war, into which they did not hesitate, for a second time in a generation, to plunge all Europe. At the present time, we are told that they have 10,000,000 or 12,000,000 prisoners or foreigners used as

slaves in Germany who will . . . be restored to their own homes and lands when victory is gained.[11]

Finally, the Potsdam Conference explicitly recognized the necessity of the transfers:

> The Three Governments, having considered the question in all its aspects, recognize that the transfer to Germany of German populations, or elements thereof, remaining in Poland, Czechoslovakia and Hungary, will have to be undertaken. They agree that any transfers that take place should be effected in an orderly and humane manner (DG, p. 41).

No one is likely to argue that the expulsions of Germans from Eastern Europe were "orderly and humane." Whether or not they were more humane than the extermination camps, slave labor camps, mass executions, and depopulation policies of the Germans in Eastern countries under Hitler seems a question impossible to answer and morally indefensible. Many Germans had declared Slavic and Jewish peoples to be "Untermenschen," had treated them like beasts rather than humans, had slaughtered, enslaved, tortured, starved, and degraded millions of Poles, Czechs, Russians, Jews and other "non-Aryan" peoples. When the moment came, the "non-Aryans" turned upon the Germans, innocent and guilty alike, with the bestiality unleashed or imposed upon them by those experiences. The dream of a Third Reich greater than all others was replaced by a nightmare: the *House of the Dead* writ large across the face of Europe.

Yet for the Germans, unlike their former victims who were deported only to be enslaved or exterminated, there were reasons to be glad amidst the fear, pain and confusion. Günther Grass, the novelist, described the exodus in *Dog Years:*

> . . . everybody who has a nose to smell with runs, swims, drags himself away: away from the Eastenemy toward the Westenemy; civilians on foot, on horseback, packed into former cruise steamers, hobble in stocking feet, drown wrapped in paper money, crawl with too little gas and too much baggage;

---

[11]*Ibid.,* pp. 9–10.

... Left behind: mounds of bones, mass graves, card files, flagpoles, party books, love letters, homes, church pews, and pianos difficult to transport.

... All are eager to forget the mounds of bones and the mass graves, the flagpoles and party books, the debts and the guilt.[12]

Indeed, all were very "eager to forget the mounds of bones and the mass graves, the flagpoles and party books, the debts and the guilt." But eager as they were to start out fresh, many were reluctant to forget the rest of what they had left behind. They remembered the "love letters, homes, church pews, and pianos difficult to transport," and they refused to be reconciled to the loss. The most significant long-range effect of the expulsions of the Germans was therefore not self-examination, but self-pity and the formation of a stubborn "revisionist" faction which long wielded a profound influence upon West German foreign policy and the prospects for German reunification.

Expellees formed a number of organizations, including the Central Association of Expelled Germans and a political organization, the "Block of the Expelled and Dispossessed." Such groups, though never large in numbers, claimed to speak for the growing numbers of refugees who made their way to West Germany in the postwar years, variously estimated as between eight and twelve million persons. They exerted significant influence as a pressure block, implacably opposed to acceptance of the Oder-Neisse line as the Polish-German boundary.

In the Soviet zone, opposition to the Oder-Neisse line was at first permitted and freely expressed. In 1950, however, after the establishment of the two German states, the German Democratic Republic recognized the Oder-Neisse line as the definitive boundary between Germany and Poland.

In the Federal Republic, a large majority of the population gave its assent, for many years, to the position taken by the expellees. In March 1951, more than five years after the end of the war, eighty percent of West Germans interviewed by opinion pollers were firmly opposed to acceptance of the Oder-Neisse line. Even in December 1956, more than ten years after the eastern territories had been taken over by Poland, seventy-three percent contin-

---

[12]Günther Grass, *Dog Years* (New York, 1965), p. 360.

ued to oppose recognition of that line. Ludwig Erhard, during his term as Chancellor of the Federal Republic (1963–66), is said to have remarked that he would "hardly come out of it alive" if he told the truth to the expellees—that recovery of the eastern territories was not to be hoped for.

Nevertheless, the passage of time did gradually erode the strength and numbers of those who insisted that the eastern territories were still "German." The population of those territories was now clearly Polish, and the number of West Germans willing to admit that the Poles who had settled there had acquired a right to claim the territory as theirs gradually increased. In November 1967 it was already a majority of fifty-six percent which was willing to concede this; by November 1969 it was as much as sixty-eight percent.

Moreover, the refugees were successfully assimilating into the West German economy and society. There are indications that at first, in the years of hardship immediately following the German defeat, the refugees met with hostility from indigenous West Germans who felt them as a severe burden on an economy beset by acute shortages of jobs, food and living accommodations. At first the refugees fared somewhat worse than the rest of the West German population, for example in unemployment. But as the West German economy swung into its spectacular recovery the refugee population also found its place, made its contribution, and settled into its new homeland.

In time, the desire to forget "mounds of bones," guilt and debts, and the eagerness to start afresh came to overshadow longing for the old homeland in the individual lives of the refugees, even if not in the propaganda of their political spokesmen. Though some ninety percent of the native residents of the American occupation zone in the early postwar years apparently expected the refugees to return to the east if given the opportunity, a smaller proportion of the refugees themselves expressed the intention to do so. By April 1949, only thirty-eight percent of the expellees expressed themselves as determined to return to the territories east of the Oder-Neisse line, and as many as thirty percent rejected a return to those territories as out of the question. By November 1967, fifty percent were ready to admit that it was out of the question for them to return; two years later the percentage was up to fifty-nine percent.

Given these changes in the circumstances and attitudes of the expellees, it is not surprising that public opinion in West Germany gradually became less firm in rejecting the Oder-Neisse line. In August 1953, sixty-six percent of West Germans interviewed were persuaded that the eastern territories would some day be returned to Germany; but by May 1959, only thirty-five percent believed this, and the percentage declined steadily. By November 1967, a majority of Germans admitted that they were convinced the eastern territories were permanently lost; in November 1969, sixty-eight percent were willing to concede the loss. This trend was paralleled, though not matched, by the opinion of the West German public on acceptance of the Oder-Neisse line. In December 1956, only nine percent of those interviewed were willing to accept that boundary, but in the early 1960s the percentage gradually rose. In 1967, forty-seven percent of those interviewed expressed willingness to accept the Oder-Neisse line; in November 1969 it was a clear majority, fifty-one percent; by April 1970 it was up to fifty-eight percent.

By that time, negotiations were under way between the Federal Republic, the U.S.S.R., and Poland, for treaties which would give formal recognition to this change in West German opinion.

FROM THE "POLITICS OF STRENGTH" TO THE POLITICS OF COEXISTENCE

In the shadow of the Berlin wall, in the first years after it was built, Willy Brandt and his close associate, Egon Bahr, began to reexamine the situation of Berlin and Germany. For Brandt, Mayor of West Berlin and leader of the West German Social Democratic Party, the true significance of West Berlin lay not in those images projected by John F. Kennedy in his speech of July 25, 1961, but rather in its symbolic meaning as the "outpost of reunification."

The Social Democrats had long claimed to be more sincere advocates of reunification than the Christian Democrats. They had reason to be, since they had lost the larger part of their voting strength in the division of the country: Prussia, despite its authoritarian traditions, had had a Social Democratic government throughout the Weimar Republic. Moreover, despite intense hostility between Communists and Social Democrats the Social Democrats were, from the viewpoint of policy, less hostile to the social and economic transformations taking place in the German Democratic Republic than were the Christian Democrats. Coincidentally, the leadership of the two parties differed strikingly in geographic origin. Not only Willy Brandt, the Berliner, but also Kurt Schumacher, who rebuilt the Social Democratic Party and led it in the postwar years until his death in 1952, was a Prussian, born in Kulm, a town settled once by Teutonic Knights, in territory later disputed with Poland. In contrast, Konrad Adenauer, leader of the Christian Democratic Union and Chancellor of the Federal Republic from its founding until 1963, was a Rhinelander openly hostile to the tradition of Prussian dominance in Germany. Adenauer's fantasies favored Charlemagne, rather than the Teutonic Knights; Franco-German union, not "the road to the East."

But the Social Democrats, no less than the Christian Democrats, sought reunification only on their own terms. And as time passed, these terms came closer to those of the CDU (Christian Democratic Union), as the Social Democratic Party gave up its traditional commitment to Marxist doctrine and adopted, in 1959, the Godesberg Program of "democratic humanism." At the same time it adopted a policy, not notably democratic-humanist in character, of "bipartisanship" in foreign policy, in particular offering support for the government's adherence to NATO, for west European integration, and for West German "defense" policies. Altogether, the style and character of the Social Democrats changed greatly, conforming to the norms of West German society, and the party grew correspondingly in popular support. In 1966, the SPD (Social Democratic Party) found itself able to take a key position in the Federal government by replacing the Free Democrats (a conservative party) in a government coalition which, since it commanded no less than ninety percent of the votes in the Bundestag, was known as the "Grand Coalition."

During the Adenauer era, the Federal Republic had followed "the politics of strength" in foreign policy, placing highest priority upon west German "security" and rearmament under the wing of NATO. There were signs of change, gestures of accommodation with the East, as early as 1963, when Ludwig Erhard succeeded Adenauer as Chancellor. In 1966, with Kurt Kiesinger as Chancellor of the "Grand Coalition" government, and Willy Brandt as Foreign Minister, Brandt found himself in an excellent position to start applying the results of his meditations on the Berlin wall.

The conclusions which Brandt and Bahr had come to in those years had been expressed by Bahr in a speech in 1963:

> Today it is clear that reunification is not a single act, . . . but a process with many steps and many stations.
>
> I hold the discussion of "recognition" as too narrow . . . because it can lead us into a blind alley and obstruct every political approach.[13]

Reunification was to be sought as a long-range process of reconciliation and reintegration by piecemeal steps, in which juristic questions like "recognition," which Brandt was determined not to grant, should be avoided in favor of a more pragmatic, "political approach."

The efforts of the "Grand Coalition" to open diplomatic and economic exchanges with the countries of eastern Europe met at first with a warm reception—too warm, from the viewpoint of the German Democratic Republic. To the GDR, it appeared that the West German moves threatened to isolate it from its Warsaw Pact allies. Thus Walter Ulbricht—First Secretary of the Socialist Unity Party and the key figure in the East German government from its founding until his replacement, over two decades later, in May 1971—set out to dampen the warmth of the reception. He urged the allies of the GDR to bear in mind that any treaties they might enter into with the Bonn government should embody not only recognition of the Oder-Neisse boundary, but also of the German Democratic Republic and its boundary with the Federal Republic. In the course of the year 1967, Ulbricht secured what he wanted from Poland, Czechoslovakia, Hungary, and Bulgaria, though not from Rumania. Nevertheless the growth of friendly contacts, especially between the Federal Republic and Czechoslovakia, left Ulbricht very uneasy. Whether he had anything to do with what followed is unclear, but certainly the Soviet invasion of Czechoslovakia in August 1968 took as its pretext the threat of West German

---

[13]"Nach der Berlin-Erfolg: Die Deutschen verhandeln," *Der Spiegel*, 36:25 (30 August 1971), p. 25 (author's translation).

subversion, and the "Eastern offensive" of the Grand Coalition ended in failure.

But in 1969 a new coalition took office, composed of the Social Democrats and the Free Democrats, with the SPD now the senior partner and the CDU out of the governing power for the first time in the history of the Federal Republic. The new coalition, under Willy Brandt as Chancellor, took office at a time when public opinion in west Germany had visibly swung away from the rigid positions of the Adenauer era. Not only was the public willing to accept recognition of the Oder-Neisse boundary, but now it even seemed to prefer recognition of the Democratic Republic itself to a prolonged period of international tension maintained in hopes of achieving eventual reunification. In any case, whether or not willing to "recognize" the German Democratic Republic, a substantial majority (sixty-two percent of those polled in November 1969) had apparently given up hope for the reunification of East and West Germany in the foreseeable future. Only eighteen percent still believed in the possibility of reunification within their lifetimes.

The policy of the Brandt government was set forth in Brandt's opening speech to the Bundestag on October 28, 1969. The purpose of accommodation with the East, he explained, was not to seal the partition of Germany as a permanent reality but, on the contrary, to lay the groundwork for reunification by removing barriers to communication between Germans:

> ... no one can dissuade us from our conviction that the Germans have a right to self-determination just as any other nation.
>
> The object of our practical political work in the years immediately ahead is to preserve the unity of the nation by easing the tenseness in relations between the two parts of Germany. The Germans are not only connected by reason of their language and their history with all its splendor and its misery, we are all at home in Germany. ...
>
> Twenty years after the establishment of the Federal Republic of Germany and of the GDR we must prevent any further alienation of the two parts of the German nation; that is, arrive at a regular modus vivendi and from there proceed to cooperation (DG, p. 815).

But certain points could not be sacrificed even for this great purpose. The Federal Republic would continue to refuse formal recognition under international law to the German Democratic Republic:

> The Federal Republic and the GDR are not foreign countries to each other (DG, p. 825).

Above all, the Federal Republic would continue to insist upon

> ... the reality of West Berlin, part of a four-power city, under the unrestricted supremacy of the three powers, linked—on behalf of the three powers—with the economic, financial and judicial system of the federation and represented outwardly by the Federal Government (DG, p. 827).

This insistence upon "the unrestricted supremacy of the three powers" in West Berlin seems a very odd position to be taken by the Berliner Brandt, who at the same time was saying: "Nobody can tell us that the Germans do not have the same right to self-determination as all other peoples." But for Brandt, three-power rule in West Berlin was a holding operation, designed to prevent the Democratic Republic from swallowing the whole of Berlin. And this was not only for the sake of the freedom of Berliners, but precisely because Berlin was the symbol of the reunified German nation.

Now the Brandt government was careful to make approaches to the German Democratic Republic before seeking ties with the other Warsaw Pact nations. And this time, there was a favorable response from Ulbricht. On March 19, 1970, Brandt met with east German Prime Minister Willi Stoph in Erfurt, in the GDR. Subsequently, the two met again, at Kassel, in the FRG. No agreement on matters of substance was reached on either occasion, and the Kassel meeting was rather less cordial than that in Erfurt.

Nevertheless, these meetings were of great importance. They were the first direct meetings between the two states at a high governmental level. There had all along been contacts and negotiations between the states at lower levels of administration relating, for example, to trade, postal exchange, et cetera. But for the Chancellor of the Federal Republic to sit down with the Prime

Minister of the Democratic Republic represented a highly significant change.

And the change bore fruit for Brandt's eastern policy. On August 12, 1970, Brandt signed a treaty in Moscow with Alexei N.
Kosygin, Chairman of the Council of Ministers of the U.S.S.R., in
behalf of their respective governments. The two countries agreed
to a mutual renunciation of the threat or use of force in the settlement of disputes, and agreed to respect as inviolable existing
boundaries in Europe, including both the Oder-Neisse line and
the frontier between the Federal Republic and the Democratic
Republic. On December 7, 1970, Brandt signed a similar treaty in
Warsaw, which explicitly recognized the Oder-Neisse boundary
and, in general, the inviolability of existing frontiers "now and in
the future." Both treaties were made conditional, in terms of ratification, upon the success of negotiations between the Four Powers,
as well as between the two German states, for a viable agreement
on Berlin. This difficult goal was reached, partly through the skill
of Egon Bahr, in a Quadripartite Agreement of September 3,
1971, followed by an agreement reached directly between representatives of the Federal Republic and the Democratic Republic,
signed on December 11, 1971.

The Berlin accords confirm both the ties between West Berlin
and the Federal Republic, and the three-power "responsibility"
for the city. They permit the establishment in West Berlin both of
agencies of the Federal Republic and of a Consulate General of the
U.S.S.R. They provide for easing current restraints upon travel,
trade, and communications between the two parts of Berlin and
between the two German states. If Brandt's analysis is correct,
they open the way for the gradual process he foresees, of reunification by "steps and stations."

EPILOGUE

Yet it seems increasingly clear that the two German states are
becoming precisely what Brandt wishes to prevent: two countries,
foreign to each other in culture and even in language, each commanding the loyalty of its own citizens. This has come about partly

through the policies and choices of other nations, partly through the policies and choices of Germans themselves.

The great powers and other European nations have continuously professed their commitment to the reunification of a "peaceful, democratic" Germany. The partition has thus had the appearance of an accidental result of policies which were not intended to divide Germany, but intended for a variety of other purposes. Such were, for example, the denial of reparations from the western zones of occupation and the high level of reparations exacted from the Soviet zone, socialization of the economy in the Soviet zone and abandonment of decartelization and controlled levels of industry in the western zones, progressive integration of the two parts of Germany into their respective European bloc systems, and the hardening of opposing positions on key issues, such as Berlin, or recognition of boundaries. All these appeared to have their own internal logic, from which partition emerged only incidentally, not by design.

But the effect, as A. J. P. Taylor has noted, was to revert to "the old device of a divided Germany which saved Europe trouble over many centuries":

> The partitioning Powers profess to regret the division of Germany, and even claim to be working for her reunion; but I suspect that they encourage each other's obstinacy behind the scenes. . . .[14]

In any case, it is clear that reunification of Germany is low on the agenda of all the great powers, and indeed that it would be unacceptable to them under present conditions. Thus George F. Kennan wrote in 1959:

> The fearful European wars of this century have been the expression of the failure to find—and perhaps the impossibility of finding—any acceptable place in a community of fully sovereign European states for a united Germany likewise fully sovereign.
>
> . . . Germany could conceivably go only one of two ways: backward, by process of partition, to a point where sovereignty would be tolerable because it was not united; or forward, to-

---

[14]Taylor, *The Course of German History,* p. 9.

ward membership in a broader and higher system of political loyalties—in some sort of European federation, where unification would be tolerable because it was not truly sovereign.[15]

For Kennan in 1959, the alternative of partition still seemed "anachronistic, . . . and pregnant with possibilities for a reenactment of the unhappy past." Even A. J. P. Taylor conceded that partition was neither a good nor a permanent solution. Partitions breed resentments, friction, irredentas, enmities, fears, and finally violence—so the theory goes. Certainly in the context of the Berlin crises it appeared that this particular partition might prove utterly disastrous for the world. And even after that danger faded, there remained the fear that some day, the dismembered German nation might revive its nationalist fervor, divest itself of foreign entanglements—both East and West—and bring about reunification through a new era of "blood and iron."

One might even speculate that it is really this fear which lies behind the many proposals for reunification put forward over the years by several of the non-German nations involved. Such proposals have an air of placatory ritual about them, giving assurance of good will and holding out hope of eventual satisfaction of the Germans' imagined desire for unity. Certainly no nation has dared to incur the wrath of the Germans by openly favoring partition.

At the same time, all proposals for reunification have been calculated for rejection; all have carried with them propositions known to be unacceptable to the opposing parties. Thus proposals by the western powers for reunification on the basis of free elections throughout Germany were bound to be rejected by the Soviet Union and the German Democratic Republic, because, given the greater prosperity, more traditional character, and much larger population of the Federal Republic, the Democratic Republic was unlikely to emerge well-represented from such elections.

Nevertheless, in the years 1952–55, the U.S.S.R. did indicate willingness to discuss unification on the basis of "free activity of democratic parties and organizations" throughout Germany, including "freedom of speech, press, religious persuasion, political convictions and assembly," to all persons "without regard to race, sex, language or religion"—on condition that all occupying troops and all foreign military bases on German soil be withdrawn, and that:

---

[15]Kennan's article in *Foreign Affairs,* January, 1959.

Germany obligates itself not to enter into any kind of coalition or military alliance directed against any power which took part with its armed forces in the war against Germany (DG, p. 193).

This provision, which would have prevented the united Germany from entering NATO, was naturally rejected by the West. Having every reason to believe that Germany, reunified by free elections, would be sympathetic to the West, and would add significant strength to NATO, the United States replied that "the all-German government should be free both before and after the conclusion of a peace treaty to enter into associations compatible with the principles of the United Nations" (DG, p. 194). Since this meant, freely translated, that Germany ought to be free to enter NATO, it was naturally unacceptable to the Soviet Union.

After a last-ditch effort to forestall West German entry into NATO by proposal for reunification on the basis of nonalignment and demilitarization, around the turn of the year 1954–55, the Soviet Union hardened its position on free elections. Where previously it had been quibbling about the means of verification— supervision of the elections by Four-Power rather than United Nations investigators—in 1956 the Soviet Union rejected the proposal for all-German elections outright. Since the Federal Republic had joined NATO, the situation had changed fundamentally:

In view of this, any talk about uniting Germany through the holding of all-German elections has no real foundation. There are no conditions in Germany at present for the holding of such elections (DG, pp. 302–303).

Thenceforward the Soviet Union supported the proposals of the German Democratic Republic for reunification by way of confederation, first put forward by Walter Ulbricht on February 3, 1957. But the proposal for confederation was unacceptable to the Federal Republic because it called for recognition that there were indeed two German states, which were to come together on a basis of equality. Similarly, the Federal Republic rejected the plan for reunification and central European nuclear disarmament which was proposed by Polish Foreign Minister Rapacki before the United Nations on October 2, 1957, on the basis that it presumed the existence of two German states. The Rapacki plan was also rejected by the western powers. Eisenhower, commenting on the plan to Chairman Bulganin in January 1958, argued:

> there cannot be great significance in denuclearizing a small area when, as you say, "the range of modern types of weapons does not know of any geographical limit," and when you defer to the indefinite future any measures to stop the production of such weapons (DG, p. 325).

Thus each side put forward proposals unacceptable to the other side, turn and turn about, year after year. And whether the partition of Germany was more the motive or the consequence of this otherwise fruitless cycle, is difficult to judge.

In the meantime, however, the partition was cementing itself in the lives of the inhabitants of the two states, as people developed vested interests, habits, and loyalties binding them to their respective social and political systems. In many respects this took place more readily in the Federal Republic than in the Democratic Republic. The growing prosperity of the Federal Republic—by 1964 it ranked third among the nations of the world in gross national product—its formally democratic political system, and its preservation of traditional German culture, all helped to make it increasingly secure in popular support. By 1961, there was evidence of a growing national consciousness and identification with the Federal government in the preference expressed by a majority of the population (fifty-three percent in an opinion poll of November 1961) for the flag of the Federal Republic (black, red and gold) over the flag of the German Empire (black, white and red).

For the German Democratic Republic, circumstances were at first certainly inauspicious for winning the allegiance of the populace. The Soviet Union exacted heavy reparations, not only during the initial occupation period, but for some years after the founding of the Democratic Republic, when the reparations were set at three billion Marks annually, until 1953, when all reparations payments were discontinued. There were also serious problems of adjustment to conditions created by the war and the separation of the zones, as well as by the socialization of industry and later, the collectivization of agriculture. All these kept the standard of living in the Democratic Republic quite low for at least a decade after

World War II. The influx of expellees from eastern Europe and the migration of refugees to the west also created severe problems, both economic and political. Nor did the brutality of the early denazification program in the Soviet zone, and the coercion required in the ideological and social transformations imposed on east German society, serve to endear the government of the GDR to its people.

Nevertheless, in the long run the policies which had created difficulties at first served to provide the foundation for stable support of the east German government. They have created this foundation of support by establishing new layers of personal and class interests wholly dependent on the continuance of the Democratic Republic and its character as a "workers' and peasants' state." Land distribution, national economic planning, "workers' control" in industry, expanded free public education, including higher education, and preference to workers' children in the educational system, measures to encourage women's participation in the labor force and political life, new political and bureaucratic elites: all these give to the inhabitants of the GDR—those who "stuck it out" through the bad years, and those who have grown up in the new society—a significant stake in preserving the independence and the new social system of the German Democratic Republic. Moreover, as a number of commentators have noticed, the very language of the inhabitants of the two states is tending to diverge, not only along regional lines, but also under the impact of divergent public ideologies and their modes of expression.

In consequence, the citizens of the German Democratic Republic appear today to be as ready to accept allegiance to their government as those of the Federal Republic to theirs. A middle-level functionary, for example, though stemming from the "old" technical intelligentsia and highly critical of the Ulbricht regime, refuses to accept a greeting card from a relative in the Federal Republic because the card refers to East Berlin as the "East Sector." "For me," says this person, "it is the capital of the German Democratic Republic."

A similar result emerges from a study of reporting patterns relating to the national identification of athletes competing in Olympic Games. In two major West German newspapers, usage of the designation "German" for identifying athletes decreased from an average frequency of sixty-five percent in 1956 to thirty-three percent in 1968. As time passed, the usage of local designations (cities or states) or expressions such as "our athletes" or referring directly to the Federal Republic became more frequent than the old national designation, "German." By comparison, the shift in usage in the German Democratic Republic was even more complete: from fifty-five percent in 1956 to a mere nine percent in 1964. By 1968 the east German newspaper analyzed did not identify any athlete as "German."

Despite these growing signs that there are not only two German states, but two distinct societies, developing on the territory of the former German Empire, the partition of Germany cannot be regarded as stable so long as Berlin retains its strange status as an occupied territory and, at the same time, an enclave of West Germany on East German territory, thus the symbolic embodiment of hopes for a reunified nation. Yet if we try to estimate the weight of this factor for the future, we must bear in mind that Berlin was the capital of a united Germany for less than a century, and it must bear the hostility of many Germans who had—and have today—little love for Prussia, and less love for Prussian dominance over Germans. In more immediate terms, too, West Berlin has been a dying city. It has required evermounting subsidies from the Federal Republic to sustain its economy, especially since the building of the wall. In 1961, the Federal Republic expended somewhat over one billion Marks in assistance to Berlin. Ten years later, in 1971, the amount had more than tripled: subsidies to West Berlin amounted to 3.4 billion Marks. The population of the city is also changing unfavorably: increasingly aged.

Whether the new accords on Berlin and Germany will be sufficient to put the city on a viable, independent basis, remains to be seen. If not, one must wonder how long the people of the Federal Republic will be willing to sustain the drain on their resources for the support of West Berlin as a symbolic link to a retreating past and a doubtful future. Berlin, after all, is not Jerusalem.

BIBLIOGRAPHY

The best and most interesting single work of interpretation of German society and history, including a valuable chapter on the German Democratic Republic, is by Ralf Dahrendorf, *Society and Democracy in Ger-*

many, New York, 1969. Dahrendorf's analysis is sociological and philosophical; the beginner would do well to establish some background in German history first.

A good general textbook of German history is Koppel S. Pinson, *Modern Germany,* New York, 1966. A more opinionated and stimulating account is A. J. P. Taylor's *The Course of German History,* New York, 1962. The tone of Taylor's book may be judged by his remark, in the 1961 Preface: "When the book appeared, some reviewers expostulated that it 'indicted' a nation. . . . I made no indictment; the facts made it for themselves."

For the beginner, the best introduction to the National Socialist period and its impact on the world is Alan Bullock's biography, *Hitler: A Study in Tyranny,* New York, revised edition, 1962. Among the most important interpretive analyses of the period are: Franz L. Neumann, *Behemoth,* New York, revised edition, 1944; Hannah Arendt, *The Origins of Totalitarianism,* New York, revised edition, 1966; and David Schoenbaum, *Hitler's Social Revolution,* Garden City, N.Y., 1966.

The best recent analysis of Allied wartime diplomacy and its impact on the division of Germany is by Gabriel Kolko, *The Politics of War: The World and United States Foreign Policy, 1943–1945,* New York, 1968.

Other useful works on World War II, Allied diplomacy, the origins of the Cold War, and the German problem, are: Gordon S. Wright, *The Ordeal of Total War, 1939–1945,* New York, 1968; Wilfrid F. Knapp, *A History of War and Peace, 1939–1965,* London, 1967; and Zbigniew Brzezinski, *Alternative to Partition,* New York, 1965.

A few useful general works dealing directly with the division of Germany are: Norman J. G. Pounds, *Divided Germany and Berlin,* Princeton, N.J., 1962; Carl Landauer, *Germany: Illusions and Dilemmas,* New York, 1969; and Johan Galtung, "The German Problem: Some Perspectives," in Galtung, ed., *Cooperation in Europe,* IPRA Studies in Peace Research, Vol. III, Assen, 1970; and in German, Thilo Vogelsang, *Das geteilte Deutschland,* Munich, 1966.

A helpful recent study of the Federal Republic of Germany, popular in format but cogent in analysis, is: Anna J. and Richard L. Merritt, *West Germany Enters the Seventies,* New York: Foreign Policy Association, Headline Series, 1971.

Among many other studies of the Federal Republic, we may note here a few: Peter H. Merkl, *The Origin of the West German Republic,* New York, 1963; and by the same author, *Germany: Yesterday and Tomorrow,* New York, 1965; Elmer Plischke, *Contemporary Government of Germany,* Boston, 1964; John Dornberg, *Schizophrenic Germany,* New York, 1961.

The best study of the German Democratic Republic is in German: Ernst Richter, *Das zweite Deutschland: Ein Staat, der nicht sein darf,* Gütersloh, 1964. There is also a useful collection of documents, also in German: Ernst Deuerlein, *DDR: Geschichte und Bestandsaufnahme,* Munich, 1966. A history published in the Democratic Republic itself is Stefan Doernberg, *Kurze Geschichte der DDR,* Berlin, 1964. An interesting sympathetic report in English is Franz von Nesselrode, *Germany's Other Half: A Journalist's Appraisal of East Germany,* New York, 1963. A more recent work in English is Arthur M. Hanhardt, *The German Democratic Republic,* Baltimore, 1968.

Two pamphlets emerging from the American peace movement dealing with Berlin, divided Germany, and the arms race, deserve special mention: *Journey Through a Wall: A Quaker Mission to a Divided Germany,* September 8–20, 1963, American Friends Service Committee publication, February, 1964; and *The German Problem: Roadblock to Disarmament,* prepared and published by the Disarmament Committee of Women Strike for Peace, Washington, D.C., 1964.

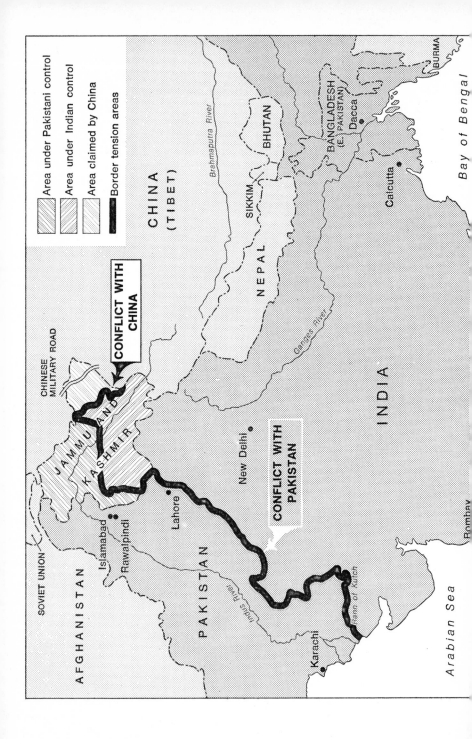

Chapter 4.

The Partition of India and Pakistan: The Emergence of Bangladesh

Michael Pearson
and
Diana Tonsich
University of Pennsylvania

PAKISTAN

On August 15, 1947, with an accompaniment of mass rioting and migration, two new nations appeared on the Indian subcontinent. After 150 years of forced unity as a British colony, the subcontinent was divided along religious lines. In 1961 India had a population of 370 million Hindus and 42 million Muslims, while Pakistan numbered 83 million Muslims and 10 million Hindus. The distribution of the two religions in the area dictated not only a partition of the former colony, but also the creation of Pakistan in two wings, separated by over 1,000 miles of Indian territory and united only by the tenuous bond of a common belief in the religion of Islam.

The Two Faiths.   Traces of the Hindu religion can be found in India as far back as the earliest civilization known in the area, that of the Indus Valley (2300–1700 B.C.). Over the centuries the religion developed and changed, incorporating new ideas and discarding some others. Its most essential characteristic was always heterogeneity, an ability to incorporate, with modifications, new beliefs and new groups of people. Thus followers of several reform movements were during several centuries reincorporated back into the all-embracing Hindu fold. Followers of the Buddha, the sixth century B.C. founder of the Buddhist religion, met this fate. Buddhism virtually disappeared in the land of its foundation. Two other reform religions, those of the Jains and the Sikhs, exist today in India, but are often regarded as being merely slightly divergent forms of Hinduism.

Both religious and political factors dictated that Islam in India would remain aloof from Hinduism. The latter has been likened to a sponge, soft-centered, fuzzy of outline, able to absorb without changing shape. Islam is fundamentally different. Like Christianity and Judaism it is hard-centered. It was founded by an historical person, Muhammad the Prophet (570–632), it possesses a sacred book, the Koran, and there are certain fundamental tenets of the religion which all Muslims must and do believe. Granted some diversity between and within different Muslim sects, and a capacity for change in response to new circumstances, Islam remained, at least by comparison with Hinduism, solid and monolithic. Hence it resisted the smothering embrace of the majority Hindu religion in the subcontinent.

In this not only the character of Islam but also political factors were of importance. The first Muslim state in India was established in the eighth century in Sind, the area around the delta of the Indus River in the extreme west of the subcontinent. A long pause followed, but from the beginning of the thirteenth century until the eighteenth century most of India was ruled by Muslims. In the north several dynasties rose and fell: the Delhi Sultanate (1206–1526) consisted of five separate dynasties, and was succeeded by the Mughal Empire, which lasted until the British conquest. Further, in the fifteenth and eighteenth centuries the imperial rulers in Delhi weakened and successor Muslim states rose not only in South India but even in the north. Yet in North India during these more than five centuries the rulers were Muslim, and with brief and ultimately unimportant exceptions these rulers employed only Muslims at the upper levels of government, patronized mostly Muslim artists, and were themselves influenced by the *ulama,* the scholars and jurists of the religion. Actual persecution of the Hindus, who remained numerically dominant, was rare; but the existence of Muslim rulers dictated some discrimination and was, in conjunction with the nature of the religion, crucial to the survival of Muslims as a distinct and relatively homogeneous group in the subcontinent.

Most Muslims in India were converts from Hinduism, and most of the conversions occurred in the northwest and the northeast. This was of basic importance, for it meant that when the subcontinent was divided on religious criteria these two areas would be the ones to be split off from the Hindu remainder. The preponderance of Muslims in the northwest, the area which today is West Pakistan, was simply a result of longer Muslim influence here than anywhere else in the subcontinent. All the many Muslim invaders of India entered, as geography dictated, through the passes of the Northwest Frontier. Sind was ruled by Muslims from the early eighth century, while the rest of the northwest was subject to periodic Muslim raids from even earlier than this, and permanent Muslim domination early in the eleventh century.

In Bengal, Muslim rule was not established until the thirteenth century, and here a different factor led to large scale conversions. Bengal had remained Buddhist long after this religion had declined in the rest of India; Hinduism was still in the process of reabsorbing Bengal when the Muslims entered. Bengal was in a state of flux, and this led to relatively rapid and widespread conversions to the Faith of Muhammad.

Different individuals converted for different reasons. For most of the time jobs under the Muslim sultans went only to Muslims, and for some Hindus conversion was thus a means to upward mobility, indeed a prerequisite. Some Hindus who worked for the Muslim rulers had to break dietary and other Hindu caste rules, and as a result were shunned by their fellow Hindus. Conversion followed easily. Most converts, however, came from low Hindu castes. For these people, subject to the rigors of existence at the bottom of the Hindu social system, conversion was a means of release, for one of the fundamental tenets of Islam is a belief in the equality of all Muslims. Granted that Muslim societies in fact are stratified, at least in theory conversion raised a low-caste Hindu from an inexorable position at the bottom of his society to equality with a sultan. This mass of low-caste converts usually entered Islam through the medium of a Muslim holy man or teacher, a follower of the *sufi*, or mystical, path. Finally, it is important not to let our secular twentieth century blinkers obscure the fact that genuine religious faith was at times the crucial determinant. To some people Islam simply seemed to be a better religion, and they converted for this reason.

These reasons were all important, but they should not be allowed to hide one basic point: conversion in India was usually not a complete break, not a total shedding of Hindu beliefs and a total adoption of Islam. Most of the converts were peasants, and it is only a slight exaggeration to argue that once a peasant always a peasant, religious conversion notwithstanding. The number of converts who actually studied their new religion and acquired any detailed knowledge of its tenets was small. Most of them were attracted to Islam by the individual piety of particular *sufi* leaders, and in this the transition was eased by the similarity between the attitudes of the *sufis* and of the Hindu devotional movement known as *bhakti*. Both strands were mystical, stressing individual devotion to and praise of a very personalized deity. Hence conversion often simply meant switching allegiance from a Hindu deity to a Muslim saint. Many Hindu social customs were retained by the converts, and indeed often a particular holy man or sacred place was venerated indiscriminately by Hindus and Muslims alike.

These superficial conversions were not of great importance in the making of Pakistan, but today they are of prime significance in the dispute between East and West Pakistan. The movement for Pakistan, as indeed the whole national movement in India, was primarily an affair of the educated. The Muslim leaders were *ulama*, lawyers, students, and landlords. To these people the differences between Islam and Hinduism were obvious, for they knew much more about their religion than did the peasants. Thus the fact of syncretism in folk Islam was of little significance beside the more sophisticated knowledge of the Muslim elite, who always knew that they were very different from the Hindus.

Given this religious, cultural, and social dichotomy among the elite of colonial India, independence had to result in partition, whether sooner or later. It was impossible ever to achieve one independent democratic nation state in the subcontinent. An historian of modern India describes how twentieth century Bengal Muslim politicians always "asserted their communities' right to a separate political existence. . . . The suggestion that the community should take its place simply as one religious and cultural group in a diverse Indian nation was never entertained. . . ."[1] More generally, a distinguished student of Islam points out that "An independent political community as the arena of religious activity is part of the very genius of Islam. The existence of such a community is not something peripheral; it lies close to the heart of the faith."[2] We have now to trace how these ideas were worked out in practice in the subcontinent.

The British and India.   Britain's policies in India became increasingly schizoid during the twentieth century. The British claimed both at the time and in retrospect that they had created a united subcontinent. This was their proudest achievement. Yet in maintaining their rule the British frequently used divisions within their colony, especially that between Hindu and Muslim. Thus while proclaiming that they had created unity the British fostered disunity. More basically, Indian unity never consisted of anything more than a common subjection to British rule. The basic Hindu-Muslim division remained. This division was exploited by the British but, as we have already emphasized, it existed long before India became their colony. As Muhammad Ali, an Indian Muslim leader, said to the British in 1930: "We divide, and you rule."

British policy was often based on using, and sometimes exacerbating, divisions in Indian society, but the heroes and the villains were not always the same. Fundamentally the British always felt closer to Muslims than to Hindus for Muslims were generally members of the much-loved martial races, as compared to many large Hindu groups which were regarded as "soft" and "effeminate". Further, Islam is much closer to Christianity than is Hinduism, for both are revealed religions, and Jesus Christ is venerated by Muslims as being at least a minor prophet. In more personal terms, caste restrictions often dictated that Hindus could not eat

[1]J. H. Broomfield, *Elite Conflict in a Plural Society: Twentieth-Century Bengal* (Berkeley and Los Angeles, 1968), p. 326.
[2]W.C. Smith, *Islam in Modern History* (New York, 1959), p. 211.

with Europeans, while for Muslim men there were no such limitations.

Nevertheless, for two decades after the Indian Mutiny of 1857 the British reversed themselves. The revolt had been largely restricted to North India, but it had been a massive challenge to British rule, and left a deep scar on the British psyche. Many of the revolt's leaders had been Muslims and this left the community under a cloud in British eyes. They regarded Muslims with deep suspicion and discriminated against them. Yet the British were not solely to blame for demoralization of India's Muslims at the time. The Muslims had failed to respond as positively as had some Hindu groups to the challenges and opportunities available under the British. "Too proud to cooperate with the victor, too sullen to adjust themselves to the new circumstances, too embittered to think objectively, too involved emotionally with the past to plan for the future, Muslim society in the decades following the events of 1857 presented a picture of desolation and decay."[3] More concretely, in Bengal at this time, where the Hindu and Muslim populations were equal, there were 773 Indians holding responsible government positions. Muslims had ninety-two of these and Hindus 681.

The man who tried both to alleviate British suspicions and to regenerate India's Muslims was Sayyid Ahmad Khan (1817–98). He wrote a pamphlet which attempted to play down the Muslim role in the Mutiny, and used his own position as a government official to lobby for his community. In religious matters, he defended Islam against attacks from Christian missionaries and others, while at the same time working among his own people to change the religion and make it more capable of responding to the fact of a western-dominated world. More important, Sayyid Ahmad campaigned tirelessly to get India's Muslims to realize that the British were in India to stay. His coreligionists had to accept this and work to secure their rightful place under the British, a place which had been usurped by certain Hindu groups. The prime necessity was education, and Sayyid Ahmad's greatest achievement may well have been the founding of the Anglo-Oriental College at Aligarh, which in the decades after its founding in 1875 turned out a stream of well-educated Muslim youths.

---

[3]C. M. Ali, *The Emergence of Pakistan* (New York, 1967), p. 7.

Some Hindus also attended this college, and Sayyid Ahmad was not anti-Hindu. Yet the logic of the situation of India's Muslims as a comparatively backward minority dictated that he oppose the growing Hindu movement for reforms in the administration of India. For example, if Indians were admitted into the Indian Civil Service[4] on a competitive basis the places would all go to Hindus. Nor could he support the embryonic nationalist movement which was institutionalized in the Indian National Congress, founded in 1885. With Hindus outnumbering Muslims four to one, self-government or any form of democracy could only produce permanent subjection for India's Muslims. Thus he favored the continuation of British rule in India for the foreseeable future: better relatively impartial British domination than a Hindu rule which he could only regard with deep suspicion. The implication of his teachings in the twentieth century is clear. If self-government were to come, the only solution for the Muslims had to be a separate state.

Sayyid Ahmad's work of regeneration, and of creating among India's Muslims a feeling of pride in their religion and their past, was taken up in the twentieth century by others. Most important were Amir Ali and Muhammad Iqbal. These two and their followers abandoned Sayyid Ahmad's essentially defensive attitude to the west, and boldly counterattacked. They stressed the past glories of Islam, and that the classical period of Muslim history, from the seventh to the thirteenth centuries, had coincided with a period when Europe had been sunk in comparative obscurity. Numerous biographies of the Prophet Muhammad appeared, presenting him as the "Perfect Man." Sir Sayyid had maintained that Islam was not inimical to liberal progress, Amir Ali presented an Islam that was such progress. "The missionaries had said that Islam degraded women; Sir Sayyid said it did not; Amir Ali said that Islam raised women from their previous degradation to a lofty pinnacle."[5]

On a more practical level, the nineteenth and twentieth centuries in India saw several attempts to purify Islam, to rid it of the numerous vestiges of Hinduism which had remained especially

---

[4]ICS; the top of the British administrative hierarchy in India, restricted to British for most of the nineteenth century.

[5]W. C. Smith, *Modern Islam in India* (Lahore, 1947), pp. 50-51. Sayyid Ahmad Khan had been knighted by the British in 1888.

important in rural Islam, and to shed from it more recent accretions. Most of these purifiers were strictly reactionary in that their aim was not to make Islam better fitted to meet the challenge of the western-dominated world, but rather to restore it to the pristine purity of seventh century Arabia. These Muslim efforts interacted with parallel movements in Hinduism. Several leaders cried "Back to the Vedas," the second millenium B.C. Hindu religious texts, but other Hindus attempted, sometimes by force, to reconvert Muslims to Hinduism. The net effect was an increase in both communities of communal feeling and, more ominously, of communal tension; that is, more and more Hindus and Muslims in India began to see themselves as members of two separate religious communities, and this in turn increasingly implied not only separation from but also distrust of members of the other community.

The British were not concerned to ease these tensions. Their aim was to maintain British rule, and a divided subject population was thus in their interest. In particular, the British used these divisions in an attempt to head off the challenge from the emerging national movement in India. This movement was dominated by Hindus and came to center in the Indian National Congress. In response the British swung back, from about 1870, to their more natural prejudice and began to favor Muslims over increasingly seditious Hindus. As an ex-ICS official, Sir John Strachey, said around 1900, "The existence side by side of these hostile creeds [Hinduism and Islam] is one of the strongest points in our political position in India." In 1926, the Secretary of State for India, Lord Oliver, submitted that "No one with any close acquaintance of Indian affairs will be prepared to deny that on the whole there is a predominant bias in British officialism in India in favor of the Muslim community, partly on the ground of closer sympathy but more largely as a make-weight against Hindu nationalism."[6]

The device which the British used most was the separate electorate. In response to pressure from the nationalists, they granted small extensions of democratic representation to India in 1909, 1919, and 1935. In each case, however, Muslim interests were "safeguarded" by reserving for them certain seats on the representative bodies created by these reforms. The Indian Councils

---

[6]Quoted in Smith, *Modern Islam in India,* pp. 199, 216.

Act of 1909 granted India representative institutions at the provincial level, but these Provincial Councils, despite their elected majority, were merely advisory bodies and had no independent legislative power. Nor were they democratic: members were chosen by indirect means. Muslims received separate representation. The Government of India Act of 1919 gave the central government of India an elected majority, although executive power remained in British hands. In the provinces the franchise was widened and some subjects were administered by ministers responsible to the elected majorities of the Provincial Councils. Separate electorates were continued. The 1935 Government of India Act gave complete provincial self-government, subject to a rarely used British veto power, and again separate electorates for Muslims were prescribed, though now on a still wider franchise.

Superficially this policy was unexceptional, for Muslims would have been hard-pressed to secure even the minority representation which their numbers required if some special measure had not been taken. Yet the separate electorates solidified and institutionalized communal divisions in India, and they represented a prime example of the way in which the British used these divisions, and their oft-proclaimed desire to protect the minorities, to delay granting self-government to India. As one official said of the separate electorates, "It is nothing less than the pulling back of sixty-two millions of people from joining the ranks of the seditious opposition." More specifically, the separate electorates of 1909 were a direct response to a delegation of Muslims to the British Viceroy in 1906, and this delegation was in fact a "command performance," suggested by British officials. In the face of an increasingly pressing nationalist demand for self-government, the British tacitly undermined their self-proclaimed greatest achievement, the creation of a united India. Nevertheless, it must be stressed that while the British certainly used Indian communal divisions for their own ends, and indeed exacerbated these divisions, they did not create them; they were present in India long before the British.

Hindu Nationalism.   Until the end of World War I the Indian National Congress was dominated by western-trained Hindu educators and lawyers, men dedicated to securing reforms by appealing to the better nature of the British. These men opposed the more truculent manifestations of nationalism produced in Bengal and Maharashtra, and indeed their methods met with some success in the Act of 1909. But from 1920 the whole tempo changed. This was largely the achievement of one man, Mohandas Karamchand Gandhi, yet ironically his success predicated his failure. His campaign led to independence, but his methods led to partition.

Gandhi was born in 1869 in Kathiawar, and studied law in London. From 1893 to 1914 he lived in South Africa for most of the time and here, while working to alleviate the discrimination under which his fellow-Indians suffered, he evolved his concept of *satyagraha,* or nonviolent (but not passive) resistance. On his return to India Gandhi quickly moved to the leadership of the Indian National Congress and from 1920 until Independence in 1947 was its leader in fact even if not always in name. Under his inspiration three civil disobedience campaigns were launched, in 1920–22, 1930–33, and 1942–43. Indians were urged to refuse all cooperation with the British government. Some renounced their British titles, some left English-run or English-oriented schools, many refused to pay their taxes, or to use goods made in England, and many others deliberately disobeyed what they considered to be unjust laws made by foreigners, and were imprisoned.

Gandhi's philosophy, and the nationalist struggle in this period, have been elaborated on in several excellent books. Generally it is clear that his work made the British move faster than they wanted toward giving greater self-government to India. For our purposes, however, it is the nature of Gandhi's appeal which must be stressed. Gandhi was quintessentially a Hindu. The masses which he occasionally could mobilize were largely Hindu. *Satyagraha* was fundamentally a Hindu concept, with some additions from European, but not from Muslim, sources. Gandhi himself dressed as a Hindu, and frequently referred to Hindus and Muslims as "we" and "they." The Mahatma ("Great Soul," a title by which Gandhi was increasingly known) himself was largely above communalism. He stressed the essential similarities of all great religions, once wrote an introduction to a collection of Muslim *sufi* poetry, and held Jesus Christ as an example. Yet his favorite book was the Hindu religious classic the *Bhagavad Gita*, and the symbols which he manipulated so dexterously were all Hindu.

The Indian National Congress, as its name implied, had always claimed to be a national body. Membership was open to anyone who accepted its aims. But the organization's methods, once Gandhi gained control, could not but appeal more to Hindus than to Muslims. Gandhi was avowedly a national, not a Hindu leader. Jawaharlal Nehru, who increasingly was seen as Gandhi's political heir apparent, and in fact was Prime Minister of independent India until his death in 1964, was a self-proclaimed agnostic in religious matters and a true secular nationalist. Nevertheless, Congress failed to become a genuinely national movement. Its goals conflicted with its methods, so that while the Muslim population of India was a little under twenty-five percent of the total, Muslim membership in the Congress never rose over fifteen percent, and in the crucial decision-making body, the Working Committee, it never exceeded ten percent.

Muslim Nationalism.   The man who emerged to challenge the Congress goal of a united independent India was Muhammad Ali Jinnah. He was an unlikely leader of India's Muslims. Until late in his life he invariably wore stylish European clothes. He never spoke Urdu, the main Indian Muslim language, at all well. He was only a second-generation Muslim himself, and was a member of a small sect within Islam, the *khojas,* which is often regarded as heretical by stricter members of the orthodox *sunni* Muslim majority. Nor was Jinnah personally appealing; his remoteness was reinforced by the failure of his private life in the 1920s, so that he was aloof and cold even toward his most devoted followers.

Jinnah was born in Karachi in 1876 and like Gandhi and Nehru studied law in London. Once he had built up a personal base as a successful lawyer in Bombay he began to engage in politics. In these years of the early twentieth century, and indeed into the 1930s, he was seen as "The Apostle of Hindu-Muslim Unity." He joined Congress in 1906. Seven years later he also joined the Muslim League. This organization had been founded in 1906, and at this time and later was small and elitist. It is typical of Jinnah's attitude before the emergence of Gandhi that he insisted, when he joined the Muslim League, that this would "in no way and at no time imply even the shadow of disloyalty to the larger national cause to which his life was dedicated."

The high point of Jinnah's career as a national, as opposed to Muslim, leader, and of Hindu-Muslim cooperation in general, came with the beginning of the *khilafat* agitation. The *khalif* was seen by most Muslims as Muhammad's successor. Since the early sixteenth century the holder of the office had lived in Turkey. During World War I his position, and the political integrity of Turkey, was threatened, for Turkey fought against the Allies, primarily Britain, France, and Russia, and later the United States, in the war. British policy toward Turkey led to considerable feeling against the British among India's Muslims, and this resulted in an agreement between the Congress and the League in 1916. A pact was signed at Lucknow by which the Congress agreed to support the League demand for separate electorates. Indeed, Congress agreed to recommend that India's Muslims receive much higher representation than their numbers in fact deserved. Jinnah was a key actor in these negotiations.

The next four years saw great Hindu-Muslim cooperation in a broadly national movement, yet in fact the alliance was built on sand. First, the aims of the two organizations were divergent, for Congress wanted self-government, while the League wanted better treatment for a defeated Turkey. Second, the leaders of Turkey after World War I cared less for the *khilafat* than India's Muslims did. Third, some Muslims (and also some Hindus) who were oriented toward constitutional opposition to the British could not support Gandhi's noncooperation campaign of 1920–22. Among them was Jinnah, who carried his opposition to the new methods of the national movement to the point of resigning from the Congress in December 1920. There was, however, considerable Muslim participation in the first noncooperation campaign. Yet the shaky nature of the Hindu-Muslim alliance was demonstrated in August 1921, when the agitation got out of hand and a Muslim group called the Moplahs launched anti-Hindu riots in South India. The final straw which ended the illusory unity was the abolition of the institution of the *khilafat* by the great Turkish nationalist leader Kemal Ataturk, in March 1924.

From 1924 until 1937, India's Muslims, except those in the Congress, played a small role in a national movement largely dominated by Gandhi's ideas. Jinnah himself spent the years from 1930 to 1934 in England and appeared to have settled there for life. In 1927 the total membership of the League was only 1,330, while the Congress in 1923 had well over 100,000 members. But outside the field of active political struggle two important developments occurred. At Cambridge University in England in the early 1930s, young Indian Muslims toyed with the idea of a separate Muslim state in India. The idea was not new, but in 1933 one of them proposed a name for this state. By taking the following letters from a list of places which had Muslim majorities, or which had influenced Indian Islam (*P*unjab, *A*fghania, *K*ashmir, *I*ran, *S*ind, *T*ukharistan, *A*fghanistan, and Baluchista*n*) a rather labored acronym was produced: PAKISTAN. Better yet, the word means in Persian "land of the pure." A little earlier, in 1930, the great poet and philosopher Muhammad Iqbal was President of the Muslim League. In his presidential address at the annual meeting he put forward a plan for an independent Muslim state in northwest India. It was, however, indicative of the state of the League at this time that this meeting was delayed for a time because a quorum of 75 members was not present.

Such ideas of a separate Muslim state carved out of India were dismissed as "students' schemes" by Indian Muslim politicians in the early 1930s. Yet in 1940 this claim was put forward as the policy of a Muslim League which by then was much bigger and more militant than it had been in 1930. In this transformation a transformed Jinnah played the crucial role.

The Government of India Act of 1935 gave virtual self-government to India's eleven provinces. Elections for the Provincial Assemblies took place in 1937, and despite a limited franchise they demonstrated clearly the relative strengths of the two political organizations. Of all the Muslim votes cast, the League won less than five percent. The League won less than one-quarter of the seats reserved for Muslims, while the Congress won nearly one-half of all the seats, and finally was able to form governments in seven provinces. But events after the elections were even more important than this demonstration of the mass appeal of the Congress. Jinnah had returned to India to lead the League campaign, and was bitterly disappointed at its failure. Nevertheless, he claimed that Congress had promised the League places in the cabinets of some provinces, especially the United Provinces. This claim was rejected by Congress under Jawaharlal Nehru and Vallabhbhai Patel.

It was a fateful decision, for a humiliated Jinnah responded by launching a campaign aimed at getting mass support for the League, and the success of this in turn gave the League a veto power over the shape of independence in India. Yet it is difficult to see how Congress could have acted differently. Congress Muslims were members of several Congress cabinets. Congress did have an absolute majority in the United Provinces, and British parliamentary practice has seldom given a minority party a place in a government which already has a majority. In any case, there were other Muslim-based parties in India which had as good a claim as the League to represent the community. In the United Provinces the League had won only twenty-four of the sixty-four seats reserved for Muslims. Finally, Nehru himself came from this province, and he was eager to promote economic and social reform there. This aim would be hindered if conservative middle class League members were admitted to the cabinet.

Once rejected, Jinnah began to launch increasingly violent attacks on the Congress, and to build up the League into a mass-based party. One example of League propaganda at this time can be given:

> The Hindu is racially deadlier and subtler than the Jews. The Hindu Fascism after establishing itself in India as the sole power will embark upon a career of economic imperialism for the strangulation of the Muslim countries by a scientific organization of an irresistible war machine backed up by a gigantic financial and industrial system which can easily beat both the Jew and the Japanese. It will be a bitterly anti-Muslim power pledged to a total war on Muslim lands and peoples.

Conservative Hindu groups replied in kind.

Jinnah was successful, and rapidly so. Muslim politicians from other parties joined the League, as did many ordinary Muslims. The party claimed two million members in 1944, and in the 1945–46 elections received seventy-five percent of the Muslim vote.

What motivated Jinnah and his followers during these last ten years of British rule in India? Their mass support owed much to appeals to religion, but Jinnah and his top political lieutenants were not thus motivated. A desire for power was no doubt there; if Jinnah could get an independent Muslim nation he would be its leader, while in an independent undivided India he could never be more than the leader of a minority. More generally, many Muslims could prosper in Pakistan as they never could in India. Hindus dominated the professions, and academic and economic life in colonial India. In Pakistan, Muslims could take over all these positions. But ultimately Jinnah and his followers were governed by the inexorable fact that democracy, which had to mean Hindu rule, was clearly approaching. Thus it was ultimately the continuing, even increasing, separateness of the Muslim community in the subcontinent which led to Pakistan. Both Jinnah and the British used this fact for their own ends, but neither created it.

Toward Independence.   The detailed political events of 1939–47 need not be treated here. The most important fact was that by the end of World War II, if not before, the League was in so strong a position as the spokesman for India's Muslims that it could veto any plan for independence not to its liking. This is what Jinnah, as the undisputed leader of the League, did. (Jinnah by now was called by his followers Qaid-i Azam, the "Great Leader.") This strong position was achieved partly by default, for Congress leaders spent most of the war years in jail. When war between Britain and Germany broke out in September 1939 the viceroy, in cavalier fashion and without deigning to consult India's leaders, declared that India was also, ipso facto, at war. The Congress provincial ministries resigned in protest. In 1942, after an attempt to get Indian nationalist support for Britain during the war had failed, Gandhi launched his third noncooperation movement. The top Congress leaders were then imprisoned. Nehru, for example, spent forty-eight of the sixty-nine war months in jail. The field was left clear for the League.

In 1940 the League had adopted as its goal the attainment of an independent Muslim state, but it was only in the flurry of negotiations after the war that even Jinnah began seriously to hope that Pakistan could be achieved. Before then, the demand for Pakistan was simply a bargaining counter to win more concessions from Congress. But in 1945, as it became clear that Britain had to leave India very soon, Jinnah began to scent victory.

The Labour Party came to power in Britain in July 1945 with a large majority, and while its foreign and colonial policies were far from radical the fact of a Labour government was important for India. The new leaders of Britain, Clement R. Attlee, Stafford Cripps, Ernest Bevin, had much more in common with the Congress leaders, and especially Nehru, than with Jinnah. Further, a

Conservative Party victory in 1945 would have left Winston Churchill as Prime Minister, and he was a "die-hard" with respect to India and the empire. He would have faced Indian nationalism with obdurate opposition all the way; Attlee was ready to listen.

British rule in India was visibly winding down in 1945. The war had left her exhausted both spiritually and financially, and the Labour government had urgent economic and social goals to pursue at home. The number of British administrators in India had fallen by forty percent between 1935 and 1946, and no recruitment had been done since 1939. British troops in India were dissatisfied, and wanted only to get home. Clearly British rule was nearly over.

In June and July 1945, as the war ended, Lord Wavell, the viceroy, tried to get India's national representatives to join him in the Executive Council of the central government. The responses from the Congress and the League indicated clearly the nature of the split in the national movement. Congress said it must be allowed to nominate anyone it liked to the Executive Council, regardless of religion, for the Congress was a national noncommunal body. Jinnah claimed that only the League, as the representative of all Indian Muslims, could nominate Muslims to the Council. Neither Wavell nor Congress could accept this, and the talks broke down.

The British were anxious to secure a clearer idea of what in fact were the bases of strength of the various Indian political parties, and so elections were held in India in 1945–46. The results substantially bore out Jinnah's claim that the League should be the sole spokesman for the whole Muslim community and demonstrated clearly the success of League work since the last elections in 1937. It won all the seats in the Central Assembly reserved for Muslims, while the Congress won all the noncommunal seats. In the provinces, the League won 439 out of 494 Muslim seats, as compared to 109 in 1937. Despite the limited franchise, the communal division in Indian politics was now plain to see.

In 1946, the British made one last attempt to preserve Indian unity after independence. A mission consisting of three Cabinet Ministers of the Labour Government spent some months in India and came up with an ingenious and complicated constitution for an independent India. In essence, the plan left India united but with a very weak central government, which would control only defense, foreign policy, and communications. Both the League and Congress accepted the plan, but Nehru and Patel for the Congress made several important reservations. In July 1946, Nehru claimed that even though Congress had accepted the plan, with reservations, it was not immutable; it could be modified after independence. To Jinnah this was intolerable. Nehru's ideas seemed to bear out Sayyid Ahmad Khan's warnings in the 1880s of Hindu domination via the ballot. The Cabinet Mission Plan was abandoned. The League now proclaimed that it had left the path of constitutional action, and was going to fight by any means for Pakistan. In August, the League-sponsored Direct Action Day was observed, which in Calcutta led to what is called the "Great Calcutta Killing." Four days of communal rioting (that is, Hindus attacking Muslims and vice versa mainly because of religious differences) left 6,000 dead, and massive destruction. From this time the politicians negotiated while appalling butcheries took place daily in North India. The massacres of partition a year later were not an innovation, they were a culmination and a result of a year's savagery.

Congress, and especially Nehru, have been heavily criticized by historians for their refusal to accept fully the Cabinet Mission Plan. Nehru was certainly maladroit, and it is true that the failure of the plan resulted in partition. Yet ultimately this was a case of petty mortals being tossed on the waves of great truths. Partition was going to come anyway, whether sooner or later. More concretely, the failure of the plan was a blessing in disguise. An India with a weak central government and bickering provinces would never have made such agricultural and industrial progress as India and Pakistan separated have made.

Independence and Partition.   The final act took place between February and August 1947, a time of frenzied activity with a backdrop of blood. Prime Minister Attlee took a final initiative and in February announced that the British were irrevocably leaving India by June 1948, come what may. Next month Lord Mountbatten arrived in Delhi as viceroy to preside over the end.

His appointment as the last viceroy is often seen as a masterstroke, as are his actions during the next few months. We will have to question this view, but Mountbatten was certainly efficient in winding up British rule. He had been in command of Allied forces in Southeast Asia at the end of World War II. To military decisiveness he added royal blood and great personal charm, a charm shared by his wife.

Mountbatten quickly decided that partition was inevitable, given the power and obduracy of the League. More important, he convinced Congress of this fact, and this was a crucial achievement. Here the mood of the Congress leaders was decisive. Gandhi had largely washed his hands of the whole mess, but he accepted partition as the better of two evils. The men who were to lead free India, the active Congress negotiators at this time, were tired of opposition and jail. Another noncooperation movement, aimed at preserving Indian unity, could only result in their imprisonment, leaving the stage clear for the Muslim League. Nehru had spent nearly nine of his fifty-seven years in jail, and had had enough. He and his colleagues wanted power, and now. Nor was this for entirely selfish ends. Nehru especially was anxious to start the far-reaching economic and social reforms which India so desperately needed, and which had not been possible under the British. The years were dragging on, and the Congress leaders were getting old. In 1947 Nehru was fifty-eight, Vallabhbhai Patel seventy-two, Naulana Azad, the great Muslim congressman fifty-nine, and Gandhi seventy-eight. If independence did not come soon they would be too old to serve their country. And by 1947 it was clear that independence could not be attained without partition.

Early in June 1947, Mountbatten announced that partition had been accepted and at the same time proclaimed that independence and the partition would both come into effect on August 15, 1947. Ten weeks were allowed to divide a country, an administration, an army, and a population. The job was done, but at an appalling cost.

The division of the typewriters, guns, red tape, and paper clips was carried out relatively painlessly, though on larger issues there was, as we shall see, some friction. It was the division of populations which was the immediate problem, for in August 1947 the population of the subcontinent was not divided up neatly into homogenous Hindu and Muslim areas. In the two provinces of Bengal and the Punjab the communal populations were roughly equal, and as part of the division of the subcontinent these two provinces were themselves divided, in accordance with a scheme worked out by an English judge. Further, in the Punjab there was another community, the Sikhs. This warlike group had a tradition of opposition to the Muslims when North India was ruled by the Mughals, and a more recent tradition of independence than any other group in India, for they had only been conquered by the British in 1849. In 1947 they were spread all over the Punjab, with many of them prospering in the western Muslim-majority area.

Communal rioting has occurred spasmodically in India for centuries, and continues today. The incidence increased greatly in the twentieth century. Nevertheless, the events in the Punjab before and after August 1947 were a holocaust on a scale never remotely approached before. In Bengal, the other province to be divided, and where a similarly even balance between Hindus and Muslims provided a cause for apprehension, the heroic actions of Gandhi had a remarkable effect. Thanks to the enormous effect of his character, and his tireless efforts, the expected repetition of the Great Calcutta Killing did not occur. But there was only one Gandhi, and he could not be in both divided provinces. In the Punjab the Sikhs butchered the Muslims in the east and the Muslims butchered the Hindus and the Sikhs in the west. The killings increased early in 1947, then ebbed at mid year, rose to an awesome peak after August 1947, and continued until late in the year. Estimates vary, but at least 500,000 died in the Punjab, and the total was probably nearer 750,000. Rape, mutilation, and destruction of property were on a comparable scale. About fifteen million people migrated, Muslims to Pakistan, and Hindus and Sikhs to India.

We have argued that partition was unavoidable, and any partition must have been accompanied by some violence. Nevertheless, this was slaughter on a large scale, even by twentieth century standards. Part of the blame rests with the propaganda of both Hindus and Muslims, which inflamed, indeed sometimes created, communal feeling amongst people who had lived for centuries in proximity and relative harmony with neighbors of a different faith. But it is hard to see how nationalism in India could be based on anything but communalism, at least in the case of the Muslim minority. We have therefore to ask only whether or not the slaughter could have been lessened. It could have been, and the British ultimately were responsible that it was not.

British historians, who have written most of the books on this period, do not see it like this. Tinker, an ex-ICS officer, writes that "1947 marked the final end of the long British policymaking effort in India: and an honorable end it was." The historian C. H. Philips agrees; "But, as if in a fairy-tale, the British hung on until the stroke of midnight, when a political masterstroke engineered by Attlee and Mountbatten enabled them to get out, not entirely without honour."[7] The use of the word "honour" is curious, for it is difficult to see any Indian, Pakistani or British leader, except Gandhi, deriving honor from 1947 in India.

The British had ruled India for 150 years, not without profit to themselves, but always, they claimed, for the benefit of the subject peoples. They did not cause the killings, but they could have lessened them, indeed had an obligation to do so. Experienced observers had predicted trouble, yet British troop strength in India had been greatly reduced by 1947, and was completely withdrawn, as it had to be, at independence. More specifically, Mountbatten's haste, the whole manic desire to get out in ten weeks, was clearly irresponsible. Better to have mobilized all available British troops, announced the line of partition early, and held on to supervise the transference of populations before independence in, say, December 1947. It was an inglorious end to an empire. As a Punjabi magistrate said in 1947: "The British are a just people. They have left India in exactly the same state of chaos as they found it."

The British were severely tested, and were found lacking. But ultimately it was only their *modus operandi* when they left which was at fault. The causes of partition lay far above the actions of any man. As a Bengali author put it: "The so-called two-nation theory was formulated long before Mr. Jinnah or the Muslim League; in truth it was not a theory at all; it was a fact of history."[8]

The New Nation.   Pakistan was formed in 1947 as a union of the Muslim-majority areas of the Indian subcontinent. Its units included Sind, Baluchistan, the North-West Frontier, and West Punjab, all contiguous territories located in the northwest corner of

---

[7]Hugh Tinker, *Experiment with Freedom* (London, 1967), p. 11; C. H. Philips, *The Partition of India, 1947* (Leeds, 1967), p. 34.

[8]N. C. Chaudhuri, *The Autobiography of an Unknown Indian* (New York, 1951), p. 227.

the subcontinent. To this was added the discontiguous province of East Bengal, a Muslim majority area located on the eastern subcontinental coast, and separated from the rest of Pakistan by over 1000 miles of Indian territory. Partition had not merely divided the subcontinent into two separate nations; it had also caused the birth of one nation, Pakistan, composed of physically, racially, culturally, and linguistically diverse components. Pakistanis had to attempt to integrate these varied units into one polity. To do so they consistently relied upon two rallying cries, Islam and India. Recent events in Pakistan suggest that these two factors were insufficiently strong integrating forces.

International Rivalry in the Subcontinent: Pakistan's Unifying Force

Pakistani leaders could hardly fail to be cognizant of India's awesome presence. Most Pakistani lands border on India and it is India that divides the two parts of Pakistan. Physically, India is four times the size of Pakistan, and the population of India exceeds that proportion. Yet, gross size and sheer numbers in themselves cannot explain why postpartition developments in the subcontinent have led to increasing international rivalry and tension between Pakistan and India. Instead, one may find a more complete answer by looking at the domestic political significance of this international rivalry.

Pakistan came into being on the basis of one common bond, Islam, and one common fear, that of Hindu domination in a democratic nation-state. The cry "Islam in danger" had frequently been heard during the Muslim League's agitation for the establishment of Pakistan. Jinnah had consistently emphasized that British India was composed of two nations, Hindus and Muslims, who could not live together amicably in a democratic nation-state. Jinnah and the Muslim League succeeded in winning for the Muslims of the subcontinent a homeland in which to establish an Islamic state. In a very real sense, it was at this moment of victory that the League became most vulnerable. During the campaign waged by Jinnah and the League for the establishment of Pakistan, very little was said as to what, in terms of economic, social and political programs, would be offered to the Muslims who chose to live in Pakistan. The League waged a battle for the establishment of a nation but, aside from its avowed Islamic nature, said little of how the new nation would be constituted. Following independence, these questions became more crucial, but the League seemed to lack the answers. Islam had served to unify the nation, and many began to ask what other integrating forces could be found to mold the diverse units of Pakistan into one polity. The factor which was most prominent and which was used as a new rallying-cry was, ironically, India.

This was not an unnatural choice, when one considers the magnitude of the hatred engendered by the massive communal slaughters of 1947. Few areas of Pakistan were totally unaffected by the carnage which preceded and accompanied independence. Pakistani politicians, bureaucrats, and military leaders began to emphasize that the greatest threat to Pakistan's existence came from India. At a time when relations between the two young nations were very strained, an issue arose further to complicate and worsen relations. The issue was over the accession of the princely states of Jammu and Kashmir.

While British India (that area directly ruled by the Government of India) was partitioned on the basis of the religious predominance of the area as well as its geographical contiguity, these principles were not applied to the princely states. Instead, the decision to accede to one of the two newly-formed nations was left in the hands of the rulers of the Indian States. In 1941 Jammu and Kashmir had a population which was more than seventy-seven percent Muslim and more than twenty percent Hindu. The ruler of Kashmir, Maharaja Hari Singh, was a Hindu. Kashmir is contiguous to both India and Pakistan. For a short while, it seemed as though Hari Singh had chosen to accede to neither new nation, preferring an independent status for Kashmir. But communalism and rioting spread from the Punjab into Jammu Province. And in October of 1947 armed Muslim tribesmen, coming through Pakistan with the knowledge and assistance of Pakistani officials, invaded Kashmir and established the *Azad* Kashmir (Free Kashmir) provisional government. On October 26, 1947, Hari Singh signed the instrument of accession to India.

With the accession of Kashmir to India, relations between India and Pakistan took a turn for the worse, resulting in armed conflict between the two nations in 1948. Pakistan began openly to aid the tribesmen, on the one hand, and to demand that the people of Kashmir be given the right of self-determination on the other. Prime Minister Nehru agreed to hold a plebiscite if the *Azad*

Kashmiri forces were withdrawn. Pakistani Prime Minister Lia-quat Ali Khan demanded that India withdraw all its troops from Kashmir, that a coalition government which included representa-tives of *Azad* Kashmir be formed, and that a plebiscite be held under international auspices. Prime Minister Nehru refused. The negotiations broke down but the issue of Kashmir remained a very live one in both nations. In August of 1965, *Azad* Kashmiri forces from Pakistan infiltrated the cease-fire line, leading to the out-break of the Indo-Pakistani war of that year.

For Pakistanis the issue of Kashmir has often been viewed as an example of what a hostile India might do to suppress the right of self-determination of Muslims. The issue has distinct ideological implications, implications which strike at the very heart of Pakis-tan's reason for existence. Pakistanis argue that the two-nation theory means that Kashmir, with its Muslim majority, must be allowed to unite with West Pakistan. India, which has never con-ceded the validity of the two-nation theory, sees in Kashmir "the chance to demonstrate the powers of nationalist sentiment to overcome in the political sphere the separatist urge of religion."[9]

The issue of Kashmir, and the refusal of the Indian government to hold the plebiscite, became and remained very real issues in Pakistani politics. Pakistani leaders took the Kashmir issue and expanded it; the struggle became not merely one for the right of self-determination of Kashmiris. Instead, Pakistanis began to see this as one issue, albeit the overriding issue, in a series which exemplified a continuing hostility on the part of India toward Pakistan. Fear of India and fear of Indian aggression became prime political tools in the hands of the leaders of Pakistan. Fear of India, augmented by the sometimes hostile attitude of India toward Pakistan, was used by Pakistani political figures in an at-tempt to unify their nation. One may see in this an extension of the prepartition struggle for independence; the Muslim League, once it had won the right to form Pakistan, continued to use India and the fear of Hindu aggression in order to unite the disparate provinces which comprised Pakistan. Thus, India became the prime ingredient in Pakistan's domestic life. The unity of the subcontinent, torn asunder by partition, was replaced by a contin-

---

[9]Keith Callard, *Pakistan: A Political Study* (New York, 1957), p. 16.

uing emphasis on this international rivalry, an international rivalry which often served to fulfill Pakistan's domestic needs.

Economic Consequences of Partition.   The economic picture of Pakistan in 1947 was a dismal one indeed. While the undivided subcontinent could hardly be viewed as economically developed or advanced, partition left Pakistan undeniably the weaker of the two nations.

At independence, West Pakistan had a good transport network and a developed irrigation system. Other than this, the new nation had very few assets. Pakistan had almost no known natural resources except for its fertile agricultural lands. It had practically no modern industry, and it had virtually no modern banking or commercial establishments. It had few technicians and few professionals. Its Muslim population consisted primarily of peasants, artisans, and soldiers.[10]

Both East and West Pakistan were lacking in industrial establishments. Prior to partition the East had produced vast quantities of jute; indeed, East Bengal provided the world with three-quarters of its jute supply. West Pakistan produced a surplus of cotton. Yet in neither province did one find industrial establishments to process these abundant raw materials. Both East and West Pakistan could be seen as hinterlands of two great industrial cities, Calcutta and Bombay which, upon partition, fell to India. The extent of Pakistan's industrial underdevelopment cannot be exaggerated. While in British India one found 14,569 manufacturing establishments employing twenty or more workers, only 1,406 of these, or less than ten percent, fell to Pakistan at partition.

Pakistan had to attempt to build an industrial base. The economic interdependence of the subcontinent had been shattered in 1947. Partition was to cut Pakistani cotton and jute-producing areas off from their former buyers and their processing plants, most of which were located in India. While Pakistan could produce abundant harvests of jute and cotton, there were almost no mills in Pakistan in which these raw materials might be processed. Pakistan, weakened by partition, struggled to establish the necessary processing plants. Her initial efforts were not very impressive.

---

[10]Gustav F. Papanek, *Pakistan's Development: Social Goals and Private Incentives* (Cambridge, Mass., 1967), p. 3.

This is not surprising when one notes that, prior to partition, the leading traders, money-lenders and businessmen resident in the Muslim-majority areas had been predominantly Hindu. With independence, most of these Hindus fled from Pakistan to India, leaving a void the struggling young nation's civil servants and migrant Muslim businessmen found difficult to fill. Pakistan's initial industrial expansion was the result of external circumstances, namely, the outbreak of the Korean War. The war led to increasingly high demands, and high prices, for both cotton and jute, Pakistan's two main products, and the profits made from the sales of these two products could be utilized in further expanding Pakistan's small industrial base.

At the time of partition, the Government of India was given possession of the cash stores of the undivided subcontinent. Of this cash, Rs. 550,000,000 was to be given to Pakistan. When tension mounted over the issue of Kashmir, some Indians advocated not giving Pakistan its share, fearing the money would be used to purchase arms which could then be turned against India. Despite this fear, Pakistan did receive its share of the cash balances, although it claimed that India withheld some money and most of the military stores due Pakistan.

Despite the receipt of its share of the cash balances of undivided India, Pakistan was economically shattered by partition. It could produce raw materials in abundance but had few mills in which to have these raw materials processed. It had only one developed port, Karachi, in West Pakistan, and it had to begin to develop another, Chittagong, to service East Pakistan. At a time when the need for development was the greatest, however, Pakistan was forced to divert vast sums of money to rehabilitating more than seven million refugees who had chosen to live in Pakistan. The economic outlook of this overwhelmingly peasant society was bleak and it was the Korean War which gave the Pakistani economy its initial boost.

A Divided Nation. Pakistan, like India, is a plural society. It is composed of a number of distinct racial, cultural, and linguistic groups, and the existing heterogeneity has often provided the major obstacle to the unification of its members into one polity. The most important division is often seen in terms of the distinction between East and West Pakistan but this should not obscure the fact that West Pakistan is far from one homogeneous unit.

The single unit of West Pakistan, created by order of the Governor General in 1955, is a broad rubric which covers at least four of the major ethnic and linguistic groups that comprise the West. The main regions within West Pakistan are the Western Punjab, Sind, the North-West Frontier Province, and Baluchistan, and the languages most commonly associated with these regions are Punjabi, Sindhi, Pushto, and Baluchi, respectively. Urdu, one of the two national languages of Pakistan, is also spoken in the West. Yet, it is striking to note that prior to 1947, there was not a single Muslim-majority province where Urdu was the dominant regional language. Prior to independence, the greatest number of Urdu speakers lived in what became, with independence, northern India. In West Pakistan, Urdu has grown in use, if not in popularity, due to the support given to it by the leaders of postindependence Pakistan.

West Pakistan was the first area in the Indian subcontinent to be affected by the Muslim invasions which began as early as the eighth century A.D. From that point on, the West experienced intermittent raids or invasions by Muslims of Turkic, Afghani, or Central Asian origin. Many of the invaders simply looted and plundered parts of the West, only to retire to their homelands in either Afghanistan or Central Asia. But many, on the other hand, settled in the regions now known as West Pakistan. Slowly but surely, the peoples of the West, under the influence of the saint as well as the sword, became predominantly Muslim. This religious conversion led to an accentuation of the cultural bond between this recently converted area and the other Islamic areas to the west of it. In many ways, the most important cultural influence on the west was of Persian origin. It was to Persia and to Arabia that the newly converted areas of the west looked for their cultural kin, often ignoring their fellows to the east.

Such a marked shift in cultural outlook did not occur in Bengal. As we have noted, conversions in Bengal occurred when the region was in a state of religio-cultural flux. By and large, the conversions in Bengal were peaceful, as many low-caste Hindus or former Buddhists turned to the egalitarian faith of Islam. Many of the new converts in Bengal retained some of the religious beliefs and practices of the faith they had recently left; a number of Hindu influences may be found in the Islam of Bengal. "Thus, while they learnt much from Islam, they at the same time modified their new religion by making it more compatible with their old beliefs."[11]

Developments in Bengal in the nineteenth century tended to reinforce the relatively peaceful coexistence which prevailed amongst its Hindus and Muslims. The Hindus of Bengal were the first group in the Indian subcontinent to benefit from the introduction of English education. The education which the elites of Bengal received, filled with ideas about liberalism and humanitarianism, tended to further strengthen a secularist trend. It should be noted that this growing secularism was not confined to Hindus alone. As early as 1915–16 Bengali *madrasahs* (Muslim religious and educational institutions), in addition to the standard, heavily religious instruction, began to offer subjects such as arithmetic, geography and English as well. This was quite unlike the west, where the hold of the *pir* and the *ulamma* on education still is strong.

Bengalis, Hindu and Muslim alike, developed a deep pride for their own distinctive cultural tradition. Bengalis expressed the belief that their language, their literature, and their music were among the most beautiful the world over. All Bengalis can and do look with pride to the works of the literary genius Rabindranath Tagore. At the same time, many can and do respect the outstanding poetry of Bengal's leading Muslim poet, Qazi Nazrul Islam. Qazi Nazrul Islam writes in Bengali but has introduced into the already rich language a wide variety of Persian words and literary forms. The power of this linguistic pride cannot be underestimated. When in 1952 the Pakistani Prime Minister, Khwaja Nazimuddin, himself a Bengali, stated that Urdu, and Urdu alone, would become the national language of Pakistan, student demonstrations in protest broke out in Dacca. Shortly thereafter Bengali and Urdu were recognized as the two national languages of Pakistan; and each constitution of Pakistan has followed this pattern.

One finds in Pakistan an almost overwhelming potential for cultural and linguistic divisiveness. West Pakistan has within it four major linguistic regions, over all of which Urdu has been superimposed. The Muslims of the west tend to be much more

---

[11] S. M. Ikram and Percival Spear, eds., *The Cultural Heritage of Pakistan* (Karachi, 1955), p. 138.

orthodox than the Muslims of Bengal. West Pakistani Muslims continue to look to Persia and Arabia for their cultural and religious sustenance.

Bengal, on the other hand, is a somewhat more homogeneous unit, composed of only the Muslim-majority areas of prepartition Bengal. While it contains the overwhelming preponderance of Pakistani Hindus (in 1961, more than eighteen percent of the population of East Pakistan was Hindu, while the comparable figure for West Pakistan was one and one-half percent), Hindus and Muslims seem to have evolved a system of peaceful coexistence. This may be the result of a number of factors. The relatively peaceful conversions in Bengal, and the syncretic form of Islam which developed, were later reinforced by secular trends and beliefs, many of which were the result of English education. Although partitioned in 1947, Bengal suffered less, in human terms, than the west; five out of every six Pakistani refugees migrated to and settled in West Pakistan. All of these factors may have contributed to a continuing strong, regional outlook amongst Bengalis who, on either side of the border, still point with pride to their homeland, its sons and its language. While West Pakistanis look to Persia as their cultural homeland, Bengalis look to their own region. In neither case does one find a successful attempt at cultural unification between the two wings of Pakistan. Indeed, the cultural and linguistic pride, found in both regions, has acted as one of the greatest obstacles to the intergration of all Pakistanis into one polity.

The Failure of Integration.   With partition and independence in 1947, Jinnah and the members of the Muslim League had achieved their long-range goal. Now the leaders of Pakistan had to begin the work of nation building. They had to attempt to integrate the various constituent units of Pakistan into one polity. This attempted integration seemed most likely to succeed in the first four years of Pakistan's existence. And yet, in this era of hope, the seeds of future discords began to germinate.

Upon independence, Muhammad Ali Jinnah assumed the post of Governor-General of Pakistan. Jinnah, successful in his quest for a Muslim-majority nation, was the single most important integrative force in the immediate postindependence era. Jinnah was not merely a political leader of Pakistan; he was not merely one among equals. In many ways Jinnah was the personification of the nation. Jinnah was Pakistan's dominant, and domineering, leader who, because of his own personal appeal, could unite the disparate parts of the country.

This was crucial to Pakistan's mere existence in the postpartition era. The Muslim League had fought its battle for Pakistan by basing its case on the fear of Hindu domination. Jinnah and his colleagues in the League had presented to their coreligionists virtually nothing in the way of social or political programs which they, as leaders of an independent Pakistan, would attempt to implement. This became a problem once independence had, in fact, been achieved. When Pakistan as a territorial and political entity was created, this void became even more prominent. At this time the League should have faced the problem of positive policy formulation.

Yet it did not, and the reason for this failure must rest with Jinnah, constrained as he was by external circumstances, and with his successor, Liaquat Ali Khan. In the days immediately following partition, the most pressing problems were those resulting from the mass migrations to and from Pakistan, accompanied, as we have noted, by mass slaughter. This was not an atmosphere in which Jinnah had much time for constructive policy formulation. Indeed, it was at this time that many must have wondered why such policies had not been conceived prior to independence. The answer to that question rests only with Jinnah, who had dominated the Muslim League but had not had the foresight to outline the policies which might be pursued when Pakistan was formed.

Within little over a year of independence Jinnah, Pakistan's most powerful leader and integrative force, was dead. Leadership was assumed by Liaquat Ali Khan, who continued to hold the post of Prime Minister. Liaquat Ali Khan was, as Jinnah had been, a dominant and popular leader. But, like Jinnah, Liaquat Ali Khan was unable to inspire the masses by offering a program of social, economic and political reforms. And under Liaquat, as under Jinnah, little was done to build grass-roots support for the Muslim League as a political party. Jinnah and Liaquat both were dominant figures, and it may have been their very dominance which blinded them to the need for finding firm, grass-roots support for their policies. Under Liaquat the nation was held together but few long-range economic or political reforms were presented. And in

1951 Liaquat was assassinated. Refugee rule in Pakistan which had provided some hope of impartial, nonregional, all-Pakistani rule, had ended, and many of the disintegrative forces within Pakistan began to come to the fore.

The death of Liaquat Ali Khan left Pakistan without a single dominant political leader. Even more than before leaders in Pakistan tended to shy away from comprehensive policy formulation. Nor could they even agree upon the sort of constitution Pakistan was to have. Indeed, it was not until 1956 that Pakistan had any constitution of its own making.

The search for integrative forces in the post-Liaquat era should have been even more intense than that which preceded it, but it was not. The Muslim League, until Liaquat's death the most prominent political party in Pakistan, could find neither a convincing social and political program nor an inspiring leader. Politics in Pakistan regressed to a state of sloganeering. As Khalid Sayeed observed, "The fact that Pakistan could be achieved in such a short time misled Pakistanis into believing that Islamic unity and slogans like faith, unity, and discipline could do the same trick in building a modern state on stable foundations."[12]   Thus the League did very little to build grass-roots support for itself and its policies. Much attention was diverted from the national scene to local, or regional, issues, a step which could hardly aid in the integration of the diverse regions. Pakistani politicians, instead of devoting themselves to nation-building, became more selfishly concerned with building up their own personal power and prestige. This led to an almost unending series of shifting political loyalties which, in turn, sometimes occasioned the fall of a government. Yet, this play for power continued and few bothered to worry about the disintegrative forces it represented. This is indeed surprising when one recalls that Pakistan had seven Prime Ministers in the period from 1950–58.

The disintegrative forces continued to grow and to infect almost all aspects of Pakistani social and political life. Ironically, Pakistanis found that their unifying bond, Islam, could itself be a disintegrative force. When Pakistanis attempted to frame a constitution along Islamic lines, they were forced to interpret what "Islamic" was. This brought to the fore the divisions found among the vari-

---

[12]Khalid B. Sayeed, *The Political System of Pakistan* (Boston, 1967), p. 83.

ous sects of Islam in Pakistan. While the majority of Pakistanis are Sunni Muslims, the Shi'a sect is also prominent, and the historical division between the two is quite pronounced. The Ahmadis are also believers in Islam but are regarded by many as heretical. Indeed, Pakistan was the scene of some violent anti-Ahmadi rioting in 1952-53, when the more orthodox Muslims attempted to pressure the government into declaring the Ahmadis a religious minority and, at the same time, into obtaining the resignation of the Ahmadi foreign minister. The divisions extend across regional lines as well. East Pakistani Muslims have often been taken to task by their more conservative and orthodox coreligionists in the west for allowing too many Hindu influences to remain within their belief system.

One sees in Pakistan's first decade of existence the collapse of many of its potentially integrating forces. Its two most prominent leaders, who had often united the nation by sheer force of personality, were dead. The Muslim League had not developed a social or political program under Jinnah or Liaquat Ali Khan and it did not after their deaths. Politics became increasingly personal and provincial; men turned from nation-building to concern themselves with building their own personal power. This was most often done by emphasizing one's regional strength. Thus, in the 1954 East Bengal elections, the Muslim League was trounced by a United Front comprised of parties concerned mainly with the articulation and solution of Bengali grievances and problems. And, in the course of constitution-making, even Islam, the bond which had united the Muslim-majority provinces, proved that it too could be divisive and further increase the nation's instability.

The two most consistently stable forces in Pakistan's first decade were the civil service and the army, both dominated by Punjabis. While there were seven Prime Ministers between 1950–58, there was only one Commander-in-Chief of the Army. When in 1958 instability seemed to have become a constant in Pakistani political life, it was not surprising that this same Commander-in-Chief, General Muhammad Ayub Khan, should step in, instituting the martial law regime. With the establishment of martial law, the constitution of 1956 was discarded, the central and provincial cabinets and assemblies were dismissed, and all political parties were banned.

Such was the state of Pakistani politics until the promulgation of a new constitution in 1962. The constitution legitimized a form of government referred to by Sayeed as a constitutional autocracy. Overwhelming political power rests with the president, who could determine provincial as well as national policies. The president and the National Assembly were to be indirectly elected, on the basis of the votes of 80,000 Basic Democrats. A presidential veto could not be overridden for the president could always refer the matter to a referendum. The Basic Democrats who did the voting were often chosen on the basis of their loyalty to the president and his policies. It was thus difficult to imagine a majority of the Basic Democrats voting against an incumbent president or his policies.

Such a system, while it provided stability, did so only in terms of the stability of one-man rule. Ayub was not successful at creating a political consensus or at accommodating the varied regional demands. During his rule, it was Ayub who provided what stability Pakistan enjoyed.

Pakistan, as we have shown, was a nation filled with centrifugal and disintegrative forces. During Pakistan's first decade, these disintegrative tendencies had become ever more prominent and threatening, leading eventually to Ayub's rule. The second decade, or Ayub's decade, was an attempt to unite Pakistan's two wings by edicts from above. But nationhood is founded at a grassroots level, a fact few Pakistani politicians and rulers seem to have grasped. Ayub's fall in 1969 was proof that even he, with all his power, could not unite the nation. His fall proved that he had not been able to eliminate the centrifugal tendencies within Pakistan. Indeed, the events which followed Ayub's demise seem to indicate that a major centrifugal trend, regionalism, had increased and not diminished in strength.

The Crisis of Bangladesh.   On March 25, 1969, while his regime was under often violent attack, President Muhammad Ayub Khan, in an act strongly reminiscent of his predecessor, peacefully abdicated office, turning control of the government over to the Commander-in-Chief of the army, General Agha Muhammad Yahya Khan. Exactly two years later West Pakistani troops entered East Pakistan in an attempt to crush what the West Pakistanis viewed as an increasingly dangerous separatist movement. This two year span was one in which the Pakistanis had the greatest hope, but, ironically, it ended in what can only be viewed as a catastrophe for the nation. Pakistan today is two nations, and it seems inconceivable that it will ever unite as one again.

Yahya Khan's martial law regime did offer Pakistanis of both wings a great deal of hope. Although the rationale for Yahya Khan's assumption of power was to provide stability for the nation, he made it clear from the very beginning that he did not intend to remain in office indefinitely. Indeed, Yahya Khan promised Pakistanis their first direct national election on the basis of universal adult suffrage. They would elect representatives to both the constituent and provincial assemblies. The Constituent Assembly would be given 120 days in which to frame a workable constitution for Pakistan. If it failed to do so, it would be dissolved and new elections would be held. Yahya Khan placed this time limit on Pakistani politicians as he wanted to avoid a long, drawn-out Constituent Assembly debate over the nature of the constitution. Excessively long debates had typified the Constituent Assembly meetings of the 1950s when, it should be noted, it took nine years to frame Pakistan's first constitution.

Pakistani politicians eagerly entered the electoral contest which spanned most all of 1970. From the very outset, the election assumed a regional, rather than a national, coloring. The two main contestants and their parties had regionally delimited power bases. Sheikh Mujibur Rahman, leader of the Awami League, found his strength in East Pakistan. Zulfiqar Ali Bhutto, head of the Pakistan Peoples Party, was prominent throughout the West. Bhutto, a Sindhi, was able to secure a power base in the Punjab as well, thus enhancing his overall strength. Bhutto's party, however, contested no elections in East Pakistan; while the Awami League did contest a few seats in the West, this was seen by many as merely a symbolic gesture.

The program put forth by Sheikh Mujibur Rahman represented a call, frequently heard in the East, for greater regional autonomy. Indeed, his call was quite similar to that presented in the East Pakistani provincial elections of 1954 by A. K. Fazlul Huq who, at that time, led the East Pakistani United Front to an overwhelming victory over the Muslim League. Sheikh Mujibur Rahman's program, not unlike that of Fazlul Huq, was aimed at decreasing the economic disparities between the two wings of Pakistan. For years the East had provided the lion's share of Pakistani foreign exchange earnings, only to have insufficient funds from these earnings channeled back into the more populous yet less developed East.

Sheikh Mujibur Rahman's Six Point Plan consisted of the demand that the new constitution provide a parliamentary form of government directly elected on the basis of universal suffrage. The federal government would deal with only two subjects, defense and foreign affairs, and all residuary powers would rest with the provinces. Pakistan would have two currencies and an attempt would thus be made to stop the flow of currency from East to West. The power of taxation would rest with the provinces and not the Center which would receive its funds from the provinces. Separate accounting of foreign exchange earnings would be instituted in both East and West; the foreign exchange requirements of the Center would come from the two wings in equal portions or at an established ratio; indigenous products would move duty-free between East and West Pakistan; and the two wings would be allowed to establish their own trade relations with foreign nations. Finally, the Six-Point Plan demanded that East Pakistan be allowed to form its own separate militia.

Had such a plan been adopted, the obvious advantage would have rested with the East. It was the more populous wing and, therefore, more of its men would have been elected to the parliament it envisaged. The East would have benefitted the most financially by the normalization of relations with India, the nation which contains it on three sides, and Sheikh Mujibur Rahman called for such a normalization during the campaign. An autonomous East Pakistan would have meant a wealthier East Pakistan, and West Pakistani politicians feared what the loss of income might do to the West. Moreover, Bhutto, the single most prominent West Pakistani politician, opposed the idea of autonomy; autonomy would only weaken the West while strengthening the East.

The elections of 1970 provided an absolute majority victory for Sheikh Mujibur Rahman. Bhutto emerged, as was expected, as the single most powerful politician in the West. The future of Pakistan called for these two leaders to meet and, if possible, to work out a compromise in the Constituent Assembly. This meeting was never held. Bhutto refused to attend the Constituent Assembly meeting. Yahya Khan, instead of applying pressure on Bhutto, went in March of 1971 to confer with Sheikh Mujibur Rahman, possibly in an attempt to get the Awami League leader to tone down his demands for autonomy. Sheikh Mujibur Rahman, flushed with victory and commanding an absolute majority in the Constituent Assembly, refused. The discussions broke down and Yahya Khan's troops entered the East, ostensibly to crush a secessionist movement.

The West Pakistani resort to force and their abrogation of the election results led to the outbreak of a full-scale civil war in Pakistan which, in turn, led to the eventual separation of East and West. The East, now called Bangladesh (Bengal Nation) by its supporters, was the scene of almost nine months of continuous fighting. A Bengali guerrilla army, the Mukti Bahini (Liberation Forces) formed and attempted to drive the West Pakistani troops and officials from the East.

With the outbreak of fighting, West Pakistani leaders attempted to extend this civil war to the international arena. They asserted that India favored secession, a highly unlikely claim, and that India overtly and covertly aided the guerrilla forces. The West Pakistanis, lacking a single strong unifying force, once again attempted to use India as a scapegoat.

The initial reply of the Government of India was a denial of the West Pakistani charges. The Government of India viewed the conflict as a civil war to be solved by a political discussion among East and West Pakistani leaders. India asserted that her role consisted mainly in caring for the masses of frightened, defenseless, and homeless refugees who had fled from East Pakistan to India. The total number of refugees who crossed the border into India was probably near ten million. The staggering economic and social burdens which the refugees imposed upon India eventually forced a change in Indian policy. Prime Minister Indira Gandhi had attempted to secure financial aid for the refugees from western nations but the grants of money or food were quite insignificant. The total annual cost of the care of the refugees was estimated between $800 and $900 million. Had India been forced to continue spending such vast sums on the refugees, the possibility of any significant expenditures on new economic development within India would have been eliminated. India's reason for involvement in the crisis, therefore, stemmed from the absolute necessity for India to free itself from the burdens imposed by the refugees. To do so would mean that the refugees would have to return home and few would leave India until peace was restored in the East. It was with this in mind that India assumed a larger role in the war in the East. India had previously trained and armed some of the Mukti Bahini. Often the guerrilla forces, after an attack on the West Pakistanis, had sought and found shelter in India. In November 1971 the Indian army itself became involved in defensive, retaliatory attacks on the West Pakistanis stationed in the East.

In December 1971, a state of war broke out between India, attempting to aid the Bengalis, and West Pakistan. The fighting was not totally confined to the East, however. In what appears to have been an attempt to divert Indian forces, West Pakistani troops attempted to capture parts of Indian-controlled Kashmir. Indian troops were not to be diverted, however; the main thrust on their part was in the East. After two weeks of battle, the West Pakistani forces in the East surrendered; and all parties honored the new cease-fire. The Indian goal had indeed been a limited one: To allow the transformation of East Pakistan into the sovereign nation of Bangladesh, a nation to which the refugees could return peacefully. In this the Indians and the Bengalis were successful.

The political arenas in both West Pakistan and Bangladesh have been filled with change and surprise since the end of the war. Yahya Khan resigned as president of West Pakistan. His post was assumed by Zulfiqar Ali Bhutto. One of Bhutto's first official actions was to place Yahya Khan under house arrest. Bhutto then disclosed that Sheikh Mujibur Rahman, leader of the Awami League and the only man who could unite all of Bangladesh, was indeed alive and would soon be released from imprisonment in the West. Bhutto and Sheikh Mujibur met and conferred. Bhutto, once an avowed opponent of regional autonomy, attempted to win Sheikh Mujibur Rahman's support for a continued, united Pakistan, of two wings, but with greater powers granted to the provinces. Sheikh Mujibur Rahman refused. He was released and flew to Dacca, the capital of the newly established nation whose government he now heads.

At this writing, Sheikh Mujibur Rahman is attempting to lead his fellow Bengalis in rebuilding their war-torn nation. The refugees in India have largely returned, lifting the phenomenal financial and social burdens which India carried for nearly a year. In the immediate future, the largest problem facing Bangladesh will be an economic one. The nation's industrial base must be built, or rebuilt. For the immediate future, and possibly over the long-run, this will result in the strengthening of economic ties between Bangladesh and India. Bangladesh is gradually being granted diplomatic recognition from nations throughout the world. Thus far, over sixty nations have recognized Bangladesh, the most prominent among them being India, the Soviet Union, the United Kingdom and the United States which waited until April 4, 1972 before according recognition to the new Asian state. Prominent due to its absence is the People's Republic of China which, like the United States, supported the West Pakistanis. The Peking Government presently remains one of the few major powers still without diplomatic representation to the government of Sheikh Mujibur Rahman.

In West Pakistan, Bhutto is attempting to consolidate the nation. The West Pakistanis stand to lose economically with the separation of Bangladesh and Bhutto cannot afford to allow these economic losses to take the form of political grievances. Thus, he has threatened to nationalize some large industries and also to confiscate some of the assets of the wealthiest West Pakistanis. Bhutto, who governs a heterogeneous polity, must also face the possibility that discontent might again raise its head in the form of Pathan or Buluchi regionalism or, perhaps, separatism.

Although both West Pakistan and Bangladesh face rather large problems in the weeks and months ahead, the separation of the two may prove to be politically beneficial to both nations. Both may become somewhat more manageable entities than the Pakistan of the partition of 1947. That Pakistan, indeed, is dead.

Editor's note: In July, 1972, India's Prime Minister Indira Gandhi and Pakistan's President Zulfiqar Ali Bhutto met in the Himalayan hill station of Simla, the same town in which twenty-five years previously plans were devised for the new nation of Pakistan to be carved out of British India. At the Simla summit, the two leaders agreed to consider the restoration of diplomatic relations and communications, suspended since the 13-day war of December 1971, and to resume air transport service between their respective countries. India, which captured most of the territory in the December conflict, made a major concession in agreeing to return some 5,100 square miles of Pakistani territory—all except a few strategic salients in Kashmir. The latter remains a source of bitter contention between the two nations. Pakistan demands that the future of the predominantly Moslem state be determined by plebiscite while India adamantly insists that Kashmir's accession to India in 1947 be accepted as legal and final. A more hopeful note was struck when both sides agreed to continue the bilateral negotiations and Mrs. Gandhi accepted President Bhutto's invitation to a September meeting in Pakistan.

Left unresolved is the matter of some 91,000 Pakistani military and civilian prisoners of war still in Indian hands. Most of the prisoners surrendered to a joint India-Bangladesh command and cannot be returned without negotiations involving Bangladesh. Thus far, Bhutto has refused to recognize the new Bengali state. The P.O.W. issue is potentially explosive since Bangladesh Prime Minister Sheikh Mujibur Rahman has said that some of the prisoners will be tried on war crimes charges. Such trials could set off reprisals against the 400,000 Bengalis who are still living and working in Pakistan.

Perhaps most significant is the seeming determination of India, Pakistan and Bangladesh to resolve their differences without reference to parties outside the subcontinent. Prior to her meeting at Simla with President Bhutto, Mrs. Gandhi traveled to Dacca for talks with the Prime Minister of Bangladesh. Since that meeting Bhutto has agreed to meet with Sheikh Mujibur Rahman and that conference could pave the way for an eventual settlement of major differences between their two countries. Despite outstanding grievances, therefore, India, Pakistan and Bangladesh appear agreed on one point: their interests will be better served if negotiations are conducted in the absence of Big Power brokers. This attitude is the result of past experiences with Big Power mediators and contains a lesson which might profitably serve other nations in the future.

BIBLIOGRAPHY

The number of books describing the partition of India, and the events leading up to this, is growing rapidly; the following titles represent only some of the more recent and scholarly books on these subjects. Most of them contain full bibliographies, in which further readings can be found. Three important collections of documents are: C. H. Philips, ed., *The Evolution of India and Pakistan, 1858–1947* (London, 1962); M. L. Gwyer and A. Appadorai, eds., *Speeches and Documents on the Indian Constitution, 1921–47* (London, 1957, 2 vols.); Aziz Ahmad and G. E. von Grunebaum, eds., *Muslim Self-Statement in India and Pakistan, 1857–1968* (Wiesbaden, 1970). Many of the participants have written books. The following are most important: H. V. Hodson, *The Great Divide. Britain, India, Pakistan* (London, 1969); Earl Mountbatten of Burma, *Reflections on the Transfer of Power and Jawaharlal Nehru* (Cambridge, 1968), a short, discreet apologia; E. W. R. Lumby, *The Transfer of Power in India, 1945–47* (New York, 1954), a dispassionate, detailed account; V. P. Menon, *The Transfer of Power in India* (Princeton, 1957) and Chaudhri Muhammad Ali, *The Emergence of Pakistan* (New York, 1967) are by two civil servants deeply involved in the events of the last few years of British rule, the former pro-India and the latter an active worker for Pakistan; S. M. Ikram, *Modern Muslim India and the Birth of Pakistan, 1858–1951* (Lahore, 1965), a series of biographical sketches of Muslim notables; Penderel Moon, *Divide and Quit* (London, 1961), by an ICS officer; Ian Stephens, *Pakistan* (London, 1967), a sympathetic survey of the country's origins and recent development; Alan Campbell-Johnson, *Mission with Mountbatten* (New York, 1953), by Mountbatten's press officer; Francis Tuker, *While Memory Serves* (London, 1950), a blood-curdling account of the riots in eastern India by the army officer responsible for quelling them.

Among recent interpretations one book stands out: C. H. Philips and M. D. Wainwright, eds., *The Partition of India. Policies and Perspectives, 1935–1947* (Cambridge, Mass., 1970), which contains a series of stimulating essays on particular aspects of the period, and sixteen short accounts by participants. Philips' earlier short account, *The Partition of India, 1947* (Leeds, 1967), and Hugh Tinker, *Experiment with Freedom. India and Pakistan, 1947* (London, 1967), are both disappointingly pro-British. A slightly more popular account is Leonard Mosley's *The Last Days of the British Raj* (London, 1961). Two good books by Muslim authors are: K. B. Sayeed, *Pakistan. The Formative Phase, 1857–1948* (London, 1968), and K. K. Aziz, *The Making of Pakistan, A Study in Nationalism* (London, 1967).

There are many biographies of the leading Indian participants, most of them too partial to be useful. Among the best are: M. H. Saiyid, *Mohammad Ali Jinnah (A Political Study)* (Lahore, 1953); Hector Bolitho, *Jinnah. Creator of Pakistan* (London, 1954); Michael Brecher, *Nehru. A Political Biography* (London, 1959); Erik H. Erikson, *Gandhi's Truth. On the*

Origins of Militant Nonviolence (New York, 1969); Joan V. Bondurant, *Conquest of Violence; The Ghandian Philosophy of Conflict* (Princeton, 1958); B. R. Nanda, *Mahatma Gandhi; A Biography* (Boston, 1959). Two general surveys of Islam in India are: Muhammad Mujeeb, *The Indian Muslims* (London, 1967) and I. H. Qureshi, *The Muslim Community of the Indo-Pakistan Subcontinent* (New York, 1960). For studies of Muslim thought during the last hundred years, see Aziz Ahmad, *Islamic Modernism in India and Pakistan, 1857–1964* (London, 1967) and W. C. Smith, *Modern Islam in India; a Social Analysis* (Lahore, 1947).

The best single study which provides an overview of the causes of partition as well as a discussion of subsequent events is W. Norman Brown, *The United States and India and Pakistan* (Cambridge, Mass., 1963).

For a sympathetic and scholarly discussion of the foreign affairs of Pakistan, the reader is referred to Wayne Wilcox, *India, Pakistan and the Rise of China* (New York, 1964). G. W. Chowdhury, *Pakistan's Relations with India 1947–1966* (New York, 1968) provides a Pakistani official's account of the anxieties and fears of Pakistan toward India and how these anxieties and fears have dominated Pakistani foreign policy decisions. One of the best accounts of the conflict over Kashmir, although an account with somewhat of a pro-Indian bias, is Sisir Gupta, *Kashmir: A Study in India-Pakistan Relations* (London, 1966). For a discussion of South Asian affairs in a broader perspective, see Norman D. Palmer, *South Asia and United States Policy* (Boston, 1966).

The reader interested in economic developments in Pakistan since independence is referred to two sympathetic and sound volumes, J. R. Andrus and A. F. M. Mohammed, *Economy of Pakistan* (Stanford, 1958), and Gustav F. Papanek, *Pakistan's Development: Social Goals and Private Incentives* (Cambridge, Mass., 1967).

For a study of the cultural development and divergences within Pakistan, one finds the work of S. M. Ikram and Percival Spear, eds., *The Cultural Heritage of Pakistan* quite useful as an introductory study. More specific works dealing with distinctly delimited geographical and cultural entities are available as well, but their sheer number precludes listing here.

The role which religion has played within Pakistani politics is discussed in a series of excellent essays in Donald Eugene Smith, ed., *South Asian Politics and Religion* (Princeton, 1966). An intensive study of the concepts of an Islamic state and the modifications of these concepts during the attempt at constitution-making is lucidly presented in Leonard Binder, *Religion and Politics in Pakistan* (Berkeley, 1963).

The best volume concentrating on political developments in Pakistan since independence in Khalid B. Sayeed, *The Political System of Pakistan* (Boston, 1967). Although published during Ayub's presidency, it contains many detailed discussions of the fundamental, underlying problems which Pakistan is still facing today; a noteworthy example is Sayeed's extensive discussion of the problems which regionalism pose for the Pakistani government. Another equally excellent work, although dated in some respects, is Keith Callard, *Pakistan: A Political Study* (New York, 1957). A thorough discussion of the attempted integration of Pakistan's princely states into the polity is provided by Wayne A. Wilcox, *Pakistan, the Consolidation of a Nation* (New York, 1963). For an analytical framework within which national political development may be viewed, see Karl Von Vorys, *Political Development in Pakistan* (Princeton, 1965).

In perusing the volumes cited above, the reader should keep in mind, however, that the nature of such contemporary subjects as political integration, economic growth, or foreign affairs is constantly changing. Thus, it is possible that some sources listed may be somewhat outdated within a short period of time. To redress the balance, the reader is referred to more contemporary periodicals, specifically the monthly editions of *Asian Survey* (Berkeley).

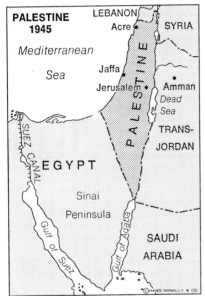

PALESTINE 1945

LEBANON
Acre
SYRIA
Mediterranean
Sea
Jaffa
PALESTINE
Jerusalem
Amman
Dead
Sea
TRANS-
JORDAN
SUEZ CANAL
EGYPT
Sinai
Peninsula
Gulf of Suez
Gulf of Aqaba
SAUDI
ARABIA
©RAND McNALLY & CO

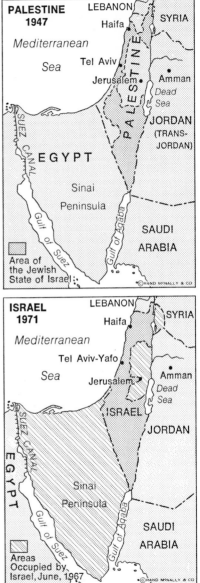

PALESTINE 1947

LEBANON
Haifa
SYRIA
Mediterranean
Sea
Tel Aviv
PALESTINE
Jerusalem
Amman
Dead
Sea
JORDAN
(TRANS-
JORDAN)
EGYPT
Sinai
Peninsula
Gulf of Suez
Gulf of Aqaba
SAUDI
ARABIA
Area of
the Jewish
State of Israel
©RAND McNALLY & CO

ISRAEL 1971

LEBANON
Haifa
SYRIA
Mediterranean
Sea
Tel Aviv-Yafo
Jerusalem
Amman
Dead
Sea
ISRAEL
JORDAN
SUEZ CANAL
EGYPT
Sinai
Peninsula
Gulf of Suez
Gulf of Aqaba
SAUDI
ARABIA
Areas
Occupied by
Israel, June, 1967
©RAND McNALLY & CO

Chapter 5

The Partition of Palestine: Conflicting Nationalism and Great Power Rivalry

Robert Freedman
Marquette University

The issues involved in the partition of Palestine are among the most complex and emotion-laden historical problems of the twentieth century. Not only is the student of the period confronted with the conflicting claims of Arab and Jew, he must also deal with the conflicting policies of the great powers. For it was primarily the rivalry among the great powers of Europe which brought the mandate of Palestine into existence after World War I and it was also as a result of great power rivalry that the mandate was dissolved in 1948.

The close relationship of European developments to the conflict over Palestine is further reflected in the growth of Zionism and Arab Nationalism, because both nationalist movements were heavily influenced by similar movements in nineteenth century Europe. Although there had been periodic Jewish immigration to Palestine prior to the nineteenth century, Zionism—as a political movement to reassert Jewish sovereignty over Palestine—did not become an active force until the success of German and Italian nationalists in regaining control over their national homelands suggested a similar program to Jewish leaders. Similarly, as the European powers made increasing political and economic inroads in the decaying Ottoman Empire in the nineteenth century, their political ideas—of which nationalism was perhaps the most important—began to have an increasing effect among the Arabs who formed the majority of the polyglot Empire. By the end of the century, both Arab Nationalism and Zionism had attracted a number of followers, although they had not yet become popular mass movements.

In World War I nearly all the belligerent powers sought to exploit the two nascent nationalist movements, and at the close of the War Britain and France had succeeded in substituting their rule for that of the Turks over much of the Ottoman Empire, including Palestine. The interwar period was marked by a number of uprisings against British and French domination of the Middle East, and following World War II both Zionism and Arab nationalism succeeded in breaking the shackles of British and French control. One of the tragedies of the situation, however, was that Zionism and Arab Nationalism, instead of cooperating against the colonial control of Britain and France, became bitter enemies. Indeed, this factor has continued to keep the region as a whole weak and open to foreign penetration, since even today the great powers are exploiting Arab-Israeli enmity.

The Arab-Israeli conflict over Palestine has now lasted for more than a half-century, and anyone seeking to understand the origin and development of the conflict must evaluate the Arab and Jewish drives for national independence against the background of great power intrigue and interference.

THE DIPLOMATIC BACKGROUND AND THE RISE OF ZIONISM AND ARAB NATIONALISM

In the century prior to World War I, the Ottoman Empire, which had controlled Palestine since 1517, was in a state of serious decay. Once the master of a large section of Europe as well as the Middle East, the Empire was now the prey of more powerful European nations. While England had sought to shore up the "Sick Man" of Europe against Russian incursions from the north, she was not unwilling to help herself to a share of the Ottoman Empire's southern provinces, particularly towards the end of the century. Uppermost in British strategy was the protection of Britain's communication lines to India. Following completion of the Suez Canal, the British gained control over Egypt, and pressured Turkey to cede Cyprus as well. Expanding from their base in Egypt, the British conquered the Sudan in 1898 and acquired most of the Sinai Peninsula by 1906.

Britain's penetration of the western sections of the Ottoman Empire was accompanied by inroads into its southern and eastern territories. As early as 1869 the British had negotiated a protectorate over the sheikdoms of the Persian Gulf, and in 1880 secured control over Muscat and in 1890 over Kuwait. Thus, by the start of World War I, England was already in control of much of the Middle East, and during the War British diplomats endeavored to secure most of the rest of the area.

While the British were concentrating on territorial aggrandizement at the expense of the Ottoman Empire, France's penetration of Turkey's Middle Eastern holdings was primarily economic. French interest was concentrated in Lebanon and Syria, areas the French were later to claim in the diplomatic negotiations held during World War I. Germany's approach to the disintegrating Ottoman Empire differed from that of France and England. The main German goal was to secure influence within the Turkish government. The Germans obtained the Sultan's consent to build a railroad between Constantinople and Baghdad, part of the Berlin to Baghdad railway, and were also called upon by the Sultan to help train the Turkish army. Kaiser Wilhelm II underlined his nation's growing interest in the Middle East by several trips to the region, including one to Palestine in 1898. The growing influence of the Germans within the Ottoman Empire was a matter of increasing concern to the British as World War I approached, since Ottoman territory lay along the land route to India. Indeed, fear of Germany had become so strong by 1907 that the British signed an agreement with the Russians delimiting their mutual spheres of influence in Iran, with Britain getting the southern part of the country as a virtual protectorate.

Thus, by the start of World War I, the entire Ottoman Empire had become a major arena for big power politics, although the final dismemberment of the Empire was to await the peace settlement following the war.

As the Ottoman Empire began to disintegrate under the blows of Western imperialism, nationalist stirrings began to appear among the Arabs who were the most populous of the peoples of the Empire. Up until the "Young Turk" revolution of 1908, however, Arab nationalism faced a serious dilemma. Since the Turks were fellow Moslems, many Moslem Arabs felt reluctant to challenge the concept of Islamic unity which was one of the pillars of the Ottoman Empire. It is for this reason that the first major moves toward a purely secular Arab nationalism on the European model came from Christian Arabs. Influenced both by the success of the Christian princes in the Balkans in throwing off the Ottoman yoke, and also by the western colleges and universities run by Christian religious orders which began to appear in Syria and Lebanon in the middle of the nineteenth century, a number of Christian Arabs began to advocate independence for the Arabs of the Ottoman Empire. Yet the movement was slow to catch on either with the Arab masses or with the Moslem elite although, by the turn of the century, a number of Moslem intellectuals had been converted to the nationalist creed.

The real impetus to Arab nationalism came with the "Young Turk" revolution of 1908. While many Arabs hoped for reform from Turkey's new leaders, especially after the ouster of the corrupt Sultan Abdul-Hamid, their hopes were dashed when the "Young Turks," after some hesitation, embarked upon a policy of Turkification of the Ottoman Empire. One facet of this policy was the suppression of all non-Turkish political groups, including many of the newly formed Arab societies which had come into existence after the revolution of 1908.

Faced by Turkish negativism toward their demands which included autonomy for the Arabs of the Empire, a number of Arabs began to contact the Western powers for support against the Turks. Several Arab organizations contacted the French, and one group of Arabs even went to Cairo to suggest to the British that they annex Syria, despite the fact that British rule was becoming more and more stringent in Egypt itself. In addition, Abdullah, the son of the important Arab ruler of Mecca, Sherif Hussein also sounded out the possibility of British support against the Turks. Nonetheless, while many Arabs, both Moslem and Christian, now opposed their Turkish rulers and called for total Arab independence, many others remained loyal and fought in the Turkish armies during World War I. Thus, while Arab nationalism had clearly become an active force by the start of the War, it was still in the very early stages of development; it was not until the collapse of the Ottoman Empire at the close of the War and the subsequent crisis over the peace settlement that Arab nationalism became a truly popular movement.

The Zionist movement, in its early stages, bore many similarities to Arab nationalism. Arab nationalists looked back to a much earlier period one thousand years before when the Arab Empire flourished, and Jews looked for inspiration to the period almost two thousand years before when they exercised sovereignty over the land of Israel. Similarly, both Zionists and Arab nationalists protested against conditions which kept them in cultural and political subservience to alien rulers. But unlike the Arabs whose nationalist slogans before World War I called for the establishment of a single Arab state encompassing the huge land mass occupied by the Arabs, the Zionists concentrated their attention on a relatively small area—Palestine. Thus, while Arab nationalism fractionized after World War I in the face of European occupation of Arab territories under separate mandates, the Zionists did not have to suffer through a difficult reevaluation of their cause as did the Arabs.

Zionism was very much the child of the liberal and national movements of nineteenth century Europe. Released from forced residence in the ghettoes of Western European cities as a result of the French Revolution, many Jews seized the opportunity held out by the tenets of liberalism to assimilate and become full members of their national communities. Indeed, many Jews became active in the German and Italian drives for national unity. This situation changed, however, toward the end of the century when the nationalism of the European states grew much more exclusive, and the question arose as to whether the Jew had a place either in the newly united countries, Germany and Italy, or in the newly nationalistic ones, France and Russia. The rise of anti-Semitism brought with it the implicit question: was assimilation possible for the Jew of Europe?

The incident which can be considered the precipitating factor in modern Zionism was the Dreyfus affair, since it converted a hitherto assimilated Austrian Jew, Theodore Herzl, into the foremost advocate of Zionism in the nineteenth and early twentieth century. Having viewed the violent anti-Semitic outbursts which accompanied the Dreyfus trial in Paris, Herzl despaired of the Jew's ever being accepted as an equal citizen in Europe. Herzl's solution for the "Jewish problem" was the creation of a Jewish state which he felt could be done with the help of the European powers. Herzl's appeal received its strongest support in Eastern Europe where Jews had suffered the most serious persecution. As early as 1881 the Czarist government of Russia had embarked on a semiofficial policy of encouraging mob attacks on Jewish communities in an effort to divert the increasingly revolutionary fervor of the Russian peasant masses. This policy led to an influx of Jews to Palestine which augmented the existing Jewish community in the country.

Just as the Arabs did not unite behind the drive for Arab independence during the early stages of the Arab nationalist movement, so too did Zionism prove to be a divisive force among Jews. Thus Jews who were extremely orthodox in their religious beliefs completely rejected Zionism, claiming that the Jewish state could only be reestablished with the coming of the Messiah. Other opponents included those Jews, primarily of Western Europe and North America, who were comfortably established in their homelands and felt no need for a Jewish state.

Even within the Zionist movement there were some serious disagreements. One Zionist leader, A'had Ha'am, advocated the establishment in Palestine of a spiritual center for the enrichment of Judaism. He, therefore, opposed the idea of a Jewish state erected on the European model which Herzl had advocated. Others, disagreeing with Herzl's hope of convincing the European powers to help establish a Jewish state, planned to settle in Palestine and gradually to develop a Jewish state through the growth of the Jewish community in the country. These Zionists came to be known as "Practical Zionists" while the followers of Herzl were called "Political Zionists."

In 1897 Herzl convened a conference of Zionist leaders at Basel, Switzerland, which adopted a platform calling for "the creation for the Jewish People of a home in Palestine secured by public [international] law." Herzl's efforts to seek international acceptance of his program, however, proved unsuccessful. He died in 1904, one year after his followers had repudiated a British plan, which he had supported, for utilizing the British colony of Uganda as a possible site for Jewish settlement. The vast majority of Zionists opposed him on this issue, asserting that for historic, cultural, and religious reasons only Palestine could provide the necessary mystique for a viable homeland.

With the death of Herzl, the "Practical Zionists" took over leadership of the Zionist movement and the Jewish community in Palestine began to grow rapidly as settlers arrived from Eastern Europe. Political Zionism, however, was not dead and the outbreak of World War I was to give the political Zionists, like the Arab nationalists, a chance to realize their dreams.

The outbreak of World War I, and especially the entry of Turkey on the side of Germany and Austria, the Central Powers, caused a major transformation in the Arab and Zionist drives for national independence. From minority movements possessing very limited influence in world politics both Zionism and Arab Nationalism became important factors in the diplomacy of the War and in the ensuing peace settlement.

The diplomatic maneuverings with regard to the Middle East during World War I were both highly complex and rather sordid. The British, in desperate need of support throughout virtually all of the conflict, appealed both to the Arabs and to the Zionists for assistance. In return for their support, the British promised sections of the Ottoman Empire's Middle Eastern holdings to the two nationalist movements. Unfortunately, the British were to make rather vague and contradictory promises concerning the disposition of this territory.

On the one hand, the British promised, in the Hussein-McMahan correspondence, an "independent Arab state" to Sherif Hussein of Mecca. The exact boundaries of this proposed state were never defined, however, and the question of whether the state was to include Palestine was never fully clarified. On the other hand, the British, in the Balfour Declaration, promised the Zionists a "national home" for the Jews in Palestine; neither the exact nature of the "national home" nor its boundaries was ever spelled out. To make matters even more complicated, the British also concluded the Sykes-Picot agreement with the French which divided the

Middle Eastern holdings of the Ottoman Empire, including the proposed Arab state and Palestine, between Britain and France with certain portions to be allotted to Italy and Czarist Russia as well.

Thus at the end of the War the Arabs came to the Paris Peace Conference looking for their "independent Arab state" and the Zionists came to the conference seeking their "national home" in Palestine. At the same time, the British and the French, severely exhausted by their war efforts, sought to reap the benefits of victory by dividing between themselves the colonies of the defeated powers, including the Ottoman Empire's holdings in the Middle East. Reconciliation of all the conflicting claims was to prove impossible.

The final peace settlement which was the legacy of the conflicting promises made during World War I did not satisfy the aspirations of either the Zionists or the Arab nationalists. As might have been expected both from the record of prewar diplomacy as well as from the nature of the diplomatic maneuvers during the War, the British and French satisfied their thirst for territory before consideration of any other claims in the area. The basic result of the peace settlement was the replacement of the Turkish overlords of the Middle East by the British and French; this was to have a tragic effect on relations between the Zionist movement and Arab nationalism.

In the initial stages of the peace talks, however, there was a great deal of Arab-Zionist cooperation. Hussein's son Faisal, who represented the Arabs, and Chaim Weizman, the leader of the Zionists, signed an agreement pledging cooperation in fulfilling the objectives of their two nationalist movements. Article Four of the Faisal-Weizman Agreement is of particular interst in light of the subsequent conflict over Jewish immigration to Palestine:

> All necessary measures shall be taken to encourage and stimulate immigration of Jews to Palestine on a large scale, and as quickly as possible to settle Jewish immigrants upon the land through closer settlement and intensive cultivation of the soil. In taking such measures the Arab peasant and tenant farmers shall be protected in their rights and shall be assisted in forwarding their economic development.[1]

---

[1] Walter Laqueur, ed., *The Israel-Arab Reader: A Documentary History of the Middle East Conflict* (New York, 1969), p. 19.

Despite the cordial tone of the agreement, however, Faisal added a final reservation in which he disclaimed any responsibility for carrying out the agreement should the proposed Arab state fail to materialize. Unfortunately for both Faisal and the future of Arab-Zionist cooperation, the Arab leader's premonitions turned out to be correct. Nonetheless, in the early stages of the peace negotiations, Arab-Zionist relations continued to be very cordial. Faisal wrote the following letter to the American Zionist leader Felix Frankfurter in March 1919:

> ... We feel that the Arabs and Jews are cousins in race, having suffered similar oppressions at the hands of powers stronger than themselves, and by a happy coincidence having been able to take the first steps toward the attainment of their national ideals together.
>
> We Arabs, especially the educated among us, look with the deepest sympathy on the Zionist movement. Our deputation here in Paris is fully acquainted with the proposals submitted yesterday by the Zionist Organization to the Peace Conference and we regard them as moderate and proper. We will do our best, insofar as we are concerned, to help them through: we will wish the Jews a most hearty welcome home.
>
> With the chiefs of your movement, especially with Dr. Weizman, we have had and continue to have the closest relations. He has been a great helper to our cause, and I hope the Arabs may soon be in a position to make the Jews some return for their kindness. We are working together for a reformed and revived Near East, and our two movements complete one another. The Jewish movement is national and not imperialist. Our movement is national and not imperialist, and there is room in Syria for us both. Indeed, I think that neither can be a real success without the other. ...[2]

Faisal's comment, "there is room in Syria for us both," is an interesting one because he saw Palestine to be one of the provinces of Syria. Virtually all of the Arab nationalist leaders of the time, including those of Palestine, held the same view. Unfortunately, while there might indeed have been room in an enlarged Syria for both Zionist and Arab, this possibility was predicated on

---

[2] *Ibid.,* p. 21.

the establishment of an independent Arab state in Syria—a development which was aborted due to the rapacity of British and French imperialism.

It had become clear by the end of 1919 that the British and French had no intention of permitting an independent Arab state in any area except the arid wastes of the Arabian Peninsula. For, after some intensive bargaining, the two European nations reached an agreement dividing the most productive areas of the Middle East between themselves. France received "mandates" over Lebanon and Syria while England acquired Palestine, the boundaries of which were drawn to include the territory of present-day Jordan and Iraq. The French enforced their claims by landing troops in Lebanon and proceeding to drive Faisal's army out of Syria.

Opposition to British and French control and the failure to grant the promised Arab state took the form of rioting by Arabs throughout the Middle East. The most serious uprisings took place in Egypt, Iraq, and Syria. The Arabs of Palestine also rioted although their anger was primarily directed against the Palestinian Jewish community. The Palestinian Arabs saw the Jews who emigrated from Europe after the War not as fellow members of a common race seeking national independence, but rather as part of the European imperialist wave which was then engulfing the Middle East. The reaction of the Palestinian Arabs to the Zionist movement in the critical years following the Balfour Declaration must therefore be viewed as part of the general Arab opposition to European encroachment and the denial of Arab independence. If an independent Arab state had ever come into being within the boundaries advocated by Faisal, it is quite possible that an autonomous or even independent area for the Zionist Jews in Palestine would have been acceptable to the Arab leaders. It was the nullification of their nationalist dream, however, which was to make the Arabs bitterly opposed to Jewish settlement in Palestine.

While the Arabs had been treated contemptuously during the peace settlement, the Zionists did not fare much better. Their "national home" took the form of a mandate under British control, and the British were soon to manage a large part of the promised territory in a rather cavalier manner. In an effort to assuage the rising tide of Arab anger over the peace settlement, the British took the area of Palestine east of the Jordan River and established a separate Arab state under Hussein's son Abdullah. Jews were forbidden to own or to purchase land in Abdullah's kingdom, which came to be known as Transjordan.

At one stroke, some eighty percent of the land in which the Jewish national home was to be developed disappeared. As a result of this act, a group of militant Zionists established the Revisionist Party which called for the return of Transjordan to the Jewish homeland.

All in all, the British Empire appeared to have profited greatly from the peace settlement. It had gained large areas of territory and extended its sway in the Middle East from Egypt to Iraq. The road to India was now protected by land as well as by sea, and the lifelines of the Empire seemed more secure than ever. While the British held the upper hand in the Middle East at the time of the proclamation of the Palestine Mandate in 1922, they had already aroused the ire of both Zionists and Arab nationalists. These two nationalist movements were to be a source of increasing problems for the British in the interwar period.

THE PALESTINE MANDATE BETWEEN THE WARS

Much has been written about the British experience in Palestine from the time of General Allenby's victorious entry into Jerusalem in December, 1917 to Britain's ignominious withdrawal from the country in May, 1948. The British have been blamed both for showing favoritism to the Arabs and to the Zionists, and the partisans of these two groups have not been reticent in criticizing British policy. Yet the student of the period would be well advised to note that the primary British intention was neither to side with Zionist against Arab, nor with Arab against Zionist. Instead, the British were chiefly concerned with their own interests, both in Palestine and in the Middle East as a whole. It is much easier to understand the convolutions of British policy in Palestine, policy which often angered both Zionist and Arab, if this is kept in mind.

Prior to publishing the terms of their mandate for Palestine, the British sought to acquire support among the Arabs. The English

Colonial Secretary, Winston Churchill, forbade Jewish settlement in Transjordan. In addition, Churchill sought further to allay Arab fears by issuing a memorandum in July 1922 which limited Jewish immigration to the "economic capacity" of the country to absorb new arrivals. This was to prove a very difficult and politically explosive issue in British-Zionist relations. The British tried simultaneously to reassure the Zionists by stating, in the same declaration, that the Jews were in Palestine as a matter "of right and not on sufferance."

In attempting to be fair to both sides, however, Churchill was vague about the issue of ultimate Jewish sovereignty over Palestine. The same was true of the text of the Mandate which was published several weeks later. The key sections for Jewish-Arab relations are Articles Two, Four, and Six:

Article Two: The Mandatory shall be responsible for placing the country under such political, administrative, and economic conditions as will secure the establishment of the Jewish National Home, as laid down in the preamble, and the development of self-governing institutions, and also for safeguarding the civil and religious rights of all the inhabitants of Palestine, irrespective of race and religion.

Article Four: An appropriate Jewish Agency shall be recognized as a public body for the purpose of advising and cooperating with the Administration of Palestine in such economic, social and other matters as may affect the establishment of the Jewish National Home and the interests of the Jewish population in Palestine, and, subject always to the control of the Administration, to assist and take part in the development of the country. The Zionist organization, so long as its organization and constitution are in the opinion of the Mandatory appropriate, shall be recognized as such Agency. It shall take steps in consultation with His Britannic Majesty's Government to secure the cooperation of all Jews who are willing to assist in the establishment of the Jewish National Home.

Article Six: The Administration of Palestine, while ensuring that the rights and position of other sections of the population are not prejudiced, shall facilitate Jewish immigration under suitable conditions and shall encourage, in cooperation with the Jewish Agency referred to in Article Four, close settlement by

Jews on the land, including State lands and waste lands not required for public purposes.[3]

Other Articles of particular interest in the Mandate are Article Twenty-five, which sanctioned previous British action in Transjordan, and Article Twenty-seven, which stated that the consent of the Council of the League of Nations was required for any "modification of the terms of this Mandate."

Both the Churchill Memorandum and the terms of the Mandate left open the questions of Jewish sovereignty and Arab sovereignty within Palestine. The Palestinian Arabs, who formed the majority of Palestine's population at the time of the Mandate, were particularly incensed because the term "Arab" was never once used in the text of the Mandate. Instead, the Mandate referred to "other sections of the population" when discussing the non-Jewish inhabitants of Palestine. A basic problem had already become clear at the time of the Mandate's publication. Because of British wartime promises, both the Jewish and the Arab communities felt that theirs was the only legitimate claim to Palestine, and any possibility of a compromise diminished rapidly as British rule became firmly established.

Prior to World War I, the Jewish community was a rapidly growing, but still relatively small, proportion of the population of the area later to be called Palestine. J. C. Hurewitz, in his excellent study *The Struggle For Palestine,* places the Jewish population at 85,000 in 1914, or about twelve percent of the total population. The Jewish population of the area declined during the War, as did the Arab, but inspired by the Balfour Declaration's promise of a "National Home" in Palestine, Jews began immigrating in fairly large numbers after the hostilities. By 1936 the Jewish population of the Palestine Mandate totaled 404,000, approximately thirty percent of the population of the Mandate. Interestingly enough, however, in absolute numbers the growth in the Arab population exceeded that of the Jewish by 1936. Thanks to immigration from surrounding Arab countries, a continued high birth rate, and a sharply declining death rate due to the increased availability of medical care, the Arab population of Palestine had climbed to

---

[3]J. C. Hurewitz, ed., *Diplomacy in the Near and Middle East* (Princeton, 1956), II. 107–108.

968,000. The proportion of Arabs in the population had, however, dropped to seventy percent.

Intent on increasing the size of the Jewish settlement in Palestine, called the *Yishuv,* the early Zionist leaders were often insensitive to the national aspirations of the Palestinian Arabs. This attitude was met with hostility on the part of Arab nationalist leaders who, after their hopes for the inclusion of Palestine into an independent Arab Syria had failed, opposed the Zionists with heightened intensity. Much of the problem was psychological. Under the Turks, the Jewish community in Palestine was clearly of a second class status. Hence, with the arrival of the British, the Zionists appeared to have acquired a privileged position. Also, the previously mentioned influx of Jews was perceived by many Arabs as part of the wave of European imperialism which was engulfing the area. Few Arabs were actually displaced by Jewish settlement because the greater part of the land purchased by the Zionist movement was unoccupied wastelands or malarial swamp. Nonetheless, the Arabs viewed the incoming Jews as a threat to their national existence, however ill-defined.

Differences in language, ideology, and socioeconomic structure exacerbated the conflict. Jews took pride in their newly revived Hebrew language and relatively few of the new immigrants learned Arabic. Even fewer Arabs, whose mother tongue was Arabic, learned Hebrew. The Jewish immigrants came to Palestine with western ideas, of which perhaps the most important, after nationalism, was socialism. The new settlers established numerous *Kibbutzim* or communal farm settlements whose ideological base was a mixture of utopian socialism and self-defense. The Arabs still lived in a relatively feudal society ruled by a small number of Moslem landed gentry families, primarily the Husseinis and Nashashibis. The small urban middle class of the Arab cities was, however, primarily Christian. The relative economic positions of the two groups constituted an additional problem between Arab and Jew. Coming from Europe, the Jews endeavored to achieve the European standard of living to which they were accustomed, while both the indigenous Arabs and those who immigrated to Palestine from the surrounding Arab countries were primarily concerned with raising their incomes above the subsistence level.

Given the differing claims of the two communities, and the cultural, linguistic, and socioeconomic differences between them, the task of the mandatory power would have been difficult even if its primary purpose were the reconciliation of the two communities instead of the fostering of its own interests. It should be pointed out, however, that the first British High Commissioner, Lord Herbert Samuel, came closest to achieving the former end. Even Anthony Nutting, a strong advocate of the Arab cause, could say of Samuel: "He was scrupulously fair in his dealings with the Arabs during his term of office (1921–25) and unlike some of his Gentile successors showed no favoritism to the Zionists."[4] Indeed, it was precisely because he was a Jew and had the reputation in England of being a Zionist, that Samuel hit upon an ingenious, if ultimately tragic scheme, to win Arab acceptance of British rule.

In 1921 Samuel appointed a young Arab nationalist, Hajj Amin Al-Husseini, a member of the dominant Husseini family, to the powerful and lucrative position of Grand Mufti, or supreme religious leader, of the Palestine Moslems. Husseini had been one of the leaders of the riots against the Jews the year before and had fled to Transjordan to escape a ten year prison sentence for his role in the disturbances. Although Husseini was only fourth in line to the position of Mufti, Samuel nevertheless appointed him to the position, which paid $120,000 per year. In naming a militant Arab to such a key position, after pardoning him for his role in the riots which took a number of Jewish lives, Samuel was evidently trying to appease the Palestinian Arabs and to demonstrate that their interests concerned the British. The choice of Husseini, however, turned out to be a most unfortunate one, both for the British and for the Arab community of Palestine.

Hajj Amin Al-Husseini, an unprincipled schemer, used his new position to gain control over the Arab nationalist movement in Palestine and did not hesitate to murder any opposing Arab. Under Husseini's leadership, the Arab community rejected political cooperation with the British, including the British offer of an "Arab Agency" to parallel the Jewish Agency established by the Mandate. The Arabs also refused to join a legislative council, claiming that participation in the mandatory government would

---

[4]Anthony Nutting, *The Arabs* (New York, 1964), pp. 317–318.

mean recognition of the legitimacy of the Mandate, and of the Jewish "National Home."

In addition to the tactical mistake of failing to cooperate with the British politically, the constant conflict within the community itself further hurt the cause of the Palestinian Arabs. Don Peretz, a sympathetic Arab observer has written:

> ... Continual bickering and infighting among the family factions vitiated what effectiveness they might have had in rallying mass support in opposition to the Mandate and the *Yishuv.* While their political goals were nearly identical and the means for obtaining them differed little, the absence of unity led to the failure by any group to attain an independent Arab Palestine.[5]

By the mid-1920s it was clear that the Jewish and Arab communities were developing independently of one another. As one observer, H. J. Simson, remarked: "both the Jews and Arabs have succeeded in growing crocodile skins around their respective communities through which the rule of the government of Palestine hardly penetrates at all." Although both Arab and Jew profited from advancements in sanitation, construction of roads, and other public works of the British, neither was particularly satisfied with the actions of the mandatory authorities and each claimed that the other was receiving favored treatment from British officials. For all intents and purposes, two independent communities were developing in Palestine, and in the spirit of rising nationalism which affected both communities it was almost inevitable that a clash would occur. Such clashes were to come in 1929 and again in 1936.

The riots of 1929 began when Arab mobs, whipped into a religious frenzy by false reports that the Palestinian Jews were about to seize control of the Arab holy places in Jerusalem, attacked Jewish communities all over Palestine. The worst slaughter took place in Hebron where sixty Jews, most of whom were old people living on charity, were murdered. One result of the riots, and the British authorities' failure adequately to protect the Jewish community, was the development by the Jewish Agency of the *Haga-*

---

[5]Don Peretz, "The Palestine Arabs: A National Entity" in *People and Politics in the Middle East* ed. Michael Curtis (New Brunswick, 1971), p. 74.

nah or Jewish self-defense force. The *Haganah* was to form the basis of the future Israeli Army.

Although the British High Commissioner, Sir John Chancellor, found the Arabs guilty of starting the riots, the Arab community, paradoxically, made substantial, if temporary, political gains from the disturbances. According to the British custom a Royal Commission, the Shaw Commission, was called to investigate the causes of the riots and to make recommendations for the prevention of similar outbreaks in the future. While the Commission agreed with Chancellor that the Arabs were responsible for the riots, it also determined that the underlying cause of the disturbance lay in Arab opposition to the Jewish National Home, and especially to Jewish immigration and land acquisition. The Commission found no fault with the manner in which the Jews had acquired land and even noted that the Jews had in fact paid compensation to the relatively few dispossessed Arabs, despite the fact that this was not required by law. Nonetheless, the majority of the Commission, returning to the 1922 Churchill Memorandum statement on "economic capacity," concluded that Palestine could not support a larger agricultural population. Acting upon the recommendation of the Colonial Secretary, Lord Passfield, the British severely limited further Jewish immigration into Palestine.

This decision evoked a major outcry from the Palestinian Jewish community which denounced the very limited evaluation given to the "economic capacity" of Palestine to absorb new immigrants. The halt in Jewish immigration would have ended the rapid growth of the Palestinian Jewish community, and the Jewish Agency lodged a strong protest to the Government in London. Chaim Weizman, Britain's best friend in the *Yishuv,* resigned in protest from his position of President of the Jewish Agency. A great deal of pressure from the Zionists and their supporters, including influential non-Jews in London, caused the British Government to retreat. In a letter to Weizman in February, 1931, Prime Minister Ramsay MacDonald reversed Passfield's ruling. Now it was the Arab's turn to protest; they called MacDonald's action the "Black Letter which canceled the White Paper."

Several lessons could be drawn from the riots of 1929 and their political repercussions, not the least of which was that disturbance and disorder in Palestine could force the British Government to act to appease the rioters. While there was Zionist influence sufficient to alter a ruling of the Colonial Office within British Government circles in 1930, and the world situation was so quiet that Britain did not have to concern herself with a possible shift of either the Arabs or the Jews towards one of her enemies, this situation was to change radically with the rise of Hitler.

One major effect of Hitler's 1933 takeover in Germany, in addition to the threat which Germany began to pose to British security, was the large exodus of German Jews to Palestine due to the overtly anti-Semitic policies of the Nazis. In 1935, 61,854 Jews arrived, the largest annual figure since the establishment of the Mandate. The rapid increase in the number of Jews arriving in Palestine had a predictable psychological effect on Palestine's Arab community. While many of the new immigrants brought with them capital sufficient to establish themselves comfortably and to make a substantial contribution to the economy of the country and while the vast majority of the new immigrants settled in the cities of Palestine and hence were no threat to Arab landholdings in the countryside, the Arabs nonetheless increasingly feared that their claims to Palestine were being overrun by the large Jewish immigration.

The Arab leaders declared a general strike to protest the immigration, stating that the general strike would last until the British Government acceded to their demand to halt all Jewish immigration. With the general strike came riots and terrorist attacks on Jewish settlements and on British military installations. With the aid of the Arab leaders of Iraq, Jordan, and Saudi Arabia, all more or less under British influence at the time, the British Government persuaded the Mufti to halt the general strike until the Royal Commission, established to investigate the situation, made its report. This was to be the first intervention by other Arab governments in the affairs of the Palestinian Arabs and it was to set a most unfortunate precedent for the Palestinian Arab community.

The Royal Commission (hereafter called the Peel Commission) conducted a detailed examination of the situation in Palestine and, in 1937, released a report accurately describing the situation as it had existed in Palestine since the mid 1920s and recommending the partition of Palestine, which was to become a reality ten years later. In its description of the relations between the two communities, the Peel Report stated:

An irrepressible conflict has arisen between two national communities within the narrow bounds of one small country. About 1,000,000 Arabs are in strife, open or latent, with some 400,000 Jews. There is no common ground between them. The Arab community is predominantly Asiatic in character, the Jewish community predominantly European. They differ in religion and in language. Their cultural and social life, their ways of thought and conduct, are as incompatible as their national aspirations. These last are the greatest bar to peace. Arabs and Jews might possibly learn to live and work together in Palestine if they would make a genuine effort to reconcile and combine their national ideals and so build up in time a joint or dual nationality. But this they cannot do. The War [World War I] and its sequel have inspired all Arabs with the hope of reviving in a free and united Arab world the traditions of the Arab golden age. The Jews similarly are inspired by their historic past. They mean to show what the Jewish nation can achieve when restored to the land of its birth. National assimilation between Arabs and Jews is thus ruled out. In the Arab picture the Jews could only occupy the place they occupied in Arab Egypt or Arab Spain. The Arabs would be as much outside the Jewish picture as the Canaanites in the old land of Israel. The National Home, as we have said before, cannot be half national. . .[6]

The report goes on to recommend partition as the only possible solution to the problem:

Manifestly the problem cannot be solved by giving either the Arabs or the Jews all they want. The answer to the question "which of them in the end will govern Palestine?" must surely be "Neither." We do not think that any fair-minded statesman would suppose, now that harmony between the races has proved untenable, that Britain ought to hand over to Arab rule 400,000 Jews whose entry into Palestine has been for the most part facilitated by the British Government and approved by the League of Nations; or that if the Jews should become a majority, a million or so Arabs should be handed over to their rule. But

---

[6]The Esco Foundation, *Palestine: A Study of Jewish, Arab and British Policies* (New Haven, 1947), pp. 840–841.

while neither race can justly rule all of Palestine, we see no
reason why, if it were practicable, each race should not rule part
of it . . . It seems to us possible that on reflection both parties will
come to realize that the drawbacks of partition are outweighed
by its advantages. For if it offers neither party all it wants, it
offers each what it wants most, namely freedom and security.[7]

In rejecting the possibility of the Jewish Community's enjoying
minority rights in an Arab Palestinian state, the maximum concession the Arabs would make to Jewish national aspirations, the Peel
Report cited the slaughter of the Assyrian minority in Iraq, which
occurred despite England's treaty with Iraq explicitly protecting
that minority. The fierce and open hatred of the Arab politicians
for the Jewish National Home was also adduced by the Report.

However logical the suggestion of partition may have been,
both sides rejected the plan although the Zionist leaders were
willing to use the Commission's boundary recommendations as a
basis for negotiation. The Arabs persisted in their refusal even to
consider the possibility of an autonomous Jewish state in Palestine,
while many Jews, still unhappy over the severing of Transjordan
in 1922, opposed the further truncation of the area open to Jewish
settlement. Emotions ran high on both sides; the Arabs signaled
their rejection of the Peel report by resuming guerrilla warfare
against the British and Jews. The Mufti threatened death to any
Arab leader unwilling to denounce the partition proposal and,
during this period, Husseini seized the opportunity to murder
many of his political opponents within the Arab community. The
murder of the British District Commissioner of Galilee by one of
Husseini's agents ended the British Government's toleration of
the Mufti; Husseini was forced to flee to Lebanon to escape arrest.

The Arab uprising which lasted until 1939, unlike that of 1929,
had help from abroad. Not only did money and supplies flow into
the Arab guerrilla forces from neighboring Arab countries, especially Syria and Iraq, but aid also came from as far away as Italy
and Nazi Germany. The Italians, who had successfully invaded
Ethiopia in 1935, now appeared to be challenging British and
French domination of the Eastern Mediterranean as well, as they
exploited the possibilities afforded them by the Arab revolt in

---

[7]C. H. Dodd and M. G. Sales, *Israel and the Arab World* (London, 1970), p. 72.

Palestine and sent the guerrilla forces arms and equipment. In addition, following the publication of the Peel Report, Nazi Germany began a limited flirtation with the Palestinian Arabs. Members of the Palestinian Arab High Committee visited the German Envoy in Baghdad and, on July 16, 1937, the Mufti himself visited the German Consul in Jerusalem seeking support. The Germans initially refused to ship arms to the Arabs, fearing to antagonize the British over an area still peripheral to Nazi strategy. One year later, however, as the Czechoslovakian crisis boiled over and British and French appeasement policies became evident, the Germans grew bolder. In the summer of 1938 they sent arms to the Palestinian Arab guerrillas by way of Iraq and Saudi Arabia, and the Nazi-controlled German organizations in Palestine also began to aid the guerrilla bands. Then in April 1939, Hitler himself made a speech attacking British policy in Palestine.

After German troops marched into the rump of Czechoslovakia in March, 1939, the British leadership finally realized that Hitler could not be appeased and that war with Germany was inevitable. As war approached, the British leaders reached a crucial decision about Palestine and the defense posture of the British Empire in the Middle East. The Peel Commission's recommendation for partition having long since been abandoned, it was now decided, very much in the spirit of Munich, to try appeasing the Arabs to gain their neutrality, if not their active support, during the coming War. The British strategists decided that, since the security of the Empire's communication lines depended upon the degree of tranquility in the Arab world, some concession to Arab nationalism was necessary. During World War I, the British had promised the Arabs independence, at the expense of the Ottoman Empire, in return for their support. Now the sacrifice was to be made by the Palestinian Jewish community which did not possess the option, as did the Arabs, of turning to Nazi Germany for aid.

Thus the British Government decided to acquiesce in one of the most cherished demands of the Arab nationalists: the termination of Jewish immigration to Palestine. In what the Zionists and their supporters were to call the "infamous" White Paper of May 17, 1939, the British restricted Jewish immigration to a total of 75,000 over the next five years and, in effect, terminated it thereafter. The White Paper stated that, at the conclusion of the five-year period, there was to be no further immigration without the consent of the Palestinian Arabs. In addition, the British sharply restricted the area open to Jewish land purchase in Palestine. England also tentatively promised independence to a Palestinian State which would clearly have an Arab majority after a ten-year period, although the promise was hedged by a number of restrictions giving the British the option of retaining control.

The strategic decision on which the British White Paper was based, as well as its moral and legal implications, met with considerable criticism in England. The Labour Party, then in opposition, passed the following declaration:

> The White Paper, by imposing minority status on the Jews, by departing from the principles of economic absorptive capacity governing Jewish immigration, by making Jewish entry dependent on Arab consent, and by restricting Jewish land settlement violates the solemn pledges contained in the Balfour Declaration and the Mandate. . . . This conference calls upon the government to rescind the White Paper and reopen the gates of Palestine for Jewish immigration in accordance with the country's absorptive capacity.[8]

Even some of the British military men had reservations. Orde Wingate, who had helped train the *Haganah* into a force capable of offensive action against the Arab guerrillas, contended that the Jews were better soldiers than the Arabs and the British should therefore base their military position in Palestine on them. Furthermore, argued Wingate, only power, not appeasement, would prevent rebellion in the Arab world. The League of Nations Mandate Commission joined the chorus of opposition to the White Paper by ruling unanimously that the policy delineated in it was not in accord with the interpretation which the Commission had placed upon the Palestine Mandate.

Whether or not the White Paper was in fact illegal, the British proceeded to implement its policy. In all fairness to Britain, it would appear that the White Paper served at least partially to lessen Arab enmity toward Britain, especially in Palestine, although a pro-Nazi coup would take place in Iraq in 1940. In Pales-

---

[8]Harry Sacher, *Israel: The Establishment of a State* (London, 1952), p. 28.

tine the more moderate Nashashibi family accepted the White Paper while the Mufti and his followers rejected it and went over to the side of the Germans. Husseini himself spent most of the War in Berlin actively helping the Nazi war effort.

While the Palestinian Arab community split over the White Paper, the Jewish community was united in opposition to it. With the gates of Palestine now all but closed to the hundreds of thousands of Jewish refugees fleeing Hitler, who faced extermination because they could be admitted nowhere else, many hitherto pro-British Palestinian Jews turned violently anti-British. The feeling grew in the Jewish community that when the Arabs made trouble, as in the riots of 1936–1939, they got what they wanted; hence it was now time for the Jews to make trouble and so to balance the score. In 1938, as a result of the Arab terrorist attacks on Jewish towns and villages, the *Irgun,* a Jewish terrorist organization, was formed. Its avowed goal was to match indiscriminate Arab terrorist attacks against Jewish civilians with similar Jewish terrorist attacks against Arabs. While the Jewish Agency and the *Haganah* opposed the *Irgun's* policy of terrorism as immoral, the publication of the White Paper spurred support for the *Irgun* and led to the development of an even more radical terrorist organization called *Lehi.*

The coming of World War II brought a temporary end to Jewish terrorist attacks against the British as the Jewish community in Palestine joined England in the fight against the common enemy, Nazi Germany. Nonetheless, Jewish opposition to British White Paper policy remained strong and, as the War came to an end, it was to burst forth with renewed vigor.

THE IMPACT OF WORLD WAR II
AND THE TERMINATION OF THE PALESTINE MANDATE

World War II was to have a major effect on the destinies of both the Arab and Jewish Communities in Palestine as well as on the British Empire. With nowhere else to turn, the Palestinian Jews rallied to the Allied cause and joined the British Army in large numbers. The Arabs, however, were either lukewarm to the Allied War effort, or, like the Mufti, actively supported the Nazis. This support was to damage severely the Arab position in postwar diplomacy. British officials, despite growing evidence of the Nazi slaughter of European Jewry, clung to the White Paper restrictions on immigration. Thus they heightened the frustration of Palestinian Jews, who then increased their support of leaders calling for complete independence from Britain. Finally, Great Britain was severely weakened by the War; the growing power of the United States and the Soviet Union was to result in the active intervention of these two powers in Middle Eastern affairs at the close of the War, and lead to the termination of the mandate in 1948.

Britain's White Paper policy restricting Jewish immigration and land sales to Palestinian Jews weakened the political position of Chaim Weizman in the Zionist movement and resulted in the emergence of David Ben-Gurion as leader of the Palestinian Jews. Far less willing to rely on British good will than Weizman, Ben-Gurion declared at the start of the War that the Palestinian Jews would fight the War as if there were no White Paper and the White Paper as if there were no War. In practice this meant large Jewish enlistments in the British army coupled with intensive efforts "illegally" to bring in Jewish refugees from Nazi-occupied Europe. British opposition to the entry of the "illegal immigrants" led to such tragedies as the sinking of the refugee ship S. S. *Struma* in 1941 with the loss of 768 lives, an event which served further to inflame the feelings of the *Yishuv*.

The fact that large numbers of Palestinian Jews served in the British armed forces during the War was to have important military and political repercussions. Approximately 50,000 Palestinian Jews served in Allied armies during the War, accumulating very valuable military experience which was to serve the Jewish community well in its battle against the invading Arab armies in the 1948 Arab-Israeli war. By contrast, very few Palestinian Arabs enlisted in the British Army. As a result, the Arab armies of 1948, although superior in manpower and equipment to the army of the Palestinian Jews, suffered from a grave lack of combat experience. Perhaps even more damaging to the Arab cause was the fact that Hajj Amin Al-Husseini, the former Mufti of Jerusalem, actively sided with the Germans and helped recruit Moslem soldiers for

Nazi S.S. units. By the close of the War, this, coupled with the pro-Nazi coup in Iraq in 1940 and pro-Nazi feelings among the Arab leadership in Egypt, greatly diminished the Arab standing in the United States and the Soviet Union.

Despite their service in the British armies, the Palestinian Jews became increasingly frustrated by British war time policy in Palestine. The rigid application of White Paper policy, it was felt, led to the deaths of hundreds of thousands of Jews in Nazi-occupied Europe who otherwise could have found a refuge in Palestine. Such tragedies as the sinking of the *Struma* led the leaders of Palestinian Zionism, with the exception of Weizman, to decide that they needed their own sovereign state in which to control their own immigration and their own destiny. Consequently on May 11, 1942, the leaders of the Palestinian Jewish Community, meeting together with American Zionist leaders, proclaimed what was later to be called the Biltmore Program:

> . . . This Conference urges that the gates of Palestine be opened, the Jewish Agency be vested with control of immigration into Palestine and with the necessary authority for upbuilding the country, including the development of its unoccupied and uncultivated lands, and that Palestine be established as a Jewish Commonwealth integrated into the structure of the new democratic world.[9]

As might be expected, the British did not greet this program warmly since it conflicted with their policy in Palestine and throughout the Arab world as well. As early as May 29, 1941 Anthony Eden, Churchill's Foreign Secretary, in an effort to win the Arabs who were wavering between the Allies and the Germans, declared that Britain would give full support to any scheme of Arab unity which commanded general approval. As Allied fortunes improved following the British victory at El-Alamain and the Russian victory at Stalingrad, a number of Arab leaders who had been fence-sitting slowly began to support the British proposal.

As World War II drew to a close, the Soviet Union, Britain's wartime ally, increasingly appeared to be a postwar enemy.

---

[9]Hurewitz, p. 235.

Britain's Middle Eastern policy then assumed a more defined form. Unsure of American support in the postwar situation, the British resolved to mold the Arab states of the Middle East into a barrier against Soviet southward expansion. Consequently, on March 22, 1945 the Arab League was formed under British auspices. In such a *cordon sanitaire* of Arab states there was clearly no room for a Zionist state, for it was feared that any concessions to the Jews of Palestine might drive the Arabs into the arms of the Russians. Hence the British Colonial Office advocated the continuation of the White Paper policy despite all that had happened in World War II. There was clearly no room for a French presence in the Middle East, either. The British, exploiting the weakness of the French position in Lebanon and Syria, moved to oust French influence from the two former French mandates following anti-French riots in Damascus in May, 1945. It became clear that Britain hoped to become the sole great power in the Arab Middle East, dominant from Egypt to the Persian Gulf, and including in her sphere of influence Lebanon and Syria, countries which had gone to France in the post-World War I settlement.

Unlike the situation following World War I, when Britain and France divided the Middle East without outside interference, the end of World War II saw a sharp rise in Soviet and American influence in the region. Throughout the war, Zionist leaders had sought both American and Soviet support for their cause, and a combination of American and Russian pressure on a Britain weakened by World War II eventually led to the partition of Palestine and the establishment of the state of Israel.

American political pressure began on July 2, 1945 when a letter sent to President Truman by a majority of the membership of both houses of Congress, called upon the President to use his influence with the government of Great Britain to open the doors of Palestine to unrestricted Jewish immigration. The letter went on to urge the establishment of Palestine as a "free and democratic Jewish Commonwealth at the earliest possible moment." Truman responded by sending Earl Harrison as his personal representative to investigate the condition of the displaced persons in the refugee camps in Germany and to discern their wishes for a future home. Not surprisingly, after the horrors of Nazi concentration camps, most of the survivors, whatever their prewar views, had become ardent Zionists. Harrison recommended that Palestine be opened as a haven for the oppressed Jews.

Acting on Harrison's recommendation, Truman then appealed to the newly elected British Prime Minister, Labour Party Leader Clement Attlee, to grant 100,000 immigration certificates to the Jewish refugees in Germany to enable them to enter Palestine. Although the Labour Party's 1944 platform had strongly endorsed unrestricted Jewish immigration into Palestine and had clearly repudiated the White Paper of 1939, both Attlee and his Foreign Minister, Ernest Bevin, decided to continue existing British policy in the Middle East. The new British leaders, facing severe domestic problems, apparently hoped to consolidate Britain's position in the Arab states and prevent their turning to the Russians. The Arab leaders were continually threatening such a move if alterations in favor of the Zionists were made in the White Paper.

Consequently, Attlee and Bevin did not take kindly to Truman's suggestion which they considered to be motivated more by domestic political considerations than by a humanitarian regard for the refugees. The British were, however, mindful of the need for Anglo-American cooperation in the postwar reconstruction and defense of Europe and they could not merely ignore the President's suggestion. Both to gain time and to involve the United States in some of Britain's Middle Eastern problems, Bevin hit upon the idea of establishing a joint Anglo-American Committee to investigate the situation in the refugee camps of Europe as well as in Palestine. When the Committee, approved by Truman, arrived in England, Bevin pledged that he "would do everything in his power to put into effect a unanimous report," a pledge he later repudiated.

The Anglo-American Committee, consisting of six Englishmen and six Americans, took testimony in Washington and London before proceeding to the European refugee camps and to Palestine. Throughout its investigation, the members of the Committee were constantly reminded of the "Russian menace" by British officials and they were told that any report sympathetic to the Zionists would throw the Arabs into the arms of the Russians.

It transpired, however, that the Committee was relatively unimpressed with the possibilities of Arab loyalty in any case, remembering the Arab position during World War II. Several members of the Committee doubted that the feudal leaders of the

Arab world would ever risk an alliance with the Soviet Union, lest they lose their thrones in an ensuing revolution. In March, 1946 the Committee delivered a unanimous report which called for the issuance of 100,000 immigration certificates to Jewish refugees in Europe and for the elimination of the 1939 White Paper restrictions on Jewish immigration to Palestine and land purchase. Given the evident conflict between the Arab and Jewish communities in Palestine, the Committee opposed giving one community sovereignty over the other. Instead it recommended continuation of the mandate under Britain pending a trusteeship agreement with the United Nations.

Despite Bevin's earlier promise to put any unanimously agreed upon recommendations into effect, the British Foreign Secretary strongly opposed the proposals of the Committee. While Truman hailed the Committee's suggestions on immigration, Bevin categorically refused to act unless two prior conditions were met. The first was a guarantee of American financial and military support for the British mandate. Although the United States was willing to assist economically in bringing the 100,000 refugees to Palestine, there was no wish either by Truman or by Congress for military involvement in the conflict between Jew and Arab. An even more impossible condition was Bevin's call for the disarmament of the *Haganah* and the suppression of the *Irgun* and *Lehi.* Given the memory of Arab riots in 1929 and 1936 and current threats by Arab leaders including the Mufti, who had slipped out of Germany and into British-controlled Egypt, the Palestinian Jews considered disarmament tantamount to suicide. Since it was evident that neither condition would be fulfilled, Bevin completely disregarded the report of the Anglo-American Committee, much to the anguish of its authors, although this action was to cost him support in the United States.

The Anglo-American Committee failed to settle the Palestine imbroglio in a manner satisfactory to British interests. The strategic value of Palestine, with its excellent port at Haifa, grew in importance as Soviet-British relations deteriorated. In March 1946 Transjordan had been given its "independence" although, like Iraq, it was tied to England by a defense treaty. British plans to evacuate Egypt made the retention of a base in Palestine even more desirable at the time. The British Government's next move was a forcible attempt to break Jewish opposition to the White Paper.

Between 1945 and 1946, Palestinian Jewish opposition to curbs on immigration had risen in intensity, and such unfortunate comments by Bevin as, "if the Jews, with all their sufferings, want to get too much at the head of the queue, you have the danger of an anti-Semitic outbreak through it all," led to further deterioration of relations between the British and Zionist leaders. In addition to the activities of the *Irgun* and *Lehi* who felt that the best way to oust the British from Palestine was to kill British soldiers, a policy morally opposed by the Jewish Agency and the *Haganah,* the *Haganah* itself adopted a policy of attempting to foil all British efforts to halt the "illegal" immigration of Jewish refugees into Palestine. This included attacks on British radar installations and naval craft, although efforts were made to avoid loss of life. The British troops, however, saw little difference between the activities of the *Haganah* and those of the terrorist groups; relations between the British army and Jewish citizens of Palestine had almost reached the breaking point by June 1946.

Following the *Haganah's* destruction of eight bridges on the borders of Palestine on June 16, 1946 which paralyzed British land communications with other Middle Eastern states, the British moved to crush the Jewish Agency and the *Haganah.* On June 29, 1946 the Jewish were arrested and placed in internment camps in Latrun. In addition, Jewish *Kibbutzim* were raided, and often severely damaged, in arms searches by British troops. If the British policy aimed, as some Zionist partisans contend, to replace men whom the British saw as the extremist leadership of the Jewish Community with moderates willing to cooperate with British policy, the attempt was a failure as the Jewish community rallied around its imprisoned leaders. Furthermore, the heavy-handed British policy was becoming an increasing embarrassment for Bevin in Anglo-American relations. The British were eventually forced to terminate their policy of force against the Palestinian Jewish community and release the imprisoned Zionist leaders because of the very negative image that Britain was projecting to the United States, at a time when she was heavily dependent on American economic aid.

Perhaps the most important effect of the British policy of force against the *Yishuv,* however, was its result for Soviet-Zionist relations. From the time of the German invasion of Russia, Zionist representatives had been contacting Soviet officials all over the world in an effort to gain the support of the Soviet Union. The U.S.S.R., however, courted also by Arab leaders on the Palestine issue, gave little indication of its position. Increasing numbers of Russian agents and diplomats toured Palestine in 1944 and 1945 to obtain a firsthand view of the situation, and in 1946 the Soviet consul at Beirut, Daniel Solod, asked the Jewish Agency for a Russian translation of its testimony before the Anglo-American Committee; the request was speedily fulfilled.[10]

From the birth of the Soviet State in 1917, Soviet leaders had considered Zionism "a tool of British Imperialism," and all Zionist activity in Russia was proscribed. The British attacks on the Jewish Agency and on the *Haganah* evidently caused a reassessment of the Soviet position. With the weakening of the leadership of Weizman, the Zionist leader most closely associated with the British, and the emergence of such figures as Ben-Gurion who demanded independence for Palestine, Soviet support for the Zionist position began to grow. Both the Russians and Zionists favored an independent Palestine unencumbered by military ties to Britain. For the Palestinian Zionists, the departure of British troops would mean an opportunity for complete Jewish sovereignty. For the Russians, the establishment of an independent Jewish state would mean the breaking of the chain of pro-British Arab states on the southern flank of the Soviet Union, and the removal of a very important strategic area from British control. Thus the British crackdown on the Jewish Agency in 1946 served not only to alienate public opinion in the United States, it was also to lead to Soviet support for the establishment of an independent Jewish state.

With the failure of its policy of force, and after several subsequent attempts at a favorable diplomatic settlement had failed as well, the British brought the problem of Palestine to the United Nations. Some commentators have argued that the British Government had concluded that the cost of remaining in Palestine had become too great and therefore brought the problem to the United Nations in an effort to seek a graceful means of withdrawing from a disagreeable situation. More suspicious observers have contended that the British hoped a Cold War clash between the

---

[10]*Zionist Archives* (Jerusalem), Document No. S/25/486/30/1/46.

United States and the Soviet Union on the issue would prevent any settlement in the U.N. and that, in despair, the United Nations would legitimize further British presence in Palestine in the form of a trusteeship as the only solution. With such an international sanction, Britain could then keep her military bases in Palestine and her alliance with the Arab states, while the United States would have a diminished basis for intervention in British policy once it had received a U.N. sanction.

If the British had in fact counted on Soviet-American discord, so prevalent on every other issue of the Cold War by the spring of 1947, they were to be sorely disappointed. The Russians surprised the world by declaring their support of Zionist aspirations. The Soviet-American agreement on this issue was too great for the British to overcome, although there were attempts to sabotage the final U.N. resolution.

The special United Nations Committee UNSCOP, similar in many respects to the Anglo-American Committee and the Royal Commission which preceded it, was appointed to visit Palestine to investigate the situation. Upon its return, a majority of the Committee recommended, much as the Peel Commission had ten years earlier, the partition of Palestine into Jewish and Arab states while a minority of the Committee favored a federated binational state. Even before the United States and the Soviet Union had officially endorsed the partition scheme, Lord Creech-Jones, Britain's Colonial Secretary, commented on September 26, 1947, that, "in the absence of a settlement, the British must plan for the early withdrawal of British forces and British Administration from Palestine," and that "if the Assembly should recommend a policy which is not acceptable to the Jews and Arabs [partition was clearly unacceptable to the Arabs] His Majesty's Government would not feel able to implement it."[11]

There was a great deal of diplomatic activity at the United Nations prior to the vote on partition; both the United States and the Soviet Union exercised their influence in behalf of the partition proposal while the British strenuously opposed it. Then, on November 29, 1947 the partition proposal was approved by a vote of 33 to 13 with ten abstentions. The partition decision gave to the Jewish state the central coastal regions along with part of the

---

[11]Sacher, pp. 91–92.

southern desert, the Negev, and part of the Northern Plain, the Galilee. The central section of the country was to go to the Arab state along with the northern and southern coastal strips. Jerusalem and Bethlehem were to form an international zone.

The United Nations decision on partition was accepted with enthusiasm by the Palestinian Jewish community. Although they had now seen their National Home partitioned for the second time since the separation of Transjordan in 1922, the Jews were nonetheless willing to have a smaller state, as long as they could be sovereign in it. The Palestinian Arabs, however, rejected the decision and in this rejection they were joined by the members of the Arab League who pledged their support in case of war. Unfortunately for the Palestinian Arabs, the Arab countries were to prove less than altruistic in offering their support.

Guerrilla warfare between the Arab and Jewish communities in Palestine broke out immediately after the U.N. vote on partition. The British, who refused to cooperate with a U.N. commission sent to implement partition, were considerably less than even-handed in their treatment of the two combatants. There is little question that the Palestinian Arabs, after six years of pro-Arab policy by England, expected British support. Indeed, the British High Commissioner for Palestine, Alan Cunningham, was later to comment:

> At first the Arabs were firmly convinced that our armed forces were on their side, a conviction which placed the soldiers in many embarrassing situations.[12]

The primary British aim seems to have been to withdraw in such a way as to enable their close ally, King Abdullah of Transjordan, with his British-trained and British-led Arab Legion, to control as much of Palestine as possible.

As the British plotted with Abdullah, the Palestinian Arabs were left little voice in the events which were to shape their future. At the start of the now inevitable conflict with the Jewish community, the Palestinian Arabs suffered from a severe lack of organization.

Abdullah was not the only Arab leader with designs on Palestinian territory. The Egyptians and Syrians, as well as a number

---

[12]Alan Cunningham, "Palestine—The Last Days of the Mandate," *International Affairs,* XXIV No. 4 (October, 1948), 487.

of Arab adventurers, also wished to take over the Palestinian Arab state and as much of the proposed Jewish state as possible. Thus although the Arabs were greatly to outnumber the Palestinian Jews at the start of the war, the rivalry among the Arab leaders would be an important factor hurting the Arab war effort.

The British officially terminated the mandate on May 15, 1948. On that same day, seven Arab armies invaded Palestine in an effort to destroy the State of Israel which had just been proclaimed by the Palestinian Jewish community and immediately recognized by both the United States and the Soviet Union. The results of the war are well known and need not be retold in any great detail. Owing partly to military and diplomatic support from the Soviet Union as well as to diplomatic assistance from the United States, the Palestinian Jews were able to defeat both the Palestinian Arabs and the invading Arab armies. Three of the invaders, Egypt, Jordan, and Iraq, received British military aid and diplomatic support throughout the conflict. After repulsing the Arab armies, the Israelis, as the Palestinian Jews now called themselves, were able to increase the size of the territory given to them in the U.N. partition decision by occupying part of the proposed Palestinian Arab State.

The Palestinian Arabs were not so fortunate. They not only lost the war but also disappeared entirely as a political entity as King Abdullah of Transjordan annexed the remainder of the eastern part of the proposed Palestinian Arab State and King Farouk of Egypt annexed the Gaza Strip. A bitter Palestinian Arab, Musa Alami, commented:

> In the face of the enemy the Arabs were not a state, but petty states; groups, not a nation; each fearing and anxiously watching the other and intriguing against it. What concerned them most and guided their policy was not to win the war and save Palestine from the enemy, but what would happen after the struggle, who would be predominant in Palestine, or annex it to themselves, and how they could achieve their own ambitions. Their announced aim was the salvation of Palestine, and they said that afterward its destiny should be left to its people. This was said with the tongue only. In their hearts all wished it for themselves; and most of them were hurrying to prevent their neigh-

bors from becoming predominant, even though nothing remained except the offal and bones.[13]

In addition, many Palestinian Arabs were made refugees as a result of the war and, languishing in refugee camps, they were to provide part of the fuel for future Arab-Israeli wars. It was not until 1967, following the defeat of the Egyptian, Syrian and Jordanian armies in the Six-Day War that the Palestinian Arabs were to reemerge as a potent political force in the Middle East.

Thus partition came to Palestine, not by an agreement between the Arab and Jewish communities, nor even by the force of the United Nations' Resolution, but by war. Both the Palestinian Jews and the Palestinian Arabs had drawn on British promises made during World War I to legitimize their claims to Palestine, and each community developed independently of the other during the British mandate. The British, who had exploited both nationalist movements to gain control over Palestine, administered their mandate with the primary purpose of strengthening their strategic position in the Middle East. Thus, partition was inevitable.

The tragedy of partition lay partly in the means used to effect it: a war. A further aspect to the tragedy was the fact that one of the two communities, that of the Palestinian Arabs, was deprived, primarily by the intrigues of fellow Arabs, of its share of a divided Palestine.

EPILOGUE

The conflict between Arab and Israeli did not end with the armistice agreements which terminated the Arab-Israeli War of 1948. Indeed, on November 16, 1948, when the war was all but over, there was a meeting of the Arab League which declared that the Arabs would never agree to partition and would never recognize Israel or have any relations with that state. This declaration was later echoed in the Arab statement at the Khartoum Conference of July, 1967 which convened after the Arab defeat by Israel in the

---

[13]William R. Polk, *The United States and the Arab World* (Cambridge, 1969), p. 192.

Six-Day War; it, too, maintained the position of no recognition and no peace with Israel. Thus the Arab-Israeli conflict, punctuated by wars in 1948, 1956, and 1967, continues to the present, with the Arabs refusing to recognize Israel as they pledge to destroy it and the Israelis constantly girding for the next battle.

There have, however, been some changes since the 1948 partition of Palestine. Israel has emerged as an important power in the Middle East, although it is dependent on the United States for high quality armaments. The Arab states have succeeded in casting off British control, although the United States in Jordan, Lebanon, and Saudi Arabia, and the Soviet Union in Egypt, Syria, and Iraq, have intervened with military and economic assistance in an effort to increase their influence among the Arabs.

Another major change has been the reemergence of the Palestinian Arabs after two decades of political inactivity. Following the defeat of the armies of Egypt, Jordan, and Syria in the June, 1967 War against Israel, which resulted in Israel's occupation of the areas seized by Egypt and Jordan from the abortive Palestinian Arab state in 1948, the Palestinians decided to do for themselves what the Arab states had proven unable to do for them. Forming a number of guerrilla organizations under the umbrella of the so-called "Palestine Liberation Organization" they launched attacks against Israel. Unfortunately for the Palestinian Arabs their attacks served, not to demoralize, but only to rally the Israelis around their government.

Even worse for their cause, however, was the threat which the Palestinians, who had become a popular force in the Arab world, posed for the narrowly-based Arab governments in the Middle East. The stronger Arab states soon sprouted their own guerrilla forces and refused to tolerate the activities of any guerrilla organization not under their direct control. The weaker Arab states, Lebanon and Jordan, faced political disintegration as the guerrilla organizations operating on their soil became more and more "a state within a state." Finally, King Hussein of Jordan, great-grandson of Sherif Hussein of Mecca who started the Arab revolt against the Turks, resolved to crush the guerrillas before they crushed him. In battles in September, 1970 and July, 1971 Hussein eliminated the Palestinian guerrillas as an effective political and military force in Jordan and severely damaged their prestige throughout the Arab world.

There is, perhaps, one ray of hope in this otherwise bleak picture of Arab-Israeli relations. A dialogue of sorts has begun between Arabs and Israelis in areas occupied by Israel after the June, 1967 war. This is particularly true of the West Bank area which was to have been part of the Arab state in 1948 but was instead annexed by Jordan. It is not entirely inconceivable that the Israelis may one day decide to allow the Palestinian Arabs to establish their own state in the West Bank; they already have limited autonomy in local affairs. It would indeed be ironic if Israel were to restore to the Palestinian Arabs the political sovereignty which other Arabs had seized, but this might be one road to a settlement of the Arab-Israeli conflict.

BIBLIOGRAPHY

Perhaps the most balanced book on the partition of Palestine is J. C. Hurewitz, *The Struggle for Palestine* (New York, 1950). The student of the period is also indebted to Dr. Hurewitz for his collection of documents, *Diplomacy in the Near and Middle East* (Princeton, 1956), which contains most of the documents pertaining to developments in Palestine and the Middle East leading to partition. Another useful collection of documents is found in Walter Laqueur, ed., *The Israel-Arab Reader: A Documentary History of the Middle East Conflict* (New York, 1969). An excellent sourcebook containing a great deal of material on the Palestine problem is the Esco Foundation's, *Palestine: A Study of Jewish, Arab and British Policies* (New Haven, 1947).

There have been numerous books written in support of the Arab and Jewish claims to Palestine. Among the best are: Fred J. Khouri, *The Arab-Israeli Dilemma,* (Syracuse, 1968), which argues the Arab case; and Ben Halpern, *The Idea of the Jewish State* (Cambridge, 1969), which supports the Jewish case. Given the bitter acrimony over Britain's role in Palestine, the student should also consult Christopher Sykes' study, *Crossroads to Israel* (Cleveland, 1965), which defends British policy and Harry Sacher, *Israel: The Establishment of a State* (London, 1952), which is severely critical of the British. For a study placing the various claims to Palestine in historical perspective, see James Parkes, *Whose Land? A History of the Peoples of Palestine,* (London, 1970).

For an early study of Arab nationalism, see George Antonius,' *The Arab Awakening: The Story of the Arab National Movement* (New York, 1938). Other useful studies of Arab nationalism include Zeine N. Zeine, *Arab-*

Turkish Relations and the Emergence of Arab Nationalism, (Beirut, 1958), and Majid Khadduri, *Political Trends in the Arab World* (Baltimore, 1970). A collection of the writings of Arab Nationalist leaders is found in Sylvia G. Haim, *Arab Nationalism* (Berkeley, 1962).

Among the best studies of Zionism are Halpern, *The Idea of the Jewish State* (Cambridge, 1969), and Arthur Hertzberg, ed., *The Zionist Idea: A Historical Analysis and Reader* (New York, 1960), which contains selections from the writings of the leading Zionist thinkers as well as a useful introductory analysis of the development of Zionist thought. See also Israel Cohen, *Theodore Herzl, Founder of Political Zionism,* (New York, 1959).

For a general overview of the complex diplomacy of World War One and the immediate postwar period, see William R. Polk, *The United States and the Arab World* (Cambridge, 1969). More detailed studies include: Jon Kimche, *The Second Arab Awakening* (New York, 1970); Leonard Stein, *The Balfour Declaration* (New York, 1961); and Aaron S. Klieman, *Foundations of British Policy in the Arab World: The Cairo Conference of 1921* (Baltimore, 1970).

Diplomatic maneuvers during World War Two are discussed in: Yehudah Bauer, *From Diplomacy to Resistance: A History of Jewish Palestine 1939–1945* (Philadelphia, 1970); Lukasz Hirszowicz, *The Third Reich and the Arab East* (Toronto, 1966); and Elie Kedourie, *The Chatham House Version and Other Middle Eastern Studies* (New York, 1970). The student of the period should also consult the memoirs of Winston Churchill and Charles de Gaulle.

There are a number of books written by participants in the diplomacy of the 1945–47 period which led to the United Nations vote on partition.

There are two reports available in book form of the impressions of participants on the Anglo-American Committee. Bartley Crum, an American member, has written *Behind the Silken Curtain* (New York, 1947), which clearly reflects his American background and point of view. A report more sympathetic to British problems, though not to the British officials in Palestine, written by Labour M. P. Richard Crossman, is *Palestine Mission: A Personal Record* (London, 1950). The Guatemalan member of the UN Special Committee on Palestine, Jorge Garcia Granados, has written a record of his experiences in Palestine on the investigatory committee in *The Birth of Israel: The Drama as I saw It* (New York, 1949). A survey of the American position on the Palestine problem is found in Herbert Feis, *The Birth of Israel: The Tangled Diplomatic Bed* (New York, 1969).

Histories of the Arab-Israeli war of 1947–49 abound. Among the best are Edgar O'Ballance, *The Arab-Israeli War, 1948* (London, 1956), and Dan Kurzman, *Genesis, 1948: The First Arab-Israeli War* (New York,

1970). For two differing viewpoints on Arab-Israeli relations in the 1948–68 period, see Fred J. Khouri, *The Arab-Israeli Dilemma* (Syracuse, 1968), and Nadav Safran, *From War to War: The Arab-Israeli Confrontation 1948–1967,* (New York, 1969).

For an analysis of the problems encountered by the United States and the Soviet Union in their attempts to increase their influence in the Arab World, see William Polk, *The United States and the Arab World* (Cambridge, 1969), and Robert O. Freedman "The Soviet Union in the Middle East: The High Cost of Influence" in *Naval War College Review* (January, 1972).

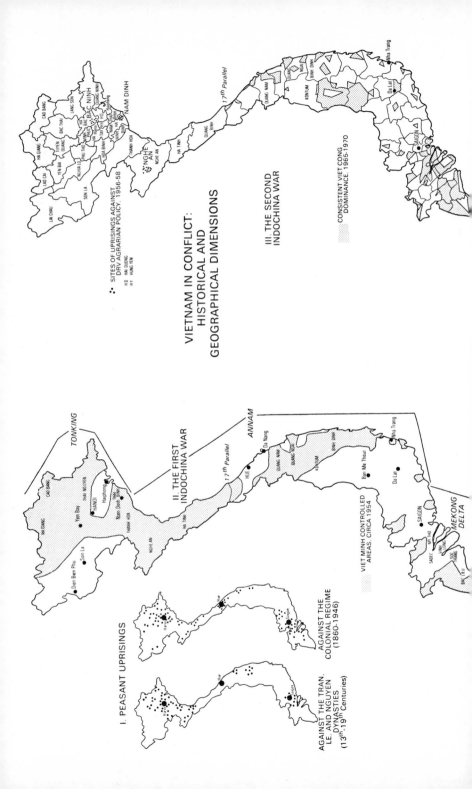

VIETNAM IN CONFLICT:
HISTORICAL AND
GEOGRAPHICAL DIMENSIONS

I. PEASANT UPRISINGS

AGAINST THE TRAN,
LE, AND NGUYEN
DYNASTIES
(13th-19th Centuries)

AGAINST THE COLONIAL REGIME
(1860-1946)

II. THE FIRST
INDOCHINA WAR

VIET MINH CONTROLLED
AREAS, CIRCA 1954

III. THE SECOND
INDOCHINA WAR

CONSISTENT VIET CONG
DOMINANCE, 1965-1970

SITES OF UPRISINGS AGAINST
DRV AGRARIAN POLICY, 1956-58

HD HAI DUONG
HY HUNG YEN

Chapter 6

The Partition of Vietnam and the Unfinished Revolution

Allan E. Goodman
Clark University

PARTITION AND VIETNAM'S UNFINISHED REVOLUTION*

The Communists finally came to our village. We had heard from neighbors that their rule was against our traditions, but we didn't leave earlier because we really wanted to stay. We couldn't; so we dressed in our worst clothes and hid what money we had on the bellies of our ducks and walked for two nights to the border. Grandmother died from the strain along the way; younger sister was killed the second night by a Viet Minh patrol. It was then that we decided to fight the Communists. But in the South we found ourselves different than most people living there: we had experienced Communism. Now, almost twenty

---

*I am grateful to Lawrence Franks and Nguyen Van Hien for their contribution of original materials on the diplomacy of the 1954 Geneva Conference and current South Vietnamese attitudes toward partition. This chapter is necessarily historical and interpretative; as much as possible, I have let Vietnamese speak for themselves.

215

years later, the experience of living under and escaping from Communism is still the basic political division in South Vietnam.

As these remarks, made by a South Vietnamese Congressman in a 1970 interview, suggest, partition divides people and countries. But too often, analyses of the partition of Vietnam have focused upon the differences between the northern and southern regimes and the deadly struggle since 1954 between them. But how divided are the Vietnamese people? Despite almost two decades of war, reunification remains a goal of each side and, in their views, a likely prospect.

The partitioned country, like Topsy, often just grows. What begins as a temporary expedient becomes a permanent condition reinforced by the tensions of international and regional conflicts. Vietnamese believe, however, that while the intervention of foreign powers caused partition, the future depends upon the resolution of conflicts beyond the ability of great power politics and diplomacy to influence. Seen from this perspective, the map of Vietnam is striking in two respects: the 17th parallel is a poor guide to the dimensions of the conflict, and the conflict itself predates 1954. Throughout Vietnamese history, the consistency of control over certain regions in the north and the south by anticolonial and then antigovernment forces has proven vexing to imperial and then to communist and noncommunist regimes alike. Ho Chi Minh's most profound reforms faced their stiffest opposition in areas of the countryside that had traditionally opposed government intervention of any sort; Ho's provincial birthplace (Nghe An) was so reticent to accept collectivisation that a bloody campaign of terror and assassination was required to put such programs into effect. In the South, similarly, Ngo Dinh Diem's birthplace, the city of Hué, had long been a prime site of opposition to his rule and remains today a stronghold of the militant An Quang Buddhists and their opposition to the government of Nguyen Van Thieu. The significance of partition lies not in its geographical features, but in the political struggle taking place between governments and the countryside.

Is Vietnam a divided whole? As the focus of this chapter shifts from the historical and personal dimensions of partition, to its consequences for politics in the future, no single question is more prominent or perplexing. And no answer is clear: present-day

Vietnam has never been a single country; *vis à vis* those foreign powers who have sought to dominate Indochina, however, the Vietnamese have responded as one people. But once the threat is past—or even once it becomes a *fait accompli*—the Vietnamese return to a mélange of political groups and movements, each pursuing similar goals in divisive ways. In the process, Vietnam becomes again vulnerable to manipulation by foreign powers. By the end of the 1960s, for example, many Vietnamese political leaders realized that the war had lost its *raison d'être*. As one opposition group in Saigon declared in an editorial of the *Cap Tien* party paper:

> To protract the current war is to lead the Vietnamese people to self-destruction. For this reason, we think time is at hand that we Vietnamese must have another look at our fate and seek a path fitted to our survival. Historical mistakes caused the partition of our beloved country and repeated efforts to reunify it by force only brought devastations to the motherland. Being the guinea-pig in the world arena for a quarter of a century is enough; so the crucial task of the genuine Vietnamese patriot is to put an end to that unfortunate role.

Rather than view Vietnam as a divided whole, therefore, I shall suggest that it is, in fact, the "whole" that the present parties to the conflict are trying to create. This is the task of Vietnam's unfinished revolution.[1]

THE HISTORICAL DIMENSIONS OF THE CONFLICT

The partition of Vietnam at the 17th parallel came relatively late in history; the tradition of division, however, is relatively old. The practical significance of this tradition lies in the opportunities it creates for contending political forces to fashion an ideology apart

---

[1]As such, its origins lie in what the August Revolution—actually those events that took place from June to September 1945, culminating in the proclamation of the Democratic Republic of Vietnam (DRV)—was not: ". . . the August Revolution was a revolution of administrative structures, not a socio-economic revolution." David J. Steinberg, et al., *In Search of Southeast Asia* (New York, 1971), p. 358.

from the complexities and parochialisms of both Vietnamese history and society. The issue of partition to Vietnamese is part of a larger question: the rather consistent preoccupation of Vietnamese nationalists with protecting their country from foreign domination. The message of Vietnam's recent history is clear:

> The scholar-gentry generation that came to political maturity around 1900 was haunted by the image of *mat nuoc*, of "losing one's country" not merely in the political sense, but more critically in terms of their future survival as Vietnamese. They struggled desperately to bring new meaning and ethnic salvation *(cuu quoc)* out of a developing sense of loss and despair.
>
> By 1945 salvation from the foreigner was taken by the peasantry to include salvation from hunger, tenantry, and taxes—a merging of activist and reformist ambitions that fueled the deadly struggle that ended at Dien Bien Phu and that continues to motivate many in the conflict now under way.[2]

No other single force has been as potent a unifier of diverse peoples and classes as has the threat of foreign domination. While the Chinese in the first millenium of the Christian era, and the French and the Americans in the twentieth century, have sought, in the Vietnamese view, to dominate Vietnam by means of fostering social and political divisions, the task of the nationalist has been to provide a basis for social and political unity. Such unity, however, had to be created rather than inherited, for present-day Vietnam was never a unified whole.

The acquisition and settlement of the territory that is now the two Vietnams was not completed until this century. For the almost three thousand years of the early kingdoms, Vietnam did not extend further south than the 20th parallel. In the first millenium, and under Chinese domination for most of that time, Vietnam's northern border with China was uncertain and the empire extended southward, to the vicinity of Hué. By 1470, under Emperor Le Thanh Ton, the overthrow of the Champa kingdom resulted in the annexation of the territory of present day Binh Dinh prov-

---

[2]David Marr, *Vietnamese Anticolonialism, 1885–1925* (Berkeley, 1971), pp. 4, 277.

ince, the northernmost province in South Vietnam's II corps region. Hué did not become the center of the empire until 1687, and the "Southern Kingdom" of the Nguyen family became a reality seventy years later with the annexation of Cochin China in 1757. Present-day Saigon, annexed by the Nguyens in 1698, never became the capital of the empire; it grew in importance largely as a result of French colonialism. For almost four thousand years, Vietnam meant primarily northern Vietnam, and even within the confines of this territory, ascendant kingdoms were vexed by the problems of political divisions and internal conflict.

The history of a Vietnam formally divided is as old as the wars between regionally centered regimes. The first of these conflicts occurred in the latter part of the sixteenth century. After the establishment of Hué as the capital of the Southern Kingdom, a fifty-year war raged between the northern Trinh family and the central Vietnamese Nguyen family. A truce was based upon the division of Vietnam into two dominions, with a partition line established by building the Dong Hoi wall, close to the present-day demarcation line of the Ben Hai river. This truce lasted for almost a hundred years until a revolt in 1773 by the Tayson brothers turned into a countrywide war, moving across the face of Vietnam until 1801. From 1802 until the final conquest of all of Vietnam by the French in 1883, Vietnam was divided into three regions: the patrimony of the Nguyen formed the kingdom centered in Hué, while two other fiefdoms were established in regions known as Tonkin and Cochin China. The French preserved these basic divisions of Vietnamese territory in their piecemeal acquisition of a colonial empire in Indochina. The most recently settled areas of Cochin China, and those considered furthest from the center of the empire, were ceded to France in 1862; by 1867 the remainder was annexed. During the 1870s, French moves against the rest of Vietnam were restrained and in 1878 the Emperor had begun negotiations with Paris to regain the annexed portions of Cochin China that, due to regime-sponsored and autonomous resistance movements, had never been securely held by the French. By 1882, however, French policy-makers had—in response to the pressure of events within Vietnam and in Paris—turned decidedly procolonial, and expeditions were sent against Hanoi and into the Red River Delta. By summer 1883, a Treaty of Protectorate marked the final phase in the formal establishment of French colonialism in Vietnam.

De facto control of this territory was always in doubt for France. While he served as French Governor-General, Paul Doumer reported to Paris that

> ... the political situation in Indochina does not offer any major source of anxiety. The population of the whole country seems to have come to accept our administration, even though they had not realized the character of permanence of our domination.

It took twelve years of intermittent warfare for French garrisons to pacify Tonkin. Throughout the period thereafter, the frequent outbreak of resistance movements suggested to sensitive Frenchmen that Vietnam could never be pacified, and recalled to their minds an earlier Chinese judgment, found in the records of the Ch'ing Dynasty:

> The Vietnamese are indeed not a reliable people. An occupation does not last very long before they raise their arms against us and expel us from their country. The history of past dynasties has proved this fact.

Pacification was a problem not only for the French. The areas where anticolonial resistance was centered during the first half of the twentieth century were also those where uprisings traditionally took place against the regimes and the usurpers that tried to govern Vietnam. Indeed, the north-south division of Vietnam, such a prominent geopolitical feature of its modern history, appears to be a consequence of the local and regional uprisings that took place against a central ruler, rather than a separate dimension from them. The most serious threats to the regimes in both North and South Vietnam, from the time of the Nguyens' onward, came not across the lines of a north-south division, but from within.

Partition along a north-south axis in Vietnam appears to have served the purpose of defining the dominion of central governments and regimes, but not of resolving the conflicts over whom should govern within those areas. Indeed, one of the most distinctive features of the divisions of Vietnam has been the task of consolidation that remained afterward for the regimes on each side of the line. Either de jure or de facto partition has represented not so much a final form of settlement of conflict between two or more regimes as it has an expediency that permitted the regimes to turn inward and focus upon the need to consolidate support. Regardless of how it was achieved, partition represented as much an *assertion* of regional control as it did an accomplished fact. Nowhere is this more clear than in a consideration of the strategic significance of the 1954 partition resulting from the Geneva conference.

In area control, neither the anticolonial movements in the North nor in the South possessed the territory held by the French after their defeat at Dien Bien Phu. French forces controlled almost all of the six western provinces in North Vietnam (representing approximately one-half of the total territory in the north), and they controlled significant portions of the six provinces to the north and east that formed a border with China. In contrast, the Viet Minh controlled the fourteen smaller provinces that encircled Hanoi. Their control of territory in the South, similarly, was spotty, but closer to parity with the French. Whatever else may be said of the battle of Dien Bien Phu—ranging from the massive and perilous supply lines maintained by the Viet Minh forces to their utter dedication to victory—the situation in which the principal antagonists found themselves throughout the rest of Vietnam indicated that the French had decided to lose the Indochina war, (that is, that it was not possible, given the prevailing sentiment in Paris, to pursue it at further cost or casualty) and not that the Viet Minh had won.

The partition of Vietnam at the 17th parallel, given the area control maintained by each side after Dien Bien Phu, made no sense. Indeed, Vietnamese historians on both sides have been quick to point out that rather than represent a response to the conditions "on the ground" (that would argue against a north-south division and for an east-west, regionally-oriented solution), the partition came at the behest of the great powers. The non-Communist powers sought to prevent the loss of all of Vietnam to the Communists, given the deterioration of French will after Dien Bien Phu. China and Russia, presumably aware of the weakness of the Viet Minh forces and their likely dependency on the Communist bloc for continued support, were instrumental in forcing the DRV to accept partition as an expedient. The southern regime, however, did not sign the agreement and to this day, 20 July is celebrated by Saigon as "National Shame Day." The DRV, represented at the conference by many of the same diplomats who are now at the Paris Talks, signed only an armistice agreement with France, and have been chary ever since of the periodic announcements by spokesmen of the Geneva powers that the present war should be resolved by reconvening the conference. The DRV lost at Geneva, in its view, even though it had quite possibly neither the military strength nor the depth of organization that would have been required to pacify the South; in this latter task, even the Diem regime faced enormous difficulties. The Geneva Conference ended the war between France and the Viet Minh. In so doing, however, it could not and did not simultaneously resolve the conflict between two political and military forces—one centered in the north and the other in central and southern Vietnam —that controlled varying portions of the countryside. Vietnam came to independence in the midst of an unfinished revolution.

THE GENEVA CONFERENCE AND THE DIPLOMACY OF PARTITION

What happened at Geneva? The seventy-three days of the Geneva Conference on Indochina, 8 May—20 July 1954, resulted in a series of specific armistice agreements between France and the Viet Minh providing, principally, for a provisional demilitarized zone at the 17th parallel, the evacuation of the French Union Forces, (FUF), a supervised deescalation, and the creation of an International Control Commission. The technicalities of these provisions were contained in a single document, the "Agreement on the Cessation of Hostilities in Viet Nam," signed on 20 July by a representative of the FUF and the Vice Minister of National Defense for the DRV. Similar documents were signed, ending the war in Cambodia and Laos. The following day, the conference participants issued a Final Declaration—that none of them signed —containing thirteen principles related to the political settlement that remained to be achieved after the end of the war. These loose guidelines for a settlement, however, proved to be poor projections for those who saw (and still do see) the final declaration as a basis for ending the political conflict in Vietnam. While the great powers at the conference appeared to achieve at least a moderate consensus on the principles embodied in the final declaration, the states of present-day Indochina did not share either this consensus or a belief in the efficacy of the principles thus laid down.

The partition of Vietnam at the 17th parallel, consequently, must be viewed in the context of the limited settlement that it was: it facilitated a cease-fire and provided for an orderly transition to a political settlement should the Vietnamese antagonists so desire. The spirit of Geneva,[3] in retrospect, seems to have been embodied in the sixth point of the Final Declaration:

> The Conference recognizes that the essential purpose of the agreement relating to Vietnam is to settle military questions with a view to ending hostilities and that the military demarcation line is provisional and should in no way be interpreted as constituting a political or territorial boundary.

Indeed, there is no documentary evidence yet publicly available that suggests why the Communist delegations settled on the 17th parallel. While the concept had been privately discussed by all sides early in the conference, the Communists suggested that nothing less than a division at the 16th parallel—giving them control over Hué and Danang—was acceptable, while the French first responded to the issue by suggesting a division at the 18th parallel along with administrative control of the Hanoi-Haiphong corridor.

The prime mover for partition was Anthony Eden. His memoirs suggest that he had this form of a settlement in mind in early 1954 and that by March there had been some low-level British-Soviet discussion of partition. By May, Eden and Soviet Foreign Minister Molotov had dined, and the latter had expressed agreement on the practicability of this form of a settlement. The British view under-

---

[3]Robert F. Randle, *Geneva 1954: The Settlement of the Indochinese War* (Princeton, 1969), pp. 190–204. This comprehensive account of the Conference and its diplomatic backdrop is by far the most important and creative study on Geneva that has yet appeared.

scored the conviction of Eden and Churchill that partition might emerge as the best possible form of settlement under the circumstances. But this view was not shared initially by France, the State of Vietnam, or the United States. The latter appeared to follow the official French lead and made its own assurances known to the noncommunist delegation. France, however, appeared to waver on the issue throughout the spring and summer of 1954. On the one hand, the Laniel government's foreign minister, Georges Bidault, assured Emperor Bao Dai in early May that:

> Nothing would be more contrary to the intentions of the French government . . . than the establishment, at the expense of the unity of Vietnam, of two states each having an international status (une vocation internationale).

On the other hand, General Henri Navarre, Commander in Chief of the French Union Forces in Indochina, had written in late April in response to a series of questions posed by a member of the French delegation that:

> France could accept a line of partition only at the 18th parallel. This would enable the French to retain the cities of Hué and Tourane [Danang] and an area . . . that was militarily valuable. It would be necessary, he added, to continue, at least provisionally, the occupation of Hanoi and Haiphong and a corridor between them. . . . The enemy might not be willing to accept a line north of the 16th parallel, Navarre warned, but French acquiescence in Viet Minh demands on the location of the demarcation line would give the Viet Minh the entire zone of French authority in central Vietnam.[4]

To be sure, the French government—or at least important segments of it—had considered the idea of partition, and, like Eden, had recognized that it might prove to be the best possible solution that could be obtained. The Bao Dai government, aware of French thought on this subject, probably never believed the substance of Bidault's letter and had in late April gone on record as both opposed to partition and, in a mandate that the Diem regime would inherit to its advantage in future relations with the United States,

---

[4] Randle, pp. 200–201.

as also unwilling to consider themselves bound by the results of any conference that resulted either in direct negotiation between France and the Viet Minh "rebels" or the partition of Vietnam. The fall of the fortress of Dien Bien Phu, the war-weariness of the French, and the fall of the Laniel government changed the French position and the dynamics of the conference. While the noncommunist powers could desire partition after these events, they had little power to move the Communist side to accept partition of a territory that they had won by almost ten years of warfare. Partition was only possible if the Communist delegations would accept it.

While research into the dynamics of the Communist delegations at Geneva is, perforce, largely circumscribed by the conjectures that must be made in the absence of memoirs and archival access, there appeared to be a distinct pecking order that influenced acceptance of partition. Hanoi was not a free agent; the parameters of this order appeared to be determined by Soviet objectives in entering a new stage of the Cold War. For their purposes, Geneva would demonstrate that imperialist-capitalist aggression could be foiled by peaceful diplomacy, particularly if the socialist bloc were unified. To that end, the conference served both to introduce the Chinese People's Republic as a great power and to make clear, in contrast to the divisions existing within the non-Communist side, that such unity could be achieved. As Randle perciperntly conjectures:

> The cooperation of the Soviet Union with China at Geneva and the Soviet's championing of the rights of the CPR [Chinese People's Republic] would enhance Sino-Soviet solidarity. Also, Geneva offered more direct benefits and opportunities that the ... Kremlin sought. The Soviets wished to prevent the rearming of West Germany and the Ratification of the EDC treaty [European Defense Community]; and it was widely believed that they wished to promote disunity among the Western allies. Therefore the Soviets might offer to use their influence with the Chinese and the Viet Minh to obtain a cease-fire in Indochina in exchange for a French promise of non-ratification of EDC. They might try to demonstrate how America's China policy tended to prolong the war in Southeast Asia, and thereby further divide the Allies. They might persuade the French to deal directly with DRVN representatives, thereby securing the Viet

Minh a measure of recognition, increased prestige, and a means for demoralizing the SVN regime.[5]

The Geneva Conference was a backdrop for the larger questions that Korea and the future defense of Western Europe represented. In large part, this accounts for the belief held by the regimes in North and South Vietnam that the settlement of the current conflict is much too important to be left to the statesmen of the great powers; as one South Vietnamese diplomat observed in an interview in 1970: "Whenever we have tried to settle a war with the aid of the great powers, we have found that, in fact, they wanted to use our war to settle a variety of other questions."

At the end of the pecking-order, the agreement on the partition of Vietnam did not come easily to the DRV. Nowhere as in Hanoi would the war weariness of the French be more evident and more important to the campaigns launched by General Giap against the remaining French positions in the Red River Delta after the fall of Dien Bien Phu. In his 8 May, 1954 letter of congratulations to the Viet Minh forces that participated in the seige of the fortress, Ho Chi Minh observed:

> This victory is big, but it is only the beginning. We must not be self-complacent and subjective and underestimate the enemy. We are determined to fight for independence, national unity, democracy, and peace. A struggle, whether military or diplomatic, must be long and hard before complete victory can be achieved.

Complete victory to the Communists meant both the expulsion of the colonialists from all of Vietnam and the consolidation of the August Revolution so that Vietnam would not be prey in the future to the domination of foreign powers or reactionary regimes. To accept, therefore, partition and the presence in the South of just such a regime would thwart this vision of victory. The aftermath of Geneva and the partition made clear that the Final Declaration, in the North Vietnamese view, did not provide a basis for progress in the revolution or resolution of the subsequent conflict between the two regimes.

---

[5]Randle, p. 141.

Nevertheless by mid-May, the DRV had made it clear that it wanted to end the war with France. By 24 May, the DRV delegation announced that it would discuss a cease-fire without a prior agreement (much like it has thus far suggested to the U.S. in Paris) on the political implications of settlement proposals. The next day, at a restricted session of the conference, Randle reports that Pham Van Dong, reversing a position rearticulated only a week before:

> . . . made an even more significant statement: There should be a complete and simultaneous cease-fire throughout Indochina, . . . followed by a regroupment of regular military forces into zones or areas of regroupment established by the conference. Each zone should be economically and politically viable, and controlled by only one authority. . . . Also, they should have facilities for independent or self-sustaining economic activity and administrative control. Wherever possible, a line of demarcation between them should follow easily recognizable terrain features. . . .

As Randle concludes, "This proposal represented the DRVN's acceptance of temporary *de facto* partition." At the time this statement was made, four PAVN (People's Army of Vietnam) divisions, redeployed from Dien Bien Phu, were in the process of marching on the French defenses of the Red River Delta; other forces were engaged in offensives throughout the Annamitic mountain chain and in Laos. Popular uprisings against the French, coordinated with these divisional maneuvers, were expected in Hanoi, Phuly, and Nam Dinh. By the first week in June, the Laniel government was faltering under the pressures of its critics in Paris, the threat the new Viet Minh moves represented, and the double realizations of war weariness and the failure of their Indochina strategy. Despite the early statement of Communist willingness to consider partition by Dong, only this latter element moved France in a similar direction:

> The impending governmental crisis in Paris accomplished something the Dien Bien Phu wounded and five weeks of negotiations at Geneva had not: the acceptance by the French of the need to *consider* partition, even to the extent of a complete

withdrawal from the delta, and the willingness of the French to deal at arm's length with the Vietminh.[6]

The crisis in Paris, coupled to the increasingly favorable position the Viet Minh forces found themselves in after Dien Bien Phu, suggests that the DRV could have achieved a much better end to the war than they did. Why, then, did the DRV accept partition; indeed, why did they accept even the partition that they did, since after Dong's 25 May speech, they had clarified their position to mean a partition that extended as far south as Hué?

More intriguing, still, is the Vietnamese penchant for accepting formal agreements generally incongruent with what, if the situation on the battlefield were taken into account, it would appear they deserved. What elements played a part in the acceptance of the partition? First, the DRV might have been concerned that the defeat they could have inflicted on the French would provoke American and Chinese intervention in Tonkin. Particularly if the proposed partition were viewed as genuinely temporary, the DRV would be inclined to end the war as rapidly as possible in order to forestall a resurgence of French militancy, or what would have been in their view an irresistable urge for the U.S. to intervene in the battle of Tonkin. Part of the genius of Dulles' policy, it would appear, was his ambiguity on the American commitment, thus demonstrating that the *threat* of intervention may be more productive to end a war than its actual occurrence. North Vietnamese uneasiness over a relationship with China that would bring the latter's troops to her soil, moreover, might have been another important pressure making temporary partition in return for no intervention acceptable.

Second, the leadership of the DRV may have believed their resources—both political and military—to be so thin after the costs of Dien Bien Phu were added to the projected costs of the campaign in the delta, so that they would be unable to control all of Vietnam. What was needed, were this view correct, would be time to consolidate their organizations and their army. Partition would permit them to move at their own pace; organizational development could take place securely behind the demarcation line, while (if the Soviets had pressured for acceptance of partition as the *quid pro quo* of future assistance) the reequipping and mod-

---

[6]Randle, pp. 232; 278.

ernization of their army could be supported by Communist bloc assistance.

Underlying both sets of pressures, of course, must have been the conviction of the Communist delegations that partition was temporary, and that acceptance of it would advance rather than retard the progress of the August Revolution. As Randle observes, Pham Van Dong

> . . .would not have indicated a Viet Minh willingness to accept temporary partition unless he (and his colleagues) were convinced that the unification of Vietnam could be achieved by peaceful means. Thus Pham [on 25 May] did not announce that the DRVN would accept temporary partition, period; he was saying a good bit more. The Viet Minh would accept *de facto* partition if the conference agreed upon conditions for a settlement that, in the opinion of the Viet Minh, would enable it to unify Vietnam under the aegis of the DRVN after the cessation of hostilities. Therefore, the task of the Communist delegations at Geneva after 25 May was to secure conditions for a settlement that would later work to the political benefit of the Viet Minh in gaining a peaceful victory throughout Vietnam.

And Ho himself had said shortly after the Agreement was signed that

> The first step in restoring peace was the cease fire. In order to have a cease fire, troops of both sides have to be grouped into two different zones; this is called the readjustment of zones. The readjustment of zones is provisional, the necessary step to achieving the cease fire, restoring peace and progressing towards the unity of the country by general elections. The demarcation line is definitely not meant to divide the country . . . all of North, Central, and South are within the borders of our country, and surely our people will be united and our compatriots throughout the country will be liberated.[7]

But on each side of the demarcation line, by the end of 1954, two regimes began a process of consolidation essential to improving

---

[7]Randle, pp. 235–236. Ho's remarks are quoted in Tran Van Giau, *South Vietnam Keeps Firm the Copper Wall* (Hanoi, 1966), I. 21.

their ability to engage the other in a major war. While the "unity of Vietnam" remained the keywords of this impending struggle, the partition achieved in 1954 defined two spheres of influence that corresponded to the two distinct groupings of Vietnamese leaders who would seek to create what no other Vietnamese leader had in modern history: the transformation of a divided anticolonial struggle between elites into a single country.

PARTITION AND AFTER

A common view, and a persistent one, is that the 1954 agreement divided a hitherto unitary state. As the description of the historical development of the territory of Vietnam earlier in this chapter suggested, the Vietnamese state was considerably less than the territory represented by present-day North and South Vietnam; not until the Nguyen dynasty did a government extend itself to the present borders. If anything, there existed a core of the state —and later of several states—that roughly corresponded to the delta areas of Vietnam's two great rivers, the Mekong and the Red, in addition to the enclave of land at the country's narrow and mountainous waist that included Danang and Hué. Each of these core areas produced both their regimes and a distinctive politics. While Vietnam was only recently and for a relatively short period of time (a decade of the early 1800s vs. three thousand years of division into at least two, if not three, kingdoms) a unitary state, there existed a nationalist spirit *(tinh tan quoc gia)* as early as the first uprisings against Chinese domination in 39 A.D. Such a spirit grew in importance, however, more as legend than as fact and it remained for a nationalist intellectual, Phan Boi Chau (1867–1940) to write a tract in the early 1900s, *A New Book about the Tears of Blood of the Ryukyu Islands,* that the historian Alexander Woodside has suggested was "perhaps the *first* book ever written in Vietnam expressing the nationalistic ideal that all Vietnamese were fellow countrymen who should be united in love of country."[8]

---

[8]The book referred to the Ryukyu Islands primarily because they had recently been annexed by Japan and, to the author, poignantly demonstrated the effects of the loss of independence. Woodside's comments can be found in David J. Steinberg, *In Search of Southeast Asia* (New York, 1971), pp. 303–304.

That such a tract should appear so late, given the nationalist spirit and traditions Vietnamese historians like to emphasize, suggests, as does the experience of the anti-French movement after this period, that the bonds of a nationalist community were difficult to forge; there were too many blacksmiths. The Confucian society reinforced divisions between the elite and the masses that modern nationalism required, and the French colonial *Sûreté* were quick to quell any political movement that resembled incipient nationalism. Nationalist parties modeled on those founded in revolutionary China, eclectic religious sects, and associations of intellectuals all sought support and power in the period between 1905 when the first modern political organizations emerged and the beginning of the Japanese occupation. Indeed, nationalism itself was a contested phenomenon that gave rise to a multiplicity of groups and political organizations that often emphasized and fought over the distinctions between themselves as much as they focused their energies on winning independence from France.

But above all, social changes were crucial to the fragmentation of Vietnam's nationalism because the society lacked other sources of meaningful division. The creation of a romanized alphabet in the seventeenth century removed an important obstacle to having a literate peasantry; a middle class, and with it, social mobility, could develop free of the constraints that continued reliance upon traditional Chinese characters would have imposed. Vietnam also possessed a common family system, a shared set of folklore and heroes, and lacked, as Woodside noted, "any unconditional symbols of regional solidarity" that would have provided for the balkanization of the state. Rather, social changes in the twentieth century reflect the unevenness of the southern expansion and the consequently rapid rate of the South's development. The trends in the growth of central cities (see chart) make clear the vast differences between the regions that urbanization produced. Moreover, social life in Cochin China was not an imitation of life in Tonkin. Despite the fact that both regions possessed a fertile delta, the density of population in Tonkin was, and continues to be, much higher than in Cochin China. A thousand years of history and village traditions, a constant need for security in the face of natural disasters and military threats, and the equally constant need for intensive cultivation that characterized the settlement of Tonkin were not problems also faced on the same scale by the South. By the end of the 1930s, what could be said for the inhabi-

CHART 1

The Growth of Central Cities and the Scale of Urbanization in Vietnam

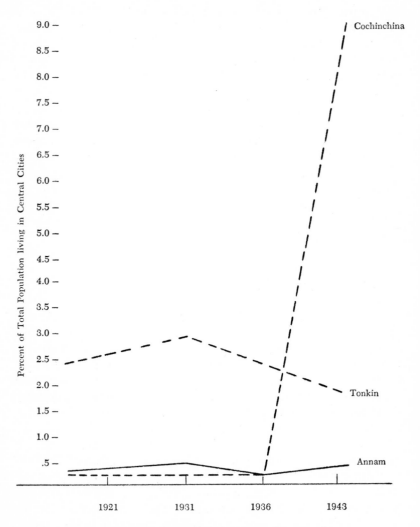

Source: Gouvernement Général de l'Indochine, *Annuaire Statistique De l'Indochine* (1923-1937) and Etat du Vietnam, *Annuaire Statistique du Vietnam* (1945-1950).

tants of the one region was exactly the opposite of what could be said for those living in the other:

> The 6,500,000 peasants of the Tonkin Delta live in a closed economy; they buy and sell little; a family subsists by consuming its own products, and reduces as much as it can the needs it cannot satisfy without the expense of money. And so, the Delta, generally considered, engaged in very paltry exchange with the regions which surrounded it. Its role in world trade, moreover, is practically nil.

So precarious was existence in Tonkin that the author of this passage concluded his study in the following terms:

> Above all care must be taken not to disrupt the moral and social stability of the peasant, this combination of traditions and customs which enables the peasant to endure strikingly wretched material conditions. If this balanced and rational civilization is to collapse, what will be the outcome? The peasant will find himself face to face with his poverty without the consolations which now are afforded to him by family and village life. . . . What would become of a people which would have a clear picture of its poverty and would center its thoughts on it, since it would have no considerations other than material ones; who, viewing material ease as the only form of happiness, would contemplate its infernal wretchedness; who would finally convince itself of the absolute impossibility of improving its lot, since a political or social change could do nothing to counter the excess population? We do not mean that we should oppose any kind of evolution; . . . development must be allowed to go forward on its own and care should be taken not to accelerate it.[9]

This remarkable counsel, so appropriate to a conservative colonialism, foreshadows also the revolution that was to come first in this backward region and then spread throughout Vietnam. For revolutionaries have a different view of the world than colonialists;

---

[9]Pierre Gourou, *Les Paysans du Delta Tonkinois: Etude de Geographie Humaine* (Paris, 1936), and republished in translation by Richard R. Miller, *Human Relations Area Files* (New Haven, 1955), pp. 639, 664–665.

they know that only when people have nothing are they willing to risk all.

The South was not so much a separate region of Vietnam as it was a frontier, a safety-valve for both social and political movements that threatened the stability of first the northern and later both it and the central Vietnamese regimes. As a frontier in the 1800s, moreover, southern Vietnam was the least well controlled by the regime in Hué, and was the first part of the country to be occupied by the French under colonialism. It was here, perhaps, that colonialism had its most profound impact, as Ellen Hammer observed in her September 1957 *Pacific Affairs* "Progress Report on Southern Vietnam:"

> ... when the French seized the south, southern officials and scholars went north rather than live under foreign occupation; and the French set up a system of direct administration which drew on inexperienced personnel only in limited numbers and at the lowest echelon of government. ... The number of the small middle class that grew up there under the colonial regime (what the Communists would later refer to as "comprador bourgeoise") was not only fairly remote from the cultural and religious traditions that prevailed farther north but, being closely linked with and wholly dependent on the French, administration tended to become much more gallicized than their compatriots in Annam and Tonkin.

Settlement in the South, thus, was fundamentally a different process than in the North, as the historian Milton Osborne suggests in the first chapter of his *The French Presence in Cochinchina and Cambodia*:

> The freedom permitted the settlers, combined with the relatively scant population of Cochinchina, resulted in a markedly different settlement pattern in the south of the country than that of the north and the center. In these older regions of Vietnamese settlement, the people clustered in village communities, population oases in the agricultural plains. Normally, the village or commune was sheltered behind a thick bamboo hedge. This was a physical representation of the social and political situation: by tradition, the authority of the central gov-

ernment ceased at the village limits. By contrast, in Cochinchina, settlement spread out along waterways, so, while the village unit was preserved for administrative purposes, it was a less closely knit group.

In such a milieu, the nationalism that did emerge, rather than rely upon the closely knit village world for support, had to create that world anew. Thus, the religious sects of the Mekong Delta sought to use religion to foster cohesion while the movements in the North could rely upon geography and traditional patterns of village settlement. Such diversity in social organization made no single nationalist movement all-encompassing. The ideology of one often proved anathema to others.

For the politics of Vietnamese nationalism, partition came at an inauspicious time. In 1954, as was true throughout the first Indochina war, there was not one nationalist movement in Vietnam, but many. In 1945, more than a dozen clandestine nationalist organizations, each specific to a particular area of the country, existed—and sometimes as much in competition with each other as in opposition to the French. Indeed, and unlike their predecessors of the 1920s and 1930s, these groups soon clustered, not around the issue of to what degree and in what manner they should oppose the French, but around the issue of communism itself. In May 1945, the Viet Minh organized six northern provinces into a "liberated zone" (Caobang, Langson, Ha Giang, Bac Kan, Tuyen Quang, and Thai Nguyen), while the Trotskyist Struggle Group was reorganized as the principal force in the urban areas. Two competing and factionated anticommunist groups, the Kuomingtang (the VNQDD) and the Dai Viet, formed a decade before, were the principal rallying points for organizations in the provinces north and west of Hanoi. A similar split occurred in the South between those organizations affiliated with the Indochina Communist Party (formed in 1929), and those who supported the movements of the religious sects of the Mekong Delta—the Cao Dai and the Hoa Hao. Together, these groups formed the United Nationalist Front. By September, these groups were affiliated with the Viet Minh in a Southern National Bloc, only to split apart during the course of the anti-French War. Throughout the anti-French struggle, united fronts at the national level were never more than temporary coalitions that the pressure of events—or lack of it—consistently undermined.

A rough indication of the diversity of groups participating in the anti-French struggle can be found by the affiliations of those elected to the National Assemblies. Vietnam's first Assembly under independence, (which the DRV had declared in September 1945), convened as a result of elections held in January 1946, and reflected the participation of at least six groups (ninety deputies or thirty percent were declared independents): Marxists (3 percent), Socialists (9 percent), Democrats (14 percent), *Dong Minh Hoi* (8 percent), VNQDD (8 percent), Viet Minh (28 percent). Between this Assembly's inauguration (25 February) and its second session in October, virtually all of the non-Viet Minh members had been purged; opposition deputies and leaders were either assassinated or went into hiding. And while this Assembly's mandate was for three years, it remained in session for ten; by 1956, of course, the National Assembly of the DRV became an appendage of the Party. The first Assembly in the South under Independence, permitted by Ngo Dinh Diem in 1956, unlike its northern competitor, never had a purge of members. No opposition deputies were elected and no opposition groups were represented. As one witness of this period, VNQDD party activist Dr. Nguyen Tien Hy, later observed in his 1970 monograph *On Political Opposition:*

> The authorities declare that they oppose communism, and the main enemy is thus chosen. But in pursuing an anticommunist policy, some other enemies secondary in importance to the communists may be encountered. . . . Because of autocratic tendencies and an uncertainty with regard to strategy, people forget that the main enemy is communism, and turn to repress anticommunist nationalist elements, who could be their temporary allies. Some prisons probably . . . contain more nationalists than communists.

In addition to declared independents, four out of the five groups represented were merely proxies for the principal party of the regime, the National Revolutionary Movement. The fifth group represented was the Dai Viet; but, as was the case for all the members of the Assembly, their candidates were personally selected by either Diem or his brother, Ngo Dinh Nhu. While the opposition was thus constrained and its effective representation circumscribed by the political philosophy of the Ngo family, there existed nonetheless more than a dozen such groups operating clandestinely.

In the North, the Communist party by 1956 was the undisputed political force that governed the country and controlled its politics. The nationalist movement was thus, with partition, divided between the two regimes and consolidation of political forces, so essential to stability after independence, proceeded separately in both parts of Vietnam. In the sense that all of Vietnam sought independence, the partition and the regimes that followed highlighted the artificial nature, not of the nationalist movement itself, but of the partition. The Vietnamese revolution—whether Communist or not—was not complete in 1954 and the regimes established in both parts of the territory "deserved" neither all of Vietnam by virtue of the extent of their political control, nor did they find the consolidation of their own regimes a facile task. Of course, domestic opposition to the Communist regime, vexing in the early days, dissipated as the Party emerged from agricultural collectivism both a hero and in full control. But the political situation in the South was different. While both regimes spent the first two years of their tenure fighting opposition forces rather than each other, the travail of Ngo Dinh Diem in the South was infinitely more difficult. Indeed, had the Viet Minh been awarded all of Vietnam, they probably would have had as difficult a time in quelling the dissidence of the religious sects and ethnic minorities as Diem did. No single political movement could claim sway over the South, including the one headed by Ngo Dinh Diem. Thus the real nature of Vietnam's unfinished revolution lies not in the division imposed by the great powers between North and South, but in the fact that the South had yet to undergo a revolution, comparable in scope to that of the North's, of either a communist or a noncommunist sort.

The direct consequence of partition for the South was extreme and almost initial dependency upon external forces for material support. While the economic consequences of the French departure were severe, the political consequences were even greater. Without the French, South Vietnam lacked a government and its regime was in flux between a system where the Emperor ruled but did not govern to one where the monarchy would be replaced

altogether. Neither as politicians nor as nationalist leaders did Bao
Dai or Ngo Dinh Diem have the stature of Ho Chi Minh. Nor was
there present at the creation of the southern regime a philosophy
of rulership or government that could compete with the one established by the leaders in Hanoi. While the North was dependent
upon the assistance it received from Communist bloc countries for
military development and industrialization it was not, like the
South, also dependent upon these external powers for political
stability. From the beginning the United States and the Diem
government were linked, in fact, in a pattern of mutual dependency. The U.S. was dependent upon the Diem regime for the
latter's goodwill and the opportunity it provided for Washington
to practice the containment policy in Asia.

While the U.S. required a reliable ally in its pursuit of anticommunism, for his part Diem derived considerable benefits from
such support. Concerned primarily about security *vis à vis* an
expected invasion from the North, the Diem government's concern matched Washington's, and the latter was more than forth-
coming—though at times in a piecemeal fashion—with assistance.
Diem must have recognized early the fact that by itself South
Vietnam could not generate the economic or political resources to
oppose the communist threat, and came to the U.S. government
in somewhat of a position of strength; neither had the communist
threat substantially materialized nor had the weaknesses of the
government itself become apparent by the later 1950s. The provision of substantial public resources, however, did not make for
dependency of a debilitating sort during this period. Able to ma-
nipulate the divisions within the U.S. mission over economic and
political issues, able to find other donors for projects not approved
by American policy-makers, and able to play upon a noticeable
U.S. reluctance to assume postures that required deep involvement in internal Vietnamese affairs, the Diem government kept
its dependency upon the U.S. within largely manageable limits.
The real significance of such dependence, however, lay not in its
relationship with the U.S. and its policies, but in the attention this
diverted from the political challenges the regime faced.

As long as the U.S. was willing to take a lion's share of the burden
(as it increasingly did throughout the 1960s) in defense of the
Southern regime, both the creation of a counter-guerrilla army
and the political mobilization of the population against the north-

ern communists were unnecessary. While, in the first six years after partition, the DRV pursued a vigorous reconstruction policy, embarked on a far-reaching industrialization program, developed a modern army, trained an entirely new generation of skilled workers, and created a political structure throughout the country-side, the Diem government spent two of its first six years fighting those who challenged its power and legitimacy, and the remaining four increasingly preoccupied not with the tremendous growth of its northern enemy, but with staying in power. Beside the achievement of the North, the early history of the Republic in the South pales, as suggested by the leader of the 1963 coup against Diem, General Duong Van (Big) Minh, in his October 1968 article in *Foreign Affairs:*

As we step back from the present conflict and look at the entire post-1954 period, we can see that our biggest mistake was to have gone too fast when we should have gone slow; and to have gone too slow when we should have gone fast. In the early days of the Republic we pressed too rapidly to destroy the political power of the sects, and in so doing turned them against the government rather than making them our allies as we gradually integrated them into the fiber of the nation. We went too quickly in building strategic hamlets, and too slowly in arming and equipping the villager to defend his home. We rushed forward with the trappings of democracy, while our government lagged in gaining the confidence of the people.

Our next big mistake was to place loyalty to self, to family, to friends ahead of loyalty to nation. This was doubly wrong when our Republic was fighting to survive in 1955, and it is close to treason to do so now as we struggle against an invasion by regular troops from the North. It is this virus of selfishness which spreads tolerance of corruption among our officials and contributes heavily to the people's lack of confidence in their government.

Another mistake which so many of the South Vietnamese made was to embrace the illusion that they could somehow stand apart from the conflict, disassociating themselves from both their government and the communists, while giving lip-service to either side as the occasion required.

The final mistake was to think, as nearly half of all Vietnamese at one time or another have done, that they and their country could ride the tiger of communism—hopefully being able to settle for a Titoist form of independence—without being eaten when they stepped down from the tiger's back.

The southern regimes lacked, simply, a level of political mobilization and awareness that would have enabled them to compete with the North. The reasons for this lay, in General Minh's view, in the tendency characteristic of most Southern regimes to concentrate, once in power, not upon increasing their power but maintaining what little they had.

As one looks back on our past experience with democracy, we can see that our central problem has been of our own making: our governments have lacked confidence in themselves. As a result, once they gain power their main efforts are focused on maintaining themselves in office rather than leading the people forward out of their troubles. Consequently, instead of broadening their base, instead of encouraging all factions, no matter how diverse their views, to join together and contribute in their own ways toward a realization of the people's dream, they have squandered most of their talent and energy in neutralizing any individual or group that is not prepared to subjugate itself completely to their direction.

Caught up thus in a defensive, introverted frame of mind, past governments have usually begun by narrowing their base. In so doing they have shut out many who might be prepared to work in their own way for the national cause. Once this process sets in, personalities become involved, rumors gain credence, suspicions absorb the creative energy of the leaders. Instead of searching for ways to move forward together, schemes are devised to eliminate those who differ even slightly on how to proceed. Those who have been excluded stand aside and criticize or plot.

While the government deludes itself and its powerful allies by giving the outward impression of authority, those responsive to its authority become fewer and fewer. Before long it finds itself balanced like an inverted pyramid and requires only a push from some other self-centered group to topple it from power.

This has happened more than once since 1954 and we have only ourselves to blame. It can happen again.

U.S. support to such a regime meant that the regime could afford to focus inward because of the American defensive umbrella. Communism from the North was never genuinely threatening and thus failed to produce an understanding both of its political potential (to this day, students in South Vietnam who study communism run the risk of being arrested as communists) and of the actions on the part of the regime that would have prepared the countryside to compete with the Viet Cong. Indeed, the Nixon Administration's policy of Vietnamization and the general mobilization that accompanied it in the South represented the first effort that noncommunist regimes in Vietnam have made that would equal any undertaken in the North. The lesson here is dramatic, but simple. Dependency on other countries for security may end up as dependency upon them for stability as well.

TWO VIETNAMS; ONE PEOPLE?

The history preceding and the diplomacy leading to partition, while important for interpretation of subsequent events and developments, obscure the human and personal meaning of that event. As one young scholar suggested to me in an interview:

> It has been over sixteen years since the movement of more than one million Vietnamese from the North to the South. Yet, the partition of the country, symbolized by the 17th parallel and the Ben Hai River, still remains in the mind of every Vietnamese as the most sorrowful event of our history.

How permanent is the territorial division of Vietnam? This is the transcendent question of Vietnamese politics, both North and South. Despite a decade of war, to most Vietnamese the existence of two Vietnams, like partition itself, is viewed as an expedient. Consider, for example, the sentiments expressed in the following statements:

Thousands of women who were born in South Vietnam are now living in the North. They long for the place of their childhood; naturally, that is the place that seems most beautiful to everyone. And so these women name their babies after a mountain, a river, or some other place near their old village. I gave one of my children a name that means "We are thinking of you South Vietnam!" The other I named after a river that flowed before our house—we called it "Perfume River." Because so many families are divided in this way, the question of reunification is emotional as well as political. Vietnam is one, her people are one.

A very significant fact to me, which speaks so eloquently and impressively of a respect for national identity, and contributes to an understanding of Vietnamese nationalism, is that, despite all the suffering due to the war in the South, due partly to the participation of North Vietnamese troops, the southerner has never developed a hatred against Vietnamese in general. Rather, they speak with enmity only of the government or the regime in the North. They ask why such a war should happen between members of the same family. Unification to them means termination of warfare between brothers.[10]

While identity with region persists, identification with a common culture and history supercedes it. The traditions of northern, southern, and central Vietnam exist on each side of the 17th parallel.

Indeed, the most immediate consequence of the partition in 1954 was the exchange of population between the two zones. Similar in scope and significance to the exchange then taking place between south China and Hong Kong, over 900,000 people left North Vietnam for the South in the space of a year. This represented a loss to the northern regime of approximately one-half of its Catholic population, and most of its industrial infrastructure. The loss in skilled human resources, however, was even greater

---

[10]The first extract is a statement by Professor Vo Thi The, representative of the Women's Union of the DRV, to the Indochina Women's Conference, Vancouver, British Columbia, Canada, 1–6 April 1971. The second extract is taken from Nguyen Van Hien, "The Meaning of Partition" (unpublished manuscript, Princeton University, 1971), p. 1.

with the departure of approximately 133,000 artisans, entrepreneurs, civil servants, professionals, and students.

In contrast, the International Control Commission estimated that only about 2,600 Vietnamese moved North in the period between the Final Declaration and the beginning of May, 1955. Clandestine movement to the North among the official class, however, had begun in 1948, and, presumably, continues through the present period.

On the whole the strictly administrative cadre tended to gravitate toward the South, while the more technically inclined tended to be divided more equally between North and South, with perhaps some preference for the North.

In summing up the significance of this transfer of skilled government personnel, one South Vietnamese official observed,

The communists got the defectors from the French and the Japanese administrations, while almost the entire ethnic staff apparatus of the French regime came South. In my particular case, I found myself, for example, different from my colleagues in the South and felt a closer affinity with my counterparts in the North. The South as opposed to the North, then, would be characterized by the divorce of intellectuals from the government machinery. . . . The point is, that the noncommunist intellectual remained *attentists* and there was and by and large still is little significant participation in the government by intellectuals.[11]

While the northern intellectual found himself under the DRV regime an important asset in the contest to inherit the cultural soul of the anti-French resistance, the absence of such a role for intellectuals in the South (and their repression by Diem and his successors) produced a literature, not so much of competing nationalism, but designed to subvert the regime itself. The parallels in current Southern Vietnamese literature with the first novels

---

[11]Both extracts are from Allan E. Goodman, ed., *Lost Revolutions: Notes on the Experience of Political and Administrative Reform in South Vietnam* (New York, 1968), pp. 4–5.

and tracts that appeared against the French in the early 1900s are striking.

Throughout the human drama of migration and resettlement, one consistent thread runs through the stories of those who came South in the exodus: all expected to return to the North. Households were left intact and family treasures buried. Between 1954 and 1956, when communication between the two zones was facilitated by special postal cards administered by the ICC, families in the South received periodic—but cryptic—messages on the status of their property. Within village leaderships, temporary movement to the South had always been considered a possibility. One Catholic priest recalled:

I came South in 1951 to explore possible sites for our temporary settlement in case the Communists won control of our area. In 1954, I studied the Geneva Accords and determined then that the outcome of the conference did not protect adequately the Catholics in the North. I then made a radio speech that contained a prearranged signal to indicate that all Catholics must immediately leave the North. But, most of us left with the impression that we would be gone at the most two or three years.

A young student recalled that

When the Communists came to our village, my father had been very disturbed by their lack of respect for the family system. He went to Haiphong to see if we could settle there until the situation in our village returned to normal. Then the letter came. He said that we must move, but this would only be for a few months. None of us wanted to leave, and I even tried to run away once we had come to Haiphong to see our village again. In Haiphong, we had learned that we were leaving North Vietnam altogether! But our father felt sure that we would be gone only a few months.

Return to the North is still today an emotionally charged issue for the older generation. But if one wanted to visit the North described in Vietnamese literature, one could see it more readily in a southern village of northern refugees than in the communes and state farms of the DRV. Indeed, as one peasant of present-day North Vietnam observed:

> In spite of the war, the transformations brought about in the past ten years are continuing. We are transforming nature, transforming human beings, transforming the pattern of living. *If the people who left in 1954 were to return today, they would not recognize the province.* There has been a radical change in outlook, and this has been brought about mainly by ideological, political means. A collective morality is beginning to take root. Each individual is working for himself and for everyone else as well. The old regime was characterized by a complete lack of democracy and the absence of all things modern. Today we have democracy, and we also have machinery, electricity and improvements in irrigation.[12]

Within the South, the children of the exodus, however, do not share the emotional referents of their parents. For them, a return to a North they never knew—and one now quite different than their fathers describe—is not a political goal, as much as it is a dream about the future, as one young student suggested:

> While there is no solid information about society in the North available to the general mass, and while northern refugees now feel compelled to take their lives in the South more seriously, the image of a return to the North still remains in their minds. For many in their fifties and even some in their forties, a return to the North is a dream they hope to see come true before they die. For younger generations, it is still fervently and enthusiastically discussed. They long to establish a new life and bring peace to the land their fathers left.

But the division within families that the exodus produced between those members who remained in the North after 1955 was,

---

[12]Tuan Doanh, member of the Provincial Committee of the Workers' Party, as told to Gerard Chailand, in *The Peasants of North Vietnam,* trans. by Peter Wiles (Middlesex, England, 1969), p. 82. Emphasis added. See also Hoang Van Chi, "Collectivisation and Rice Production," *China Quarterly* (January - March, 1962), pp. 99–100.

in the second generation, replaced by a gap between fathers and sons *vis à vis* the political organizations each supports. Indeed, Catholic politics since the middle 1960s has been split between those groups stressing return to the North as their principal *raison d'être* and those stressing the need to create a revolution in the South to compete with the Communists. At present, as one Catholic leader suggested in an interview:

> Catholic anticommunism is really stymied. Those who have experienced the Communists and know what their terror means are alienated from those who have only experienced the need for the South to create a social revolution. The former consider the latter soft, as you would put it, on communism, while the latter feel the others are hopelessly outdated and corrupted by their involvement with Diem. There is in the South not one anticommunism, but many. Too many, because when President Thieu calls for the anticommunist spirit of the people this more often serves to divide the people than to unite them.

Moreover, spokesmen for both North and South make clear that, at the present juncture, emotional commitment to reunification provides little basis for ending the present war. The position articulated by the foreign ministry of South Vietnam in mid-1968, for example, demonstrates a commitment to reunification, but at a gradual pace:

> What we want is the end of aggression and the restoration of the *status quo ante.* Once peace is achieved, we are prepared to coexist peacefully with North Vietnam. Going even further, we would consider favourably the gradual development of relations beneficial to both North and South Viet-Nam, subject only to the essential safeguards against renewed subversion. Such a course of action would lead to the ultimate reunification of our country, in peace, freedom and progress.

Such a gradualist view is also maintained by the Communists, as is evident in the important announcement by the Viet Cong delegation in Paris of their Seven Points in July 1971. Their position on reunification—one shared by Hanoi, presumably, as well—was contained in the fourth point:

> The reunification of Vietnam will be achieved step by step, by peaceful means on the basis of discussions and agreements between the two zones, without constraint and annexation from either party, without foreign interference. Pending reunification of the country, the North and the South zones will reestablish normal relations, guarantee free movement, free correspondence, free choice of residence, and maintain economic and cultural relations on the principal of mutual interests and mutual assistance.
>
> All questions concerning the two zones will be settled by qualified representatives of the Vietnamese people in the two zones on the basis of negotiations, without foreign interference.

Underlying these positions is the fact that reunification was made difficult not by the partition, per se, but by the development of two regimes subsequently and their involvement in a major war. What is striking is that each regime believes that the existence of two Vietnams after the war would facilitate rather than hinder reunification. The emotional and cultural bases for a single Vietnamese nation have not been eroded by the war; as the following extract from Tran Xuan Ly's 1969 essay, "Why North and South Vietnam Should be Reunited," makes clear:

> Vietnam . . . is a nation with its head in Hanoi, its heart in the old imperial city of Hué and its breadbasket in the fertile Mekong Delta.
> . . . the case for reunification is [thus] stronger than foreign observers may think. After all, some 400,000 Southern guerrillas have died since 1960, because they believed in reunification. The hard truth is that there is no such entity as two Vietnams; there are almost as many Southerners in the Hanoi government as Northerners in the present Saigon administration. Mai Van Bo, the senior Hanoi diplomat in Paris, is a former schoolmate of Pham Dang Lam, the ambassador from Saigon. Both are from the same Mekong delta province. Tom Duc Thang, Hanoi's vice president, is a Southerner. . . .

One major reason favouring reunification is that North and South Vietnam are so economically interdependent that neither can hope for a bright future if fresh access to the other's resources is denied him. . . . If reunification cannot be achieved, the South will continue for an indefinite period to be the economic ward of the United States, while the North—like Cuba —will be kept alive with massive transfusion of Sino-Soviet assistance. But sooner or later, the natural forces for unification will manifest themselves.

For many, reunification is viewed as something less than national integration. Despite rhetoric to the contrary, the nearly two decades of partition have produced separate societies rather than social antipathies. Particularly in the North, as the peasant leader quoted earlier suggested, social changes under communism have produced a Vietnam unrecognizable to those who left it around 1954.

What reality lies behind the dream of the unification, if not national integration? Histories of the conflict for both North and South stress one fundamental fact: that the division of Vietnam was the result of foreign intervention. Possibly more important than integration and reunification itself, after the present war ends, is the ability of both Vietnams to reduce their dependency upon foreign powers. Such a form of self-determination need not be synonymous with either integration or reunification. In fact, in countless books, novels, and political tracts, one idea persists: however dissimilar life in the two Vietnams may currently be, freedom from foreign intervention is the principal aim of Vietnam's unfinished revolution. Perhaps more than any of the distinctive and antagonistic political goals sought by the two regimes, the creation of a Vietnam free from foreign domination is the unfinished task that they both share; each part of Vietnam has always faced problems generated by the spectre of intervention. The North has constantly had to defend its border and regularize its relationship with China. The territorial integrity of the South required constant vigilance to keep at bay colonial penetrations and the aggressive designs of its martial western neighbor. Two Vietnams might, in fact, defend all of Vietnam better than one. The present Northern regime could deal as readily with China as the Southern regime could with the U.S. and other Southeast Asian powers. A blend of both regimes (assuming that the complete victory of one over the other is impossible) might weaken the strengths of each in this area or replicate patterns of dependency that presently exist to peril the viability of such a solution in Laos. The future of the conflict between the two Vietnams that began with the partition in 1954 depends ultimately upon recognition by both of shared perils and goals.

In "Kim-Van-Kieu," the early nineteenth century poem by Nguyen Du, Vietnamese friends suggest, can be found such a basis for reunification. Given the history of this country so tragically divided, the allegory of two long-separated lovers meeting at the end of hardships and miseries each accepted out of love for the other, speaks eloquently to the future:

> We pledged ourselves to each other, suddenly we were separated, as fish from water, as birds from the sky; I am sure that after all the promises exchanged, you too have suffered equally; through life and death we swore to maintain our love; now as we meet again we must make each other happy, bringing fullness to our love: . . . all through the years (of separation) has my love for you but deepened ever searching for you, even though it has been like the hopeless groping for a needle at the bottom of the sea! It is because of this great love, engraved as it is so deeply in all we treasure, rather than to any thought of lightness, that I ever dared to go on hoping somehow we two would come together once more! Surely in the face of all of this, it is unnecessary we share the same bed to be counted husband and wife.

Of course, these mature and gentle lovers are prevented from the intimacy that they longed for in their youth. The heroine, Thuy Kieu, in order to save her family, sold herself into prostitution and disappeared from the life of the melancholy scholar, Kim Trong. The words above are Kim's; they are his solution to a problem similar to the one the two Vietnams will face at the end of this bloody war: unity against the forces that drove them apart, friendship in the future, but not marriage. What is uncertain now, and perhaps with time altogether unimportant, is which regime became the prostitute.

BIBLIOGRAPHY

Vietnam—General and Pre-1945

Buttinger, Joseph, *The Smaller Dragon, A Political History of Vietnam* (New York, 1958); Gourou, Pierre, *The Peasants of the Tonkin Delta* (2 vols.) (New Haven, 1955); Hammer, Ellen, *Vietnam, Yesterday and Today* (New York, 1966); Marr, David, *Vietnamese Anticolonialism, 1885–1925* (Berkeley, 1971); Thai, Nguyen Van and Nguyen Van Mung, *A Short History of Vietnam* (Saigon, 1958).

Vietnam Since 1945

Fall, Bernard B., *Street Without Joy* (Harrisburg, Pa., 1961); Hammer, Ellen J., *The Struggle for Indochina* (Stanford, 1954); Lancaster, Donald, *The Emancipation of French Indochina* (London, 1961); Murti, B. S. N., *Vietnam Divided: The Unfinished Struggle* (New York, 1964); Randle, Robert F., *Geneva 1954: The Settlement of the Indochinese War* (Princeton, 1969); Scigliano, Robert, *South Vietnam: Nation Under Stress* (Boston, 1963); Tanham, George K., ed., *War Without Guns: American Civilians in Rural Vietnam* (New York, 1966).

North Vietnam and the Viet Cong

Chi, Hoang Van, *From Colonialism to Communism, A Case History of North Vietnam* (New York, 1964); Fall, Bernard B., *The Viet Minh Regime, Government Administration in the Democratic Republic of Vietnam* (Ithaca, N.Y., 1954); Giap, Vo Nguyen, *People's War, People's Army: The Viet Cong Instruction Manual for Underdeveloped Countries* (New York, 1961); Honey, P. J., *Communism in North Vietnam: Its Role in the Sino-Soviet Dispute* (Cambridge, Mass., 1963), and his *North Vietnam Today* (New York, 1962); Pike, Douglas, *Viet Cong: The Organization and Technique of the National Liberation Front of South Vietnam* (Cambridge, Mass., 1966).

Index

Index